Keynes's *The General Theory of Employment, Interest, and Money*

A Concordance

Keynes's *The General Theory of Employment, Interest, and Money*

A Concordance

Edited by
Fred R. Glahe

with an Introduction by
Kenneth E. Boulding

Rowman & Littlefield Publishers, Inc.

ROWMAN & LITTLEFIELD PUBLISHERS, INC.

Published in the United States of America
by Rowman & Littlefield Publishers, Inc.
8705 Bollman Place, Savage, Maryland 20763

British Cataloging in Publication Information Available

Library of Congress Cataloging-in-Publication Data
Glahe, Fred R.
Keynes's The general theory of employment, interest,
and money : a concordance / edited by Fred R. Glahe.
p.   cm.
"This concordance ... is based on the 1936 first
edition, as published in the United States by Harcourt
Brace Jovanovich"—Editor's pref.
1. Keynes, John Maynard, 1883-1946. General theory
of employment, interest, and money—Concordances.
I. Keynes, John Maynard, 1883-1946. General theory
of employment, interest, and money.   II. Title.
HB99.K38G53   1991
330.15' 6—dc20   91–23359 CIP

ISBN 0–8476–7678–1 (hardcover : alk. paper)

Printed in the United States of America

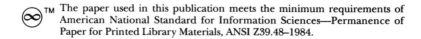 ™ The paper used in this publication meets the minimum requirements of
American National Standard for Information Sciences—Permanence of
Paper for Printed Library Materials, ANSI Z39.48–1984.

To My Sister and Brother

Contents

Preface

This concordance to *The General Theory of Employment, Interest, and Money* by John Maynard Keynes is based on his 1936 first edition, published in the United States by Harcourt Brace Jovanovich. The first American printing of this edition actually used paper that had been printed in England. The American edition continues to this day to be published by Harcourt Brace Jovanovich—one indicator of the "classical" nature of one of the most important books of the twentieth century.

This concordance lists each word used in *The General Theory,* the frequency of its occurrence, and the page and paragraph where it can be found, with the exception of the words and symbols described below.

A problem arose with frequency counts and pagination when a word was hyphenated across pages. For example, the word "employment" is split by a hyphen between pages 30 and 31 in *The General Theory*. In terms of citation in the concordance, I chose to place the word on both pages; in addition, I adjusted the frequency of occurrence so the word was counted only once. Hence, the frequency count in the concordance accurately reflects the number of times a word is used, but the actual number of page and paragraph citations will, at times, be greater.

Another minor problem presented itself in the preparation of this concordance: the definition of a paragraph. This was usually a simple matter. If a paragraph was split between pages, it was counted as a separate paragraph on each page. For example, the last paragraph on page 10 of *The General Theory* continues on page 11, where it is counted as the first paragraph on page 11. Each footnote is defined to be a paragraph; consequently, on page 8, footnote 1 is counted as the fourth paragraph on that page. There were a few instances where a footnote in the text was split across pages, as on pages 42 and 43. In this case, the portion of footnote 2 found on page 42 is counted as paragraph 3 on page 42, while the remainder of footnote 2 found on page 43 is counted as paragraph 3 on page 43.

A more complicated matter of paragraph definition occurred a dozen or so times, and I chose paragraph definitions for these cases which should improve the ease of using this concordance. On page 5, for example, the italicized subheadings associated with Roman numerals I and II end in periods and are, therefore, treated as paragraphs of one sentence each. This makes sense since each subheading is immediately followed by a paragraph. On the other hand, assumptions enumerated with arabic numbers on page 21 do not end with periods, nor are they immediately followed by paragraphs. Hence, they are considered to be part of a single paragraph which begins immediately after Roman numeral VII on page 21. This approach to paragraph definition is used in similar situations throughout the text.

While all words used in *The General Theory* are cited and their frequency of use given, not all words are indexed. This was done to eliminate obviously uninteresting words such as "a," "an," "the," and "and." In addition, numbers, with the exception of dates, and mathematical notations were not indexed or counted for frequency of occurrence.

The preparation of this concordance has been an interesting and educational exercise in the application of computer technology to the study of a controversial and revolutionary economic text. I wish to thank the Regents of the University of Colorado for providing me with the sabbatical leave during which this concordance was initiated, and Charles R. Middleton, Dean of the College of Arts and Sciences, and Larry D. Singell, Chair of the Department of Economics, for their continued support after my return from sabbatical leave. I also wish to thank Professor Rubin Rabinowitz of the Department of English (University of Colorado at Boulder) for his help in the early stages of this project, and Duane Troxel of the Graduate School of Education (University of Colorado at Denver) for technical advice in the optical scanning of *The General Theory* and assistance in the computer generation of the concordance. I am indebted to Mr. Mohammed Zebib for his very conscientious proofreading of the scanned text and to the Intel Corporation for their grant of equipment. Special thanks are due to Harcourt Brace Jovanovich for granting permission to publish this concordance and to James Shapiro for customized programming assistance. Lastly, I wish to thank my wife, Nancy, and son, Charles, for their forbearance while I spent uncounted hours before the warm glow of my trusty Sony computer monitor.

Fred R. Glahe
December 13, 1990

Introduction

The word "concordance" inevitably brings to the mind of one raised a Methodist, like myself, the great name of Cruden, whose concordance of the King James Bible (1737) is a valuable asset to anyone wanting to look up a specific section of text. In his preface Alexander Cruden says, "The earliest scripture concordance was compiled by Hugo, . . . a preaching friar of the Dominican order . . . who died in the year 1262. In the execution of his work we are informed that he was assisted by the labors of 500 monks." Dr. Glahe's work is assisted mainly by a single computer, which tells us something about the twentieth century.

While not everyone would agree that Keynes's *General Theory* is the closest thing to a bible in the twentieth century, a good case can nevertheless be made for this proposition. In his book *The Fiscal Revolution in America,* Herbert Stein points out that both Paul Samuelson and I used the great phrase from Wordsworth, "Bliss was it in that dawn to be alive, But to be young was very heaven," to describe the impact of Keynes on us, young men coming of age in the Great Depression. During the early 1930s in the United States, 25 percent of the labor force was unemployed, profits were negative, net investment was negative, and it looked as if capitalism was on the brink of collapse. At the same time, Stalin was killing and starving some five million or more people during the First Collectivization in the Soviet Union. Conventional economics seemed to have no answer to these problems, and Marxism offered an unacceptable answer. Keynes certainly did not come up with the final answer, but at least he had a view of the world which raised these catastrophes from the utterly unintelligible to the moderately understandable. The fact that we have had nothing like a "Great Depression" since the thirties and that the communist world is now hoping for a better answer to its problems than Marxism suggests that there is a prophetic quality about Keynes's work which made an enormous difference to the world.

Those who are looking for good quotations from *The General Theory* will be very grateful to Fred Glahe and his work. As an example, the word "mathematical" leads to a delightful quotation on page 298: "Too large a proportion of recent 'mathematical' economics are mere concoctions, as imprecise as the initial assumptions they rest on, which allow the author to lose sight of the complexities and interdependencies of the real world in a maze of pretentious and unhelpful symbols"—a prophetic remark which might well be placed over the lintel of most departments of economics today.

A concordance, just by revealing the number of particular words used, throws an interesting light on what a book is all about. It is interesting to note that the most frequent words used in the book are "rate" and "rates" (737), "interest" (712), "employment" (615), "investment" and "investments" (570), "money" (505), "increase" and related words (472), "change" (446), "capital" (428), "wage" and "wages" (370), "marginal" (365), "income" (346), "demand" (330), "cost" and "costs" (294), "output" (287), "price" and "prices" (278), "consumption" (275), and "supply" (187). These numbers illustrate the enormous importance of interest and the domination of supply by demand in Keynes's thinking, the importance he gives to wages, the fact that he was more interested in employment than unemployment (only 101 references), and suggest something about the quality and content of *The General Theory*. Many economists will find it very useful to have this work on their shelves.

Kenneth E. Boulding,
Distinguished Professor of Economics, Emeritus, and
Research Associate and Project Director, Institute of
Behavioral Science,
University of Colorado at Boulder

Keynes's *The General Theory of Employment, Interest, and Money*

A Concordance

1530's	(1)	346:4
1581	(1)	346:1
1598	(1)	358:3
1620's	(1)	342:1
1621	(2)	344:2; 347:2
1622	(2)	342:1; 345:2
1662	(1)	359:1
1663	(1)	344:2
1665	(1)	346:1
1668	(1)	342:1
1675	(1)	346:1
1676	(1)	342:1
1682	(1)	342:1
1686	(1)	359:1
1690	(1)	359:1
1691	(1)	346:1
1692	(1)	342:5
1695	(1)	359:1
16th	(2)	345:4; 346:4
1701	(1)	342:2
1706	(1)	342:2
1723	(1)	359:2
1752	(1)	343:4
1787	(1)	353:2
17th	(1)	346:1
1820	(2)	4:3; 308:1
1821	(2)	363:5,6
1844	(1)	364:6
1862-1930	(1)	353:3
1889	(2)	364:2; 365:3
1891	(1)	354:1
1892	(1)	365:4
1895	(1)	365:3
18th	(1)	350:2
1906	(2)	354:1,2
1911	(1)	354:2
1914	(1)	308:1
1916	(1)	354:2
1919	(1)	354:2
1919-1933	(1)	102:3
1923	(3)	334:2,5; 354:2
1924-1931	(1)	102:2
1924-1934	(1)	276:1

1925	(1)	101:1
1925-1929	(2)	104:1,1
1928-1931	(1)	102:2
1928-29	(1)	322:4
1929	(5)	100:2; 104:1; 128:1; 323:1; 327:2
1930	(3)	101:3; 140:3; 354:2
1931	(2)	113:1; 122:1
1932	(7)	9:3; 80:4; 104:1; 122:1; 128:1; 207:4; 223:5
1933	(4)	79:4,4; 101:3; 102:1
1933-1934	(1)	197:2
1934	(4)	72:5; 143:4; 176:4; 180:4
1935	(6)	38:5; 39:5; 59:4; 60:4; 101:1; 365:5
1936	(1)	364:5
a	(Count: 2646 – not included)	
abandon	(1)	360:2
abandoned	(1)	99:3
abandonment	(1)	48:1
abated	(1)	349:1
abating	(1)	179:2
abilities	(1)	150:2
ability	(2)	207:1; 369:1
able	(18)	18:5; 163:1; 173:1; 175:4; 197:2; 214:1,2; 219:3; 220:3; 250:1; 261:2; 328:1; 350:1; 354:1; 363:3,4; 378:1; 379:2
abnormal	(4)	91:1; 94:2; 154:2; 207:4
abnormally	(2)	307:1; 323:1
abolishing	(3)	294:1; 322:2,2
abolition	(1)	355:2
about	(50)	14:2; 61:2,2; 66:1; 84:3,3; 95:3; 123:4; 126:1,1,1; 148:2,2; 149:2; 158:2; 161:1; 172:2,2,2; 181:1; 186:3,3; 187:2; 188:1; 190:4; 200:2,2; 204:1; 208:4; 218:1; 221:3; 235:1; 240:3; 248:3; 249:3; 253:3,3; 264:2; 267:5; 269:2; 278:6; 293:2; 295:3; 308:1; 318:2; 324:3; 325:3; 332:1; 365:3; 379:1
above	(179)	7:3,5; 8:1; 16:1; 19:5; 24:4; 25:5; 29:1,2; 42:3; 46:3; 50:2,3,3; 55:1; 56:1,2; 57:1,1; 60:1,3; 61:2; 62:3; 63:2,2; 66:2; 67:3; 71:3; 72:4; 76:2,2; 77:1; 80:2; 83:1; 84:3; 92:2; 94:1; 98:3; 100:1; 104:1,2; 109:2; 110:3; 115:1; 118:2,2; 119:2, 2,2; 120:5; 124:1; 125:2; 126:2,3,3; 127:1,1,2; 128:2; 129:3;

above (cont.)		137:2,4; 139:2,2; 140:2,2; 146:2; 150:2;
		152:2; 159:1,1; 161:3; 164:3; 170:1,2;
		175:3; 178:1,2; 179:2; 180:1,2; 181:1,1;
		186:1; 189:3,5; 190:4; 191:2; 193:1,1;
		197:2; 202:2; 205:1; 207:3; 208:2,3; 209:1;
		212:1; 215:1,2; 216:1; 218:1,3; 219:1,1;
		221:3; 228:3; 229:1; 230:2; 231:2; 233:5;
		236:4; 237:1; 239:3,3; 240:2,4; 242:4;
		243:3,5; 244:1; 247:1; 249:2,2,3; 252:3;
		253:3; 254:3,4; 258:2,2; 263:3; 264:4;
		266:3; 269:2; 270:1; 271:2; 273:2; 274:4;
		275:3; 277:4; 278:4; 281:3; 282:2; 287:4;
		291:2; 294:1,3; 297:1; 299:3; 300:1; 302:4;
		303:3; 304:3,4,4; 305:3; 308:1,1; 315:3;
		316:3; 318:1; 319:4; 320:1,2,3; 321:3;
		327:3; 329:2; 330:2; 346:1; 353:2; 358:1,2;
		361:4,8; 363:3; 380:2; 381:4
abridged	(1)	342:4
abroad	(6)	262:6; 272:3; 336:1; 337:1,2; 360:3
absence	(7)	15:4; 151:1; 170:2; 196:5; 235:1,1; 241:2
absolute	(16)	40:2; 97:2,2,2; 111:1; 114:3; 125:3; 138:3;
		153:2; 191:2; 201:3; 207:3; 240:3; 247:2;
		301:3; 368:1
absolutely	(6)	106:1; 174:2; 216:1; 262:1; 333:1; 335:1
absorb	(7)	27:2; 100:2; 106:2; 171:2; 200:2; 202:2;
		288:1
absorbed	(15)	70:3,4; 71:4; 72:2; 100:1; 144:3; 171:2,4;
		200:2; 283:1; 288:1; 298:2,3; 301:2; 352:2
absorbing	(1)	318:2
absorbs	(1)	139:3
absorption	(5)	71:2,5; 318:2,2; 332:2
abstain	(2)	21:2; 167:2
abstaining	(3)	19:1; 210:2; 348:1
abstinence	(1)	373:3
abstract	(2)	175:4; 342:3
abstraction	(1)	149:2
abstractions	(1)	340:1
absurd	(9)	4:2; 10:2; 129:2; 154:1; 187:3; 211:2;
		323:1; 324:2; 351:4
absurdities	(1)	152:1
absurdity	(1)	346:2
abundance	(11)	131:2; 213:4,4; 220:1,1; 253:2; 315:3,5;
		321:3; 337:2; 347:1

abundant	(8)	221:2; 267:3; 307:2; 320:3; 321:2; 341:3; 349:1; 376:1
abuses	(1)	380:2
academic	(7)	3:1; 32:2; 106:3; 353:3; 355:1; 356:3; 383:3
accentuate	(3)	120:5; 153:3; 314:1
accentuated	(2)	101:1; 337:1
accept	(13)	6:1,2; 9:3,3; 10:1; 16:1,1; 18:2; 19:3; 131:2; 140:2; 178:1; 257:3
acceptable	(5)	10:3; 129:2; 307:3; 308:1; 309:2
acceptance	(3)	327:2; 355:2; 367:1
accepted	(12)	32:2; 58:2; 128:2; 129:2; 166:4; 175:1; 177:4; 203:3; 257:3; 348:3; 369:1; 378:2
accepting	(2)	11:1,3
accepts	(1)	277:3
accident	(2)	28:2; 349:1
accidental	(2)	308:1; 365:3
accommodated	(1)	106:1
accommodates	(1)	26:1
accompanied	(10)	12:1; 26:2; 97:1; 249:1; 259:2,2; 263:4; 265:2; 274:3; 369:1
accompanies	(2)	316:1; 328:1
accompaniment	(2)	17:3; 370:1
accompany	(6)	10:1; 81:1; 83:1; 248:2; 271:2; 328:1
accomplished	(4)	31:4; 215:2; 265:2; 378:1
accord	(1)	33:2
accordance	(6)	5:4; 65:1; 75:1; 169:2; 302:4; 333:1
according	(27)	6:3; 24:4; 29:5; 30:1; 109:3,3,3,3,3; 126:4; 176:4; 179:2; 188:3; 192:1; 193:1; 213:4,4; 224:3; 227:2; 239:4; 242:3; 269:4; 285:1; 320:3; 321:2; 357:1,1
accordingly	(5)	51:1; 188:1; 204:3; 321:3; 360:7
accords	(1)	252:3
account	(53)	7:2; 10:1; 33:3; 43:3; 56:1; 57:2,3,3; 58:2,2; 59:2,2; 63:1; 68:2; 75:1; 82:1; 91:1; 93:2; 95:2; 101:3; 112:1; 116:1; 119:2; 122:4; 128:1; 129:4; 131:1; 139:2,3; 146:1; 158:2; 175:1; 177:3; 184:2; 189:3,3,4; 202:1; 205:3; 227:2; 240:3; 245:2; 249:2; 271:3,3; 294:2; 299:1; 328:1; 335:1; 344:5; 347:2; 370:1; 382:2
accounting	(4)	58:2,2; 59:1; 66:2
accounts	(3)	121:3; 129:4; 160:1

accrue	(5)	43:3; 120:3; 283:1,1; 288:1
accrues	(5)	60:3; 121:1; 200:2,2; 327:2
accruing	(1)	121:1
accumulate	(5)	219:1; 221:2; 362:4,4; 363:1
accumulated	(7)	4:2; 98:1; 108:3; 188:2; 194:1; 221:2; 242:1
accumulation	(25)	31:3; 51:3,3; 97:2; 108:3; 109:1; 112:1; 192:1; 219:2,4; 221:2; 242:2; 318:2; 331:2; 335:3; 344:3,4; 362:4; 364:1; 367:2,3; 368:2; 377:2,2,2
accumulations	(4)	188:2; 189:4,4; 348:1
accuracy	(2)	114:3; 144:4
accurate	(7)	10:2; 78:1; 127:2; 187:2; 188:2; 203:3; 247:2
accurately	(3)	8:3; 40:2; 61:1
accustomed	(13)	3:2; 199:1; 204:3,3; 229:3; 232:2; 238:4; 257:1; 290:2; 292:1; 315:4; 374:2; 382:3
achieve	(3)	174:2; 270:1; 316:2
achieved	(2)	309:2; 372:2
achievement	(2)	192:1; 350:1
achieving	(1)	267:2
acknowledged	(1)	363:1
acorns	(1)	361:3
acquainted	(3)	257:2; 279:3; 353:3
acquiescence	(1)	289:3
acquire	(5)	47:2; 81:2; 97:2; 205:3; 233:4
acquired	(2)	58:2; 59:1
acquiring	(1)	81:2
acquisition	(1)	343:4
act	(30)	19:1; 20:3; 21:1,1; 64:1; 69:3,4; 70:1; 84:1; 177:2,2; 178:1,1; 187:1; 189:5,5; 210:1,1,1; 211:2,2,2; 212:1,1,1; 213:1; 261:2,2; 349:1; 370:1
action	(14)	19:5; 83:1; 108:1; 120:3; 129:4; 139:3; 161:4; 220:2; 235:1; 247:1; 267:3,3; 362:4; 381:1
actions	(1)	288:1
active	(5)	160:3; 264:1; 306:5; 319:2; 351:4
actively	(1)	212:1
activities	(17)	21:2; 33:1; 38:1; 40:2; 50:2; 52:2; 63:1; 130:1; 131:2; 159:1; 161:4; 200:2; 245:2; 294:1; 347:2; 374:2,2
activity	(20)	20:2,2,2; 44:2; 62:3; 104:3; 120:3; 158:3,3;

activity (cont.)		162:3; 163:1; 172:2; 173:1; 196:5; 197:1; 198:1; 199:1; 211:2; 249:4; 378:1
acts	(2)	108:1; 121:1
actual	(84)	4:2; 8:2,3; 9:4; 12:3; 30:2; 31:2,2; 40:1; 42:2; 48:2; 50:2; 52:4; 57:2; 58:2; 61:1; 66:2; 67:1; 68:1; 71:4; 77:1; 80:2; 93:3; 97:1; 99:2; 101:1,2; 109:1; 111:2,4; 113:1; 118:2; 119:2; 120:1; 136:4; 137:3; 149:2; 150:2; 152:1; 153:4; 155:2; 160:2; 168:1; 170:1; 174:2,2,2; 176:1; 187:3; 197:1; 203:3; 205:1; 206:2,2,2; 211:1; 219:1,2; 243:5,5; 249:2,2,3; 254:3; 260:1; 264:2; 265:3; 269:4; 270:1; 271:3; 272:1; 274:2; 275:2; 290:1; 301:3; 313:2; 335:2; 347:4; 357:1; 362:4; 367:3; 368:5; 378:2; 379:2
actually	(38)	3:1; 5:6; 10:3; 13:1,2; 20:2,2; 24:5; 34:1; 47:2; 60:3; 77:1; 81:2; 99:2; 100:1,1; 101:1,1; 110:3,3,3; 129:3; 135:2; 140:2; 144:2; 177:4; 180:1; 196:3; 206:2; 210:1; 247:2; 253:2; 278:1; 299:2; 343:4,4; 346:3; 368:2
actuarial	(3)	152:1; 169:2; 240:2
actuated	(1)	162:1
actuating	(1)	108:3
acuteness	(1)	308:2
Adam	(7)	352:2,2,3; 353:2; 361:8; 363:3; 368:2
adapt	(1)	97:1
adaptation	(2)	126:2; 146:2
adapted	(5)	9:1; 33:1; 42:1,1; 187:4
add	(14)	17:4; 56:1; 61:2; 84:2,3; 131:2; 139:3; 140:2; 156:3; 201:1; 251:2; 273:5; 321:3; 382:3
added	(6)	33:1; 144:3; 145:1; 188:2; 224:2; 330:1
addicted	(1)	374:2
adding	(1)	192:1
addition	(26)	6:2; 38:1,2; 47:1; 56:1; 62:3,3; 63:1; 64:1; 70:3; 75:1; 82:2; 130:2; 144:4; 170:1; 183:1; 230:2; 232:1; 240:3; 249:1; 301:3; 329:3; 330:1,1,1,1
additional	(38)	7:1; 17:4; 67:3; 70:2; 80:3; 82:2; 83:1,1; 97:2,2; 118:1; 119:2; 125:4; 127:1,1; 135:2; 138:2,4,4; 171:2; 177:2; 211:2; 217:2; 272:4,4,4,4,4; 273:5,5,5,5; 275:4,4,4;

after (cont.)		318:2; 319:1,1; 325:2; 331:2,2; 353:3; 383:3; 384:1
afterwards	(1)	365:3
again	(35)	20:4; 49:1; 101:1; 112:1; 120:2; 127:1; 129:3; 142:2; 176:1,1; 183:1; 191:1; 192:1; 206:2; 232:3; 243:5; 247:1; 253:2; 254:2; 261:2; 263:4; 264:2; 276:2; 288:1; 297:2; 328:2; 332:2; 336:3; 339:3; 345:3,3; 346:1; 378:2; 379:1; 382:1
against	(46)	5:7; 39:1,1; 60:1; 94:3; 99:2; 107:2; 108:1; 110:3; 135:2; 160:2; 188:2; 189:2; 226:4; 240:2; 241:2,4,4; 277:3; 319:1; 320:2,2; 326:3; 331:2; 332:2; 338:3; 339:2,2; 345:1,2; 346:3; 347:2; 351:3; 352:2; 355:2; 365:1,3,3; 368:4; 371:1; 378:2; 379:1,2; 380:2; 381:1; 382:3
age	(11)	94:1; 107:2; 109:2; 251:3; 308:1; 336:1; 340:3; 350:2; 353:2; 361:3; 384:1
agency	(1)	376:1
agents	(1)	368:2
ages	(5)	71:4; 131:2; 253:3; 348:5; 356:1
aggravate	(2)	316:1; 319:2
aggravated	(2)	100:1; 313:2
aggravating	(4)	101:1; 105:2; 128:1; 315:4
aggregate	(228)	14:1,2,3; 15:1,3,3; 17:4; 18:3; 20:2,2; 21:1; 22:1,1; 24:1,1,2,4,4,4,4,4,4,4; 25:2,2,2,3,3,3,3,3; 26:1,1,1,2,2,2,2,2; 27:2,2,2; 28:2,2,2,5; 29:2,3; 30:1,1,1; 32:2; 40:2,2,2; 41:1; 43:1,3; 44:1,2,2; 45:2,2,2; 54:1,4,4; 55:2,2,2,4,5,5,5; 56:2; 57:1,1; 60:3; 62:1,1,1; 64:1,2,2; 65:1,1; 67:3,3; 75:1,1,1,1; 77:2; 79:3; 80:1; 82:1; 83:1,2; 84:1,3; 85:2,2; 89:1,1,1,1,1,1,2; 90:2; 91:3; 92:1; 94:1; 95:2; 96:2,2,3,3; 97:2; 98:1,2; 100:1; 104:3,3; 105:1; 107:1; 110:3,3; 111:2,4; 113:1; 114:1; 115:3,5; 116:1,4; 117:2; 119:1,2; 121:1; 122:2,3; 123:2,3,3,3,3; 124:1,1; 127:1,2,2; 136:3,3; 139:1; 153:4; 167:2; 174:2; 176:1,1; 178:1,1; 185:1; 186:2,2,2; 188:1,1; 192:3; 195:1,3; 197:1; 209:1; 213:3; 215:3; 217:3; 218:2; 219:1; 221:3,3; 246:1; 248:2; 258:1,1,1; 259:2,2,2,2,2; 273:1,3; 274:3;

aggregate (cont.)		275:2; 276:1,1,1; 279:1; 280:1,1,1; 281:2,2,2,3; 282:1,2,2; 286:2,2,3,3,3,4; 293:1; 323:1; 324:1; 329:1; 330:1; 335:3,3; 367:2; 370:1; 375:2,3; 378:1,2; 381:1
aggregates	(3)	177:1; 368:2,2
aggregating	(1)	40:2
agitation	(1)	365:3
agitators	(1)	384:1
ago	(2)	40:1,1
agree	(7)	8:1; 19:3; 152:1; 258:1; 322:5; 360:7; 379:3
agreeable	(5)	61:2; 146:3; 215:2,2,2
agreed	(7)	61:2; 63:2; 152:1; 159:2; 177:3; 182:3; 257:3
agreement	(5)	8:1; 17:2; 178:1; 342:1,1
agrees	(3)	54:1; 74:2; 275:4
agricultural	(12)	241:2; 314:3; 323:1; 329:2,2; 331:1,1,1,1,2,3; 332:1
agriculture	(2)	330:1; 361:7
ahead	(7)	48:4; 109:1; 154:3; 217:1; 287:1; 332:2,2
aid	(4)	206:2; 304:3; 316:2; 367:2
aided	(1)	213:4
aids	(1)	130:1
aim	(6)	60:1; 266:1; 326:1; 352:2; 376:3; 377:2
aimed	(4)	113:1; 267:3; 288:1; 351:4
aiming	(3)	39:1; 325:3; 348:2
air	(2)	346:3; 383:3
aires	(3)	354:1,1,1
Albert	(1)	349:3
Alfred	(2)	20:4; 176:1
algebra	(2)	280:3; 297:2
alia	(1)	246:1
alike	(4)	14:1; 189:2; 219:3; 339:1
alive	(4)	180:1; 220:1; 338:3; 343:4
all	(211)	4:2; 13:1,1; 14:1; 18:5; 19:3; 20:2; 21:3; 22:1,2,2; 23:1; 25:4; 26:1,1,1,2,2; 29:4,5,5; 33:3,3; 38:1; 40:2; 42:1,2; 43:3; 46:1,1; 48:1,3; 60:2; 62:1; 63:2; 66:2; 67:3,3; 70:5,6; 71:4; 74:1; 75:1; 76:1; 80:3,3; 84:2; 90:2; 93:2; 94:1; 95:1; 97:2; 99:3,4; 103:1; 104:1,3; 105:2; 106:2; 109:3; 111:4,4; 120:4; 122:4; 129:2,4; 136:3; 137:4; 139:1; 140:3,3; 141:2; 144:3; 149:3; 152:1;

all (cont.)		156:1,2,3; 157:1; 160:1,2; 168:3,3; 171:3; 172:2; 174:2; 175:1; 178:1; 182:2,3; 183:1,1,1,1; 187:5; 189:3; 196:3; 199:1; 203:3; 205:3,3; 206:1,2; 209:3; 215:2,2; 224:3; 227:1; 228:1,3; 231:2; 232:3; 234:4; 235:1; 236:2,2; 239:4; 240:3; 252:1; 253:1,1,3; 260:1; 261:1; 264:2,2,4; 268:2; 269:4; 270:1; 273:5; 274:2,2; 275:1,4; 277:1,2; 278:4; 279:1; 289:3,3; 290:3; 292:1; 293:2,2; 294:1; 295:2,3; 296:2; 297:2,2; 298:1; 299:1; 300:3; 301:2; 302:2,4; 309:1; 313:2; 314:3; 323:1; 325:3; 327:2; 328:1,1; 329:1,2; 331:3; 332:1; 333:1; 334:2; 337:2; 338:3; 342:1; 343:1,4; 344:4; 346:1,4; 347:1,2; 348:1,1; 349:2; 352:2,2; 353:1; 359:1,1; 360:1,2,7; 361:7,7; 362:2; 363:4; 364:1; 366:1,3,4,4; 368:2,4; 370:1; 373:1; 378:1,1; 380:2,2; 381:1; 382:2
all-round	(3)	14:3; 269:3; 303:3
alleged	(2)	128:1; 369:1
allegorical	(1)	360:2
allegory	(1)	361:4
allied	(1)	351:2
allocate	(1)	67:1
allow	(24)	61:1; 64:2; 67:3; 73:2; 84:1; 120:4; 127:2; 161:2; 232:3; 240:2; 246:1,1; 253:1; 295:2; 297:2; 298:1; 308:1,2; 332:2; 352:1; 365:3; 371:1; 374:2; 376:1
allowance	(13)	59:1; 77:2; 90:2; 92:1; 99:2; 103:1; 145:2; 206:2; 208:2; 221:3; 309:2; 323:1; 375:3
allowances	(3)	99:4; 100:2; 208:2
allowed	(12)	92:1,2,3; 94:1; 118:2; 158:3; 260:1; 297:2; 307:3; 308:1; 334:2; 366:1
allowing	(19)	38:1; 59:2; 62:3; 63:1; 70:2; 73:2; 75:1; 121:3; 139:3; 140:2; 188:1,2; 203:1; 232:2; 240:2; 271:3,3; 273:5; 343:1
allows	(8)	6:2; 82:2,2; 93:2; 309:2; 356:1,2; 376:3
almost	(29)	10:1; 12:2; 19:3; 20:5; 100:2; 124:2; 171:2; 185:1; 203:2; 207:3; 211:2; 231:1; 247:2; 273:5; 307:2,3; 319:2; 333:1; 336:1; 338:2; 339:3; 346:3; 347:2; 351:3; 362:4,4; 364:2; 366:4; 375:3

12

alone	(10)	9:1; 20:5; 33:3; 67:3; 100:2; 182:3; 275:4; 335:3; 355:1; 366:4
along	(10)	70:5; 140:2; 155:1; 184:2; 193:1; 249:2; 267:2; 326:4; 355:2; 366:3
already	(35)	31:3; 37:1; 42:1; 81:1; 82:2; 89:1; 92:1; 94:1; 98:3; 99:2; 103:1; 104:2; 107:1; 115:1; 124:2; 127:1,2; 144:3; 169:4; 184:2; 186:1; 188:1; 202:1; 215:2; 228:2; 239:3; 245:3; 260:3; 267:5; 273:5; 277:1; 335:3; 345:4; 362:3,3
als	(1)	354:1
also	(123)	4:2; 6:2; 21:1; 29:6; 33:3; 49:1; 52:1; 54:3; 55:3; 56:1; 57:1; 59:1,3; 61:1; 62:3; 68:1; 70:3; 72:2; 75:1; 83:1; 84:1; 93:2; 94:2; 95:2; 97:2; 98:1,1; 102:2,3; 108:2,3; 109:2; 110:1; 117:3; 119:2; 120:5; 124:1; 125:3; 126:4; 127:1; 128:3; 129:3; 137:2; 139:1; 148:3; 150:3; 155:1; 156:3; 157:2,2; 158:2; 160:3; 170:1,3; 177:1,2; 178:1; 180:4; 181:1; 192:2; 194:1; 196:2,3; 198:1; 200:2; 202:2; 203:1; 206:2; 208:2; 209:2; 210:1; 213:4; 216:2,2; 218:2; 221:3; 223:2; 224:2,2; 226:4; 227:2,2; 230:2; 231:3; 235:1,1,1; 236:3; 238:1; 239:1,2; 249:2,3; 251:3; 252:1; 259:2; 262:5; 264:2; 266:3; 271:3; 274:1; 275:4; 276:3; 282:4; 289:3; 300:5; 302:2,3; 308:1; 314:1; 315:3,5; 319:2; 328:1; 332:2; 336:1; 338:3; 368:4; 369:2; 372:1,2; 380:2; 382:3
alter	(7)	94:1; 190:3,3; 198:2; 235:1; 289:3; 350:2
alteration	(1)	191:2
altered	(3)	186:2; 224:3; 276:2
alternate	(1)	253:3
alternative	(23)	15:3; 26:2; 32:2; 78:2; 82:1,1; 84:3; 160:2,2; 170:3; 200:2; 212:2; 216:2; 218:2; 224:3,3,3; 267:4; 271:3; 325:2; 358:2; 370:1; 374:2
alternatively	(7)	55:5; 136:3; 139:2; 181:2; 223:3; 243:5; 275:2
alternatives	(5)	163:1; 174:2; 227:2; 228:1; 327:2
although	(16)	8:3; 18:2; 33:2; 38:2; 48:2; 50:4; 58:1; 84:2; 140:3; 160:1; 178:1; 252:3; 287:1; 294:1; 316:3; 334:2

altogether	(10)	11:1; 42:1; 154:1; 279:2; 334:2; 340:3; 343:1; 355:2; 356:2; 364:2
Alvin	(1)	193:1
always	(52)	6:2; 10:1; 11:1; 12:1,2,2; 20:2; 24:4; 26:1,2; 30:1; 43:3; 48:2; 75:1; 78:2; 83:2; 99:2; 105:2; 112:1; 114:2; 142:3; 148:4; 158:3; 169:1; 187:4; 190:4; 191:1; 197:2; 201:2; 204:3; 209:1,2; 212:2; 239:4; 243:5,5; 253:2; 264:2; 267:3; 270:1; 273:3; 274:4,4; 278:1; 284:2; 291:2; 304:2; 307:2; 327:2; 336:1; 369:1,1
am	(24)	4:3; 17:3; 20:4; 24:4; 61:1; 79:2; 81:1; 127:2; 145:2; 153:2; 159:1; 164:3; 221:2; 243:2; 266:2; 270:2; 278:3; 279:3; 321:2; 325:2; 341:5; 373:3; 376:2; 383:3
ambiguities	(1)	138:2
ambiguity	(3)	103:1; 138:2; 272:4
ambiguous	(2)	188:3; 320:3
amended	(1)	38:5
America	(1)	327:2
America's	(1)	331:3
American	(8)	122:5; 154:1; 159:1,1,2; 332:2; 368:4; 380:3
Americans	(2)	155:2; 159:1
amidst	(3)	61:2; 340:3; 364:2
among	(4)	42:1; 277:4; 345:4; 363:2
amongst	(19)	4:3; 8:1; 11:2,2; 93:1; 147:2,2; 155:3,3; 226:4; 236:2,2; 297:2; 329:2; 343:4; 349:3; 351:3; 355:1; 364:2
amount	(188)	4:3; 5:5,7; 6:3; 11:2; 13:1; 14:2; 17:4; 22:2; 23:1; 24:1,1,2,2; 25:1; 26:1,1; 27:2,2,2,2,2,2; 28:2; 29:1,1,1; 41:1,1,1,1; 47:2; 49:1; 53:1; 55:2; 56:1; 57:1,1,1,3; 58:2,2; 61:1; 63:2,2; 64:1,2,2; 66:2; 68:1,1; 69:3,3,3; 70:1,1,3; 74:1; 79:3,3; 80:1,1; 82:1; 83:2; 84:2,2,2,2,3,3,3,3,3; 90:3,3; 91:3,3; 92:2,3; 96:3,3,4,4; 97:2,2; 98:1; 99:2; 101:1,1,1; 107:1; 108:3; 110:3,3; 111:1,2,2; 113:1,1; 114:2,2; 115:3; 120:4; 122:2; 123:2; 140:1; 167:2; 168:2; 171:2,4; 174:2,2; 175:2,2; 178:1,1; 179:1,1,2,2; 180:1,3; 181:2; 187:1,3,3,3; 188:1,2,2,4; 189:5,5,5; 190:3; 192:1; 195:3; 196:3,5;

amount (cont.)		197:2; 199:2,3,3; 202:1,1; 205:3; 211:1; 213:1; 214:2,2; 215:3,3; 218:2; 224:3; 226:2; 228:1,3; 247:2; 248:2; 259:2; 261:2,2; 265:2,2; 266:1; 274:3; 276:1,1; 280:1,1,1,1,1; 282:2,2; 286:2; 287:1; 288:1; 291:2,2; 299:1; 303:3,3; 331:1; 342:1; 358:3; 366:1; 378:1
amounted	(1)	101:1
amounting	(1)	337:2
amounts	(22)	15:3; 19:1; 23:1,1; 26:2; 63:2; 65:1; 80:1,1; 84:3; 110:3; 150:1; 166:3; 178:1; 179:2,2; 181:1; 199:2; 274:1,2,2; 375:2
ampler	(1)	31:2
amplitude	(1)	122:2
an	(Count: 597 – not included)	
analogous	(8)	5:6; 79:2; 84:3; 108:3; 169:4; 234:2; 241:2; 268:1
analogue	(1)	222:2
analogy	(5)	20:2; 130:1; 260:1; 301:3; 350:4
analysed	(4)	68:1; 144:1; 148:4; 353:3
analysing	(4)	43:2; 66:2; 195:2; 262:2
analysis	(59)	9:3; 30:3; 31:4; 37:2; 39:1,2,3,4; 40:1,1; 43:3; 67:1,3; 68:3; 78:2; 89:1; 107:1; 124:2; 146:1; 176:4; 177:3; 183:2; 184:1; 194:1; 195:1; 199:2; 205:2; 241:1; 243:2; 245:3; 247:1; 250:3; 257:2; 258:2,2,2; 260:1,2; 272:2; 273:5; 274:2; 275:1,3,4; 276:3; 277:4; 279:2; 296:3; 297:2,2; 298:3; 313:2; 320:2,3; 321:2; 350:1; 378:2,2; 381:2
analytically	(1)	267:4
ancient	(6)	131:2; 168:2; 333:1; 351:3,3; 362:2
and	(Count: 2123 – not included)	
animal	(3)	161:4; 162:1,2
annual	(6)	94:1; 99:3; 101:1; 102:3; 104:1; 140:2
annually	(4)	59:1; 71:4; 139:3; 368:2
annuities	(3)	135:1,2; 224:3
annuity	(2)	94:1,1
annum	(13)	104:1; 139:3,3; 140:1; 202:1,1,1; 222:2,2; 223:3; 224:3; 318:2; 357:1
another	(57)	6:2; 19:2; 20:1,2; 24:4; 25:3; 28:2; 38:1; 39:1; 42:1; 44:1; 50:4; 53:1; 62:1,1,1; 64:1; 69:2; 80:1; 81:2; 91:1; 142:2; 151:1; 159:1;

another (cont.)		163:2; 169:3; 175:2; 177:1; 179:1,2; 182:2; 184:1; 188:2; 189:3; 192:1; 195:1; 199:2; 228:1; 229:1; 238:3; 240:1; 314:1,1,2; 326:2; 329:2; 337:1; 343:4; 344:2; 356:1; 360:7; 362:3; 365:3; 366:1; 369:1; 380:3; 382:3
answer	(11)	105:1; 166:1; 243:5; 260:1; 276:2,2; 297:2; 334:2; 355:2; 369:1; 383:3
answered	(3)	156:3; 222:1; 260:3
answering	(1)	260:2
answers	(1)	165:2
anti-marxian	(1)	355:2
anti-social	(1)	155:2
anticipate	(3)	154:2; 155:3; 215:3
anticipated	(3)	76:1; 107:2; 112:2
anticipating	(4)	83:1; 100:1; 156:2; 208:3
anticipation	(3)	51:1; 54:4; 155:2
Antonio	(1)	355:1
anxiety	(2)	109:1; 333:1
anxious	(2)	148:4; 342:2
any	(Count: 242 – not included)	
anyhow	(1)	194:1
anyone	(8)	21:1; 155:3; 157:1; 168:2; 169:3; 198:2; 208:1; 328:2
anything	(9)	21:1; 100:1; 129:1; 233:2; 243:2; 265:1; 273:5; 352:2; 356:2
anytime	(1)	247:2
anywhere	(1)	182:3
apace	(1)	360:7
apart	(36)	10:2; 16:1; 20:2; 32:2; 63:1,1; 69:2,3,3; 75:2; 92:1; 94:1; 97:2; 106:3; 108:3; 150:2; 161:4; 171:2; 186:1; 214:1,2; 221:3; 225:6; 234:3; 235:1; 264:2; 268:2; 270:3; 280:2; 300:2; 328:1; 340:3; 357:1; 379:1; 381:2; 383:3
apex	(1)	305:2
appalled	(1)	367:1
appalling	(2)	104:1; 360:2
apparatus	(1)	340:1
apparel	(1)	359:1
apparent	(9)	9:3; 16:1,1; 33:1; 84:2; 229:1; 291:2; 348:3; 353:3
apparently	(8)	8:1; 13:1; 16:2; 21:1; 33:2; 277:3; 292:1; 346:4

16

appeal	(2)	32:2; 380:2
appeals	(1)	203:2
appear	(5)	21:2; 74:1; 91:2; 320:2; 326:4
appearance	(1)	364:2
appeared	(1)	350:3
appearing	(1)	366:1
appears	(11)	9:2; 19:5; 140:2; 206:2; 229:2; 258:3; 303:3; 329:2; 364:1; 367:1,3
appended	(1)	352:3
appendix	(15)	7:4; 8:4; 13:4; 18:2; 24:4; 53:3; 55:4; 66:1; 165:2; 175:4; 177:1; 184:4; 260:4; 334:3,3
appetite	(1)	349:1
applaud	(1)	382:3
applicable	(8)	3:1; 11:3; 16:2; 64:2; 73:3; 187:2; 216:1; 276:1
application	(7)	244:1; 272:2; 273:5; 284:2; 346:3; 352:2,2
applications	(1)	190:3
applied	(15)	20:2; 33:2; 40:2; 61:2; 67:3,3; 81:1; 139:3; 230:2; 250:4; 260:1; 275:3; 306:1; 327:2; 329:2
applies	(4)	106:2; 126:2; 285:2; 373:2
apply	(18)	3:1; 11:3; 16:2; 71:5; 99:2; 119:2; 151:3; 194:1; 260:2; 265:2; 266:3; 268:1; 273:5; 285:2; 357:1,2; 374:1; 384:1
applying	(10)	14:1; 114:2; 131:2; 191:2; 206:2; 248:3; 289:3,3; 290:1; 297:2
appreciable	(2)	208:2; 348:4
appreciably	(5)	93:3; 219:1; 254:3,3; 327:3
appreciate	(2)	184:3; 224:3
appreciated	(1)	99:2
appreciation	(8)	94:1; 106:3; 107:2; 142:2; 159:1; 227:2; 228:1; 349:3
apprehension	(2)	359:7; 382:3
approach	(4)	19:1; 127:1; 220:2; 329:2
approached	(3)	127:1,1; 288:1
approaches	(2)	70:4; 287:1
approaching	(3)	100:1; 203:1; 233:2
appropriate	(24)	31:3; 37:2; 39:1; 55:4; 66:1; 157:1; 158:3; 164:2; 181:1,1,1; 182:2; 195:3; 198:2; 215:3; 270:1,1; 273:5; 278:1; 324:2; 341:2; 342:1; 357:1; 382:3
appropriately	(3)	68:1; 141:2; 303:2
approval	(1)	346:1

approved	(1)	58:2
approximate	(5)	39:4; 43:2; 127:2; 241:4; 288:1
approximately	(5)	51:2; 220:3; 230:2; 250:1; 323:2
approximation	(12)	78:2; 90:2; 92:1; 93:2; 174:2; 199:2; 248:3; 286:3; 302:4,4; 377:2; 378:1
April	(1)	354:2
apt	(9)	57:3; 97:1; 100:1; 129:2; 145:2; 159:1; 324:2; 332:2; 342:3
arbeitsertrag	(1)	354:2
arbitrary	(4)	59:1; 153:2; 247:2; 372:1
arc	(1)	29:4
arches	(2)	359:1; 362:2
ardour	(1)	364:2
are	(Count: 661 – not included)	
area	(1)	138:2
Argentine	(1)	354:1
arguable	(2)	327:2; 338:2
argue	(6)	3:1; 12:2; 13:2; 55:4; 258:1; 370:1
argued	(5)	71:5; 77:2; 188:2; 191:2; 359:1
argues	(4)	177:1; 189:2; 355:3; 357:1
arguing	(4)	7:3; 152:1; 212:2; 258:1
argument	(55)	5:7; 8:3; 12:4; 17:4; 27:1; 72:5; 78:1; 109:3; 111:2; 113:1; 116:1; 137:5; 140:2,2; 171:2; 184:2; 189:5,5; 191:2; 192:2; 193:1; 228:3; 240:2; 245:1; 247:3; 257:3; 259:1,1,2,2,2; 264:5; 266:2; 272:2; 276:2; 277:1,1,3; 285:2; 320:2; 326:4; 334:1; 338:3; 344:5; 346:3,3; 353:3; 365:3; 366:1; 367:1; 368:5; 370:1; 372:2; 373:3; 374:3
arguments	(12)	3:1; 78:1; 148:5; 271:3; 322:5; 328:1; 334:2; 335:2; 344:4; 365:3; 368:3,4
arise	(11)	24:4; 43:3; 61:2; 74:2; 169:2; 183:1; 207:2,3; 213:2; 246:3; 317:3
arisen	(1)	99:2
arises	(8)	43:1; 144:2; 205:2; 206:2; 211:2; 231:5; 234:3; 308:2
arising	(5)	14:1; 191:1; 288:1; 323:1; 363:2
arithmetical	(2)	138:2; 346:1
arithmetically	(1)	152:1
arithmetick	(1)	342:1
armaments	(1)	360:2
armed	(1)	327:2
Armstrong	(1)	347:1

assumption (cont.)		304:2; 305:3; 329:1; 334:4; 368:4
assumptions	(29)	9:1; 20:4; 21:4; 22:2; 24:4; 28:2; 30:1; 42:3; 43:3; 127:1; 146:2; 190:1,4; 192:5; 209:2; 220:3; 272:2; 276:1; 277:3,3,4; 281:2; 295:3; 296:2; 298:1; 306:3; 321:4; 327:2; 378:2
assuredly	(1)	238:1
assuring	(1)	309:1
asymmetry	(4)	291:2,2; 303:3; 304:1
at	(Count: 485 − not included)	
athenaeum	(1)	334:5
Atlantic	(1)	149:4
atmosphere	(2)	155:2; 162:3
atomic	(1)	247:1
attach	(3)	148:2; 239:4; 305:3
attached	(1)	357:2
attaches	(1)	75:3
attaching	(6)	159:1; 226:2; 237:1,1; 242:1,1
attack	(2)	366:2; 367:1
attacks	(1)	347:2
attain	(6)	204:1; 212:1; 220:3; 222:1; 223:4; 382:3
attained	(7)	48:2; 97:2; 159:1; 290:3; 291:1; 309:1; 340:1
attainment	(1)	339:1
attempt	(41)	3:1; 5:7; 12:2; 13:2; 32:1; 33:1; 37:1; 38:1; 39:3; 78:1,2; 81:1,1,1; 84:2,2,2; 91:1; 118:3; 150:1; 153:1; 176:3; 183:1,1; 184:2; 187:3; 239:1; 247:3; 269:4; 274:2; 279:3; 292:1; 305:3; 332:1; 362:4,4; 363:1; 365:3; 366:1; 375:1; 383:3
attempting	(3)	43:2; 151:1; 166:4
attempts	(5)	103:1; 157:1; 189:5; 333:1; 351:4
attend	(2)	67:3; 160:1
attendant	(6)	91:1; 215:2,2,2; 298:3; 318:3
attends	(2)	39:2; 327:2
attention	(10)	72:5; 138:4; 148:4; 154:3; 157:2; 199:1; 331:2; 338:1; 340:1; 379:3
attitude	(12)	8:2; 21:3; 247:1; 248:1; 345:4; 346:1; 350:2,3; 351:4; 352:2; 372:2; 373:3
attract	(1)	288:1
attracted	(1)	33:1
attracting	(1)	236:5
attraction	(2)	110:3; 130:2

attractions	(3)	130:2; 233:3; 240:3
attractive	(3)	31:3; 160:2; 359:3
attractiveness	(1)	187:3
attributable	(3)	6:2; 52:2; 263:1
attribute	(5)	241:3,3,3; 324:2; 331:2
attributed	(2)	15:1; 225:2
attributes	(3)	225:4; 294:1,1
attributing	(1)	229:3
attribution	(1)	239:2
audiences	(1)	366:1
auf	(1)	354:2
Aug.	(1)	39:5
augment	(2)	348:1,1
augmenteth	(1)	345:2
augmenting	(1)	378:1
August	(2)	60:4; 176:4
auspices	(1)	106:2
austere	(3)	33:1; 327:3; 362:2
Australia	(3)	269:4; 270:1,1
Austrian	(1)	76:2
author	(2)	298:1; 383:3
authoritarian	(2)	269:3; 381:2
authorities	(16)	58:2; 60:1; 101:1,1,1,1,1,3; 129:4; 163:2; 204:3; 207:3; 336:2,2; 338:1; 348:4
authority	(41)	33:1,1; 106:2; 113:1; 119:4; 164:1; 177:2; 191:1,2,2,2,2,2; 202:2; 203:1,2; 204:1,3; 205:1,2,2,3; 206:2,2,2,2; 207:1,3,3; 230:2,3; 243:5; 247:2; 297:2; 317:1; 335:3; 365:3; 367:1; 374:2; 378:1; 383:3
authority's	(1)	207:2
authors	(2)	79:2; 366:2
authorship	(1)	354:1
automatic	(3)	176:1; 180:1; 264:2
automatically	(3)	31:3; 177:2,2
autonomous	(2)	349:1,2
available	(63)	4:2,2; 7:1; 10:2; 13:1,2; 30:2,2; 38:1; 42:1,1,1,2; 57:3; 59:3; 99:2,2,3; 104:2; 126:3; 127:2; 130:1,1; 145:1; 160:1,2; 161:2; 167:2,2; 171:2,2; 174:2; 183:1; 189:2,5,5; 197:3; 202:1; 212:2; 218:1; 236:2; 240:2; 245:2,2; 273:5; 274:1,2,3; 277:1; 289:2,2; 296:2; 300:4; 303:1; 309:2; 332:2; 335:1; 336:1,2; 341:1,3; 368:2;

balance (cont.)		348:4; 363:3; 374:2; 382:2,3
balanced	(4)	66:2; 99:2; 170:1; 183:1
balances	(3)	6:3; 84:3; 306:5
balancing	(3)	165:2; 174:2; 220:2
bank	(19)	81:2,2; 82:2; 167:3; 168:2; 190:3,3,3; 196:3; 198:1; 206:1,1; 208:2,2; 235:2; 247:1; 339:3,3; 374:2
bank's	(1)	189:2
bank-credit	(5)	79:2; 82:2; 83:1,1,1
bank-holiday	(1)	154:1
bank-money	(5)	188:2; 189:4; 308:1; 357:1; 358:1
bank-notes	(1)	237:1
banker	(1)	177:2
bankers	(6)	130:1; 189:2,2,2; 317:1; 339:3
banking	(23)	11:3; 81:2,2; 82:1,2; 84:3; 85:1; 190:1; 191:1; 197:2; 200:2; 201:2; 205:2,3; 206:2,2; 207:3; 208:2; 243:5; 267:3; 327:2; 336:1; 378:1
banknotes	(1)	129:3
banks	(6)	157:1; 167:3; 189:5,5,5; 200:2
bar	(1)	14:1
Barbon	(1)	359:1
Barbon's	(1)	359:2
bare	(2)	5:1; 361:3
barely	(1)	343:2
bargain	(2)	13:2,2
bargaining	(4)	6:2; 8:1; 253:1; 267:5
bargains	(7)	10:3,3; 11:2; 12:2; 13:2; 247:1; 264:2
barometer	(1)	151:1
barren	(2)	357:1; 361:5
base	(3)	51:1; 265:1; 383:3
based	(25)	5:2; 11:3,3; 20:1; 51:2; 60:1; 93:3; 121:2; 147:2; 148:3; 152:1,1; 157:1; 162:1; 179:2; 185:1; 193:1; 210:1; 253:3; 273:5; 315:3; 334:1,2; 355:2; 368:4
bases	(1)	258:3
basic	(4)	20:4; 59:1; 68:1; 378:1
basis	(31)	7:3; 38:1,2; 40:1; 59:1,1; 122:3; 148:1; 149:4,4; 152:1; 153:2; 154:2,3; 155:3,3; 159:1; 162:1; 163:1; 164:3; 180:1; 188:1; 203:1; 228:2; 247:2; 264:2; 315:3; 323:1; 346:3; 361:4; 368:2

24

Basle	(1)	354:2
battle	(1)	155:3
Bavaria	(1)	354:2
be	(Count: 1313 – not included)	
bear	(5)	69:5; 92:3; 171:2; 196:5; 232:1
bearing	(4)	275:2; 368:3; 372:1; 375:1
bearish	(1)	171:2
bearishness	(2)	173:2,2
bears	(6)	55:5; 102:2; 170:1; 223:2; 234:3; 319:4
beat	(2)	155:2; 157:1
beauty	(1)	33:1
became	(4)	100:2; 204:3; 353:3; 354:2
because	(85)	10:1; 15:3,3; 18:5; 20:2; 37:1; 48:1; 55:2; 61:1; 68:2; 69:5; 94:1; 107:2; 115:2; 121:1; 129:2; 130:1; 136:3,3; 141:3; 142:1,2; 143:2,3; 145:3; 149:1; 153:1; 171:2; 172:1; 183:2; 196:4,4; 197:2; 202:2; 203:1,1,2; 204:3; 211:2; 213:3,3; 214:2,2; 215:2; 223:4,4; 228:1; 230:3; 231:1; 232:4; 233:1; 235:2; 248:2; 250:4; 253:1,1; 258:1; 261:2; 263:3; 279:3,3; 286:2,2; 317:3,3; 321:2; 324:1; 328:1,1; 330:2,2; 333:1; 338:2; 341:5; 343:4; 345:2; 350:4; 356:1,2; 358:3,3; 366:2; 376:1,1; 382:3
become	(33)	3:2; 20:4; 25:3; 31:2; 64:1; 80:2; 82:2; 127:1,1; 129:3; 145:2; 182:2; 188:2; 204:3; 207:3,3; 213:3; 214:2,2; 215:3; 217:3; 218:2; 240:1; 292:1,1; 306:3; 317:3; 340:1; 345:2; 346:3; 349:1; 364:1; 376:1
becomes	(16)	39:3; 55:2; 72:2; 137:2; 153:1; 159:1,1; 174:2; 181:1; 184:2; 191:2; 213:3; 215:2; 217:3; 260:1; 366:4
becoming	(2)	332:2; 337:1
been	(Count: 217 – not included)	
bees	(3)	106:1; 359:2; 360:2
before	(56)	8:1; 12:2; 30:3; 48:1; 49:1,1; 50:2; 51:3; 59:2; 70:3; 71:4; 94:1,1; 98:2,3; 100:1; 101:1; 104:2; 114:1; 124:2; 131:2; 137:5; 153:1; 156:1; 162:1; 167:1; 169:2; 180:1; 184:2; 219:1; 226:1; 236:3; 250:1,1; 253:3,3; 254:2; 259:2,2; 260:2; 261:2; 288:1; 291:1; 296:2; 299:1; 301:2; 309:2; 317:2; 318:1; 331:2; 340:3; 344:1; 348:4;

before (cont.)		365:5; 376:1; 379:1
beg	(1)	347:1
began	(3)	331:3; 343:4; 365:3
begin	(13)	71:4; 138:2; 148:1; 177:3; 189:5,5; 217:1; 228:2; 245:1; 281:3; 294:1; 300:4; 336:3
beginning	(5)	49:1; 52:2; 56:1; 293:2; 315:2
begins	(5)	251:2; 276:2; 302:3; 317:2,3
begun	(3)	48:1; 290:3; 318:3
behave	(2)	34:1; 157:1
behaves	(1)	9:2
behaviour	(17)	12:3; 17:1; 24:5; 26:2; 43:2; 47:2; 63:2,2; 85:2,2; 98:1; 150:1; 152:1; 155:1; 157:1; 241:1; 248:2
behind	(5)	33:1; 109:1; 142:2; 258:2; 357:2
being	(195)	3:1; 9:2; 10:1,1; 12:2,2,2; 16:1; 20:1; 25:2,2; 31:3; 33:3; 41:1; 42:1; 43:3; 44:1; 46:2,2; 50:2,3; 51:1; 53:2,2; 54:3,3; 58:2; 60:1; 61:1; 63:1; 64:2; 67:3; 70:3,4; 71:4; 72:3; 74:1; 75:1; 76:1; 77:2; 78:1,2,2; 80:3; 81:2; 84:2; 93:3; 96:3; 97:2; 98:3; 99:2; 100:1,1; 101:1; 110:2; 115:4; 118:2,2,2; 124:1; 128:1; 129:3; 131:2; 135:2; 136:3; 138:3; 140:1; 143:1; 148:1,2; 153:1; 156:2; 161:2; 163:2,2; 165:1; 167:2; 169:2; 175:3; 180:1; 181:1; 182:2,2; 183:1; 184:1; 185:1; 186:2; 187:4,4; 189:2; 191:2; 194:1; 195:4; 198:1; 199:1,2; 201:3; 203:2,2; 204:1; 206:2; 208:2; 209:2,2; 211:2; 212:1; 213:1,3; 217:3; 218:3; 219:1,3; 225:1,3,6; 226:4,4; 228:2; 229:3; 232:4; 234:2,3,4; 235:1; 236:4; 237:1,2,2; 238:2,4; 241:4; 246:1; 247:1; 248:2,4; 250:1,4; 252:2; 260:2,3; 263:1; 265:2; 268:1; 270:1,1; 273:2,5; 274:3; 275:4; 276:2; 277:1; 278:1; 280:1; 283:1; 289:3; 291:2; 292:1; 293:2; 295:2; 300:3,3,5; 305:3; 313:2; 315:3; 319:3,3; 321:2; 322:3; 323:1,1; 328:1; 331:1; 332:1; 343:1,3,4; 345:2; 350:1; 353:3; 354:1,2,2; 355:2; 357:1; 361:7; 365:4; 367:2; 369:1; 370:1; 371:1; 373:3; 374:2; 376:3; 380:2
belated	(1)	206:2
belief	(12)	12:2; 43:2; 157:1; 177:2; 178:1; 263:1;

belief (cont.)		267:2,2; 328:1; 358:3; 372:2; 373:2
beliefs	(2)	350:1,2
believe	(17)	11:3; 12:2; 39:1; 138:2; 139:2; 152:1; 155:1,1; 156:2; 177:4; 266:2; 335:1; 348:3; 351:4; 355:2; 374:2; 383:3
believed	(14)	13:3; 170:3; 177:4; 202:1; 242:3; 265:2; 345:1; 346:1,1,4; 347:3; 358:3,3; 382:3
believes	(5)	159:1; 170:1,3; 265:2; 278:3
believing	(1)	212:1
bellicosity	(1)	381:4
belong	(1)	200:2
belonged	(1)	43:3
belonging	(2)	20:5; 203:1
belongs	(5)	43:3; 59:2; 189:3,3; 323:1
below	(73)	6:1,2; 7:4; 8:4; 9:2; 10:2; 12:4; 13:1; 15:1,3; 30:1; 31:5; 32:2; 49:1; 53:4; 68:3; 69:8; 90:2; 93:4; 97:3; 104:1; 119:5; 122:5; 124:1; 129:2; 144:1; 150:2; 170:3; 176:2; 181:1; 182:5; 202:2; 203:2; 208:2,2,3; 209:4; 211:1; 213:1; 216:2; 218:1; 229:1; 232:5; 233:2,4; 243:7; 245:2; 246:3,4; 253:3; 254:3,3; 257:3; 269:4; 270:1; 276:3; 287:2; 291:2; 301:3; 303:3; 304:1; 308:1,1,1; 309:2; 322:5; 325:1; 326:1; 332:2; 334:2; 368:2; 370:1; 377:2
benefactor	(1)	363:3
beneficial	(2)	303:3; 327:2
benefit	(5)	70:1; 120:3; 124:2; 335:2; 360:1
benefiting	(1)	339:5
benefits	(3)	161:4; 162:1,2
benign	(1)	382:3
Bentham	(8)	80:3,3; 352:2,2,2,2; 353:2,5
Bentham's	(2)	80:3; 352:2
Benthamite	(1)	81:1
bequeath	(1)	108:1
Berlin	(3)	354:2,2,2
Bernard	(1)	359:2
besides	(3)	119:2; 268:2; 376:2
best	(42)	7:2; 16:1; 33:3,3; 46:1; 64:3; 109:2; 127:2; 131:2; 141:2; 143:1; 148:3; 156:2,3; 159:1; 163:1; 170:1; 172:2; 180:1; 212:2; 216:1,1,1; 239:4; 240:2,2; 262:1; 268:2; 290:2; 305:3; 313:2; 315:2; 327:1; 345:1;

best (cont.)   347:2; 348:3; 351:2; 359:2,7; 375:1;
                                380:2,2
bestrewed   (1)   353:5
better   (32)   39:3; 40:1; 48:1,1; 59:2; 83:1; 98:1;
                                129:1,3; 130:1,2; 157:1; 158:1; 170:2;
                                190:4; 195:1; 216:1,1; 232:4; 243:3; 265:2;
                                275:2,4; 286:3; 301:2; 302:4; 316:3; 325:2;
                                335:1; 353:3; 374:2; 380:2
between   (239)   4:1; 5:6; 6:2,2; 9:4; 11:2,2; 12:2; 13:3;
                                14:2; 16:1; 21:3; 23:1; 25:2,2,3,4; 26:2;
                                28:1,2,5; 29:5; 30:1,1,1,2; 31:2; 33:2; 38:2;
                                43:3; 44:1,2; 45:2; 46:1; 51:1; 57:3;
                                58:2,2,2; 61:2; 62:1; 63:3,3; 64:1,2; 67:1;
                                68:1; 69:6; 70:1; 71:1,4; 73:2,3; 75:2;
                                77:1,2; 79:1,2,2,3,4; 80:1; 81:2; 82:2; 83:1;
                                84:2; 85:2; 90:2,2,2; 91:1; 92:1,2,2,2; 93:2;
                                94:1; 95:3; 97:1,2; 105:1,2; 107:2;
                                113:1,1,1,1; 115:2; 116:1; 118:2; 122:4;
                                123:2,4; 125:3; 130:1; 135:2,2; 138:4,4;
                                140:3; 142:2; 145:1,1,3,4; 147:1,1; 150:3;
                                151:1,1,2; 154:3; 161:2; 163:1,2; 167:1,3;
                                168:2; 173:1,2,2; 174:1; 176:1; 178:1;
                                179:2; 181:1; 182:2; 183:1; 186:3,3; 190:3;
                                191:2; 192:3; 194:1; 195:3,3,4,4; 197:3;
                                199:3; 201:1,2,3; 202:1; 205:2,3; 206:2;
                                209:2; 214:2; 216:2; 223:2,4; 224:2; 226:1;
                                227:1,2,2; 229:1; 232:3; 237:1; 238:3;
                                239:1; 240:2; 242:3; 246:1; 247:1;
                                248:1,2,2,2; 253:2; 258:3; 261:2,2; 267:4;
                                268:2; 269:4; 270:1; 271:3; 273:2; 274:3;
                                275:3,3; 277:3,4; 278:3,4; 279:2; 281:3;
                                282:1; 284:3; 286:2,3; 287:2; 291:2;
                                293:1,1,1,2,2,2,2; 294:1; 296:3; 297:2,2,2;
                                298:3; 299:1,2,3; 305:3; 306:5; 307:1;
                                308:1,1; 309:3; 317:2,2; 329:2; 330:1;
                                332:2; 335:3; 342:3; 343:1,4; 344:2,4;
                                346:1; 350:1,2,4; 355:3; 356:2; 362:4;
                                370:1; 379:1,1,1
beyond   (19)   9:2,3; 15:3; 25:3; 56:1; 66:2; 154:3; 158:3;
                                205:1; 233:2; 271:3; 290:2; 300:3; 303:3;
                                306:5; 350:2; 369:1; 375:1; 378:1
biassed   (1)   341:5
bidding   (1)   197:2

bilateral	(1)	63:3
bill	(2)	41:2; 360:5
bills	(3)	167:3; 206:1; 342:1
biography	(2)	359:2; 362:5
birds	(1)	347:3
bitten	(1)	183:1
bitterly	(1)	347:2
blame	(1)	257:1
blessed	(1)	349:2
blessing	(1)	357:1
blessings	(1)	367:1
blind	(3)	297:2; 339:3; 349:1
blindly	(1)	297:2
board	(1)	365:3
boards	(2)	101:1; 157:1
bodies	(2)	220:1; 349:3
bodily	(1)	9:1
body	(3)	6:1; 11:3; 15:3
Böhm-Bawerk	(2)	183:3; 214:3
Böhm-Bawerkian	(1)	176:4
boldly	(1)	207:3
bombarded	(1)	353:3
Bonar	(1)	350:4
bond	(4)	168:2; 171:2; 198:1; 200:2
bond-prices	(1)	199:1
bonds	(10)	171:2,2,2; 197:1,2,2,2; 198:1; 206:1; 241:2
bonus	(2)	218:2; 376:3
book	(43)	3:1; 5:7; 18:6; 31:3; 37:2; 77:2; 89:1; 90:1,1; 95:5; 103:2; 109:3; 112:2; 114:2; 119:3; 137:3; 149:2; 166:2; 186:1; 195:1; 201:4; 202:2; 260:1; 272:1; 275:2,2; 277:2; 281:1; 287:4; 313:2; 319:4; 352:4; 353:3; 355:2,2; 359:2,3; 364:4; 365:1,2,3,4; 366:1
book's	(1)	359:2
books	(4)	89:1; 103:1; 354:1; 370:1
boom	(30)	9:3; 128:1; 144:1; 145:2; 218:1; 265:2; 315:2,5; 317:3; 320:2,2,2; 321:1,2,3,3,3; 322:2,2,3,3,4,5; 323:1; 326:4; 327:2,2; 328:1; 329:1; 331:2
booms	(2)	322:2; 324:2
boon	(1)	345:1
booths	(1)	365:3
boots	(1)	210:1

bore	(1)	79:2
boring	(1)	157:1
born	(1)	353:6
borne	(1)	290:1
borrow	(6)	145:1; 151:2; 158:2; 189:5; 190:3; 207:3
borrowed	(6)	82:2; 98:1; 157:1; 187:5; 251:3; 319:2
borrower	(9)	144:4; 145:1,1,1; 208:2,2,2,2; 309:2
borrower's	(2)	144:2; 145:2
borrowers	(3)	79:3; 219:1; 309:2
borrowing	(8)	95:2; 109:2; 122:1; 128:3; 144:3; 170:1; 186:3; 196:3
borrowings	(1)	129:4
both	(82)	3:1; 15:3; 16:1; 24:2,4,4,4; 28:4; 46:1; 52:1; 53:1; 57:2; 62:2; 63:2; 67:3; 72:2; 78:1; 79:3; 85:2; 96:3,4,4; 98:1; 111:1; 118:2; 123:3; 127:2; 138:2; 145:2,2; 158:2; 179:2; 182:3; 183:3; 188:2; 196:4; 197:3; 203:1; 205:3; 206:2; 209:2; 216:1,2; 219:3; 228:2; 230:2; 234:3; 238:1; 239:3; 240:2; 248:2; 251:3; 253:1; 254:3; 262:6; 263:3; 287:2; 294:2; 315:4; 318:3; 319:1,3; 325:3,3; 331:1,2; 333:1,1; 334:4; 336:2; 341:2,4; 346:1; 348:5; 359:1; 361:7; 362:2,4; 363:2,3; 380:3; 383:3
bottle-necks	(4)	300:3,4; 301:1; 322:4
bottles	(1)	129:3
bottom	(7)	16:1,1; 104:1; 183:1; 236:1; 265:2; 279:2
bottomless	(1)	231:4
bought	(4)	38:4; 66:2,2; 369:1
bound	(8)	189:2; 225:2; 236:4; 261:2; 271:3; 274:3; 304:2; 348:5
bountiful	(1)	330:1
bounty	(1)	329:3
brains	(1)	159:1
brake	(1)	357:1
branch	(1)	189:3
branches	(1)	361:7
brave	(1)	371:1
Brazil	(1)	362:1
bread	(2)	240:1; 364:1
break	(4)	199:2; 264:2; 344:2; 378:1
breakdown	(2)	153:1; 207:4
breakfast	(1)	151:1

breaking	(2)	145:3; 192:1
breaks	(9)	8:3; 68:2,3; 165:2; 179:2; 275:1,4; 277:1; 336:3
bred	(1)	374:2
brewers	(1)	359:1
bridge	(6)	183:1,1; 195:3,4,4; 196:3
brief	(4)	27:1; 124:2; 369:1; 381:2
briefly	(5)	153:3; 195:2; 208:3; 267:4; 340:2
brigade	(1)	171:2
bring	(28)	11:2; 13:2; 18:5; 30:3; 42:1; 94:2; 111:3; 138:2; 158:2; 170:2; 176:1; 200:2; 218:1; 219:1; 220:3; 235:1,1,1; 253:3,3; 276:1; 288:1; 293:1; 318:2; 337:2; 366:1; 379:1; 381:1
bringing	(7)	71:5; 146:2; 208:2,2; 219:1; 309:2; 344:1
brings	(15)	31:3; 73:2; 160:2; 165:2; 167:2; 175:2; 176:1; 177:1,2; 178:1; 179:1; 223:2; 248:1; 302:3; 317:2
briskly	(1)	250:1
Britain	(19)	101:1; 102:2; 108:3; 122:1; 204:3; 206:2; 219:2; 263:1; 269:3; 276:1; 277:1; 323:2; 333:1; 337:2; 338:2; 339:3; 348:4; 372:2; 376:2
British	(1)	154:1
broad	(4)	39:4; 57:2; 91:1; 146:3
broader	(1)	333:1
broadly	(8)	48:2; 56:1; 59:3; 75:1; 165:2; 195:2; 205:2; 327:2
broke	(1)	89:1
broken	(2)	331:2; 379:2
broker's	(1)	360:3
brokerage	(1)	160:1
brought	(29)	3:1; 69:8; 72:3; 84:3,3; 93:3; 102:2; 123:4; 175:1,3; 177:2; 186:3,3; 196:5; 208:2; 235:1; 248:3; 267:5; 269:2; 295:3; 323:1; 335:1; 339:2; 347:1; 351:4; 364:2; 366:2; 368:2,5
Brücke	(1)	354:1
bubble	(1)	159:1
bubbles	(1)	159:1
Büchi	(1)	354:2
bud	(1)	327:2
budgetary	(2)	98:1; 129:4

Buenos	(3)	354:1,1,1
build	(6)	101:1; 107:2; 129:3; 136:3; 183:1,1
building	(10)	49:1; 50:1; 101:1,1; 131:2; 150:1; 151:1; 188:1; 220:1; 361:1
buildings	(2)	163:2; 362:2
built	(5)	99:4; 106:2; 130:2; 131:2; 355:2
bull	(2)	171:2; 309:4
bull-bear	(1)	169:5
bulletin	(1)	103:2
bulls	(1)	170:1
bunched	(1)	71:4
bund	(1)	354:2
bundle	(1)	24:5
burden	(7)	220:2; 264:3,3; 268:3,3; 271:3; 307:2
burdens	(1)	131:2
bureau	(1)	103:2
burst	(1)	100:1
bury	(1)	129:3
bushel	(4)	17:4,4,4,4
bushels	(2)	17:4,4
business	(41)	39:3; 46:2,2,2; 58:2; 59:1; 71:5,5; 103:1,1; 104:3; 108:1,3; 129:2; 149:2; 150:2,3; 151:1; 153:4; 162:3; 168:2; 170:2; 189:2,3,5; 190:3; 195:4; 210:1,1; 216:1; 221:2; 250:1; 252:2; 263:4; 264:3; 269:3; 301:2; 317:1,1; 365:3; 368:1
business-deposits	(2)	195:1,2
business-motive	(2)	195:2,4
businessmen	(1)	150:2
but	(Count: 496 – not included)	
butler	(1)	349:3
buy	(13)	18:5; 24:4; 64:2; 206:1; 210:1; 223:3,3,3,3; 328:1; 345:3,4,4
buyer	(2)	85:2,2
buyers	(1)	18:5
buying	(6)	17:4,4; 20:4; 186:3; 200:2; 316:1
buying-price	(1)	206:2
buys	(4)	55:1; 68:1; 135:1; 155:1
by	(Count: 834 – not included)	
by-product	(2)	159:1; 328:1
cabinet	(1)	354:2
Cairncross	(1)	364:2
calculable	(1)	70:3

calculate	(4)	38:2; 164:3; 184:2; 224:3
calculated	(11)	68:1; 70:1; 71:3; 72:3; 131:2; 152:1; 164:3; 169:2,2; 248:1; 382:3
calculates	(1)	157:2
calculating	(9)	39:1; 43:3; 52:2,3; 70:2; 92:3; 163:1; 226:1; 240:2
calculation	(13)	39:4; 70:3,4; 108:2; 111:4; 150:2,2; 152:2; 154:2; 162:1,2,3; 324:1
calculations	(4)	163:1; 201:3; 269:3; 294:1
calculus	(1)	40:1
call	(41)	23:1,1,1; 24:1; 27:2,2; 28:5; 41:2,2; 47:1; 53:1,1,1; 56:1; 59:1; 64:1,1,1; 68:1; 90:2; 91:1; 102:3; 113:1; 115:3,4; 135:1; 136:3; 140:3; 144:3; 222:2; 223:4; 226:2; 227:2; 272:3; 302:4; 314:2; 332:2; 358:1; 361:5,7; 377:2
called	(37)	3:1; 4:3; 6:2; 25:2,2,3,5; 29:1; 38:2; 48:2; 57:2; 72:5; 108:2; 113:1; 135:2; 142:2; 166:2; 173:2; 183:1; 192:2; 194:1; 213:4,4; 227:2; 242:3; 273:2; 282:4; 292:1; 299:2; 343:1; 352:2; 354:2; 362:2; 365:3,5; 376:1; 379:3
calling	(2)	313:2; 340:1
calls 358:3	(7)	8:2; 102:3; 140:3; 189:4; 272:3; 280:1;
calms	(1)	160:2
came	(6)	57:1; 241:4; 365:2,3,3,3
campaign	(2)	365:3; 366:1
can	(Count: 301 – not included)	
can't	(1)	361:3
canalised	(1)	374:2
cancel	(2)	75:1; 197:2
cancellation	(1)	211:1
cancels	(1)	75:1
candid	(1)	162:1
Candides	(1)	33:3
cannot	(92)	6:2; 9:1; 16:1; 17:4; 18:2; 28:2,2; 29:4; 30:1; 38:1; 39:4; 40:2; 42:3; 45:2; 51:2,2; 59:2; 64:1,1; 71:5; 73:2; 80:3; 83:1; 85:2; 95:5; 100:1; 104:3,3; 111:3; 117:2; 118:2; 138:4; 139:3; 152:1; 159:1; 160:2,2; 162:4; 166:5; 167:3; 169:2; 182:3; 184:1; 186:2; 187:2,4,5; 192:1; 202:2; 213:1; 217:2;

capital (cont.)		262:1,2; 263:3,3; 264:2; 265:1,2; 266:1; 269:2; 270:1; 273:5; 274:4; 278:3; 289:3; 307:3; 308:2; 309:2; 313:2,2,2; 314:3,3; 315:3,4,6,6; 316:1,1,1,1,1,2; 317:1,2,3,3; 318:1,1,3; 319:2,2,3,3; 320:1,3; 321:2,3; 323:1; 324:4; 325:2,2,3; 329:1; 341:3; 344:2; 351:3; 352:1,1; 355:3,3; 356:1,1,2; 357:1,1,1; 363:2; 365:3; 366:1; 367:2,2,2,3; 368:1,2,5,6; 369:1,1; 372:2; 373:1,1,1,2; 375:1,2,2,3,3,3; 376:1,1,1,1,1,1,3; 377:2
capital-asset	(14)	82:1; 135:1,2,2,2; 136:2,4; 161:2; 212:1,1; 222:1,2; 223:4; 248:1
capital-assets	(15)	135:2; 147:2,2,2; 212:2; 224:3; 228:2; 236:3; 241:2; 242:1; 246:2; 247:1; 252:2; 253:3; 316:1
capital-charges	(1)	221:1
capital-disinvestment	(3)	105:2,2,2
capital-goods	(31)	24:4; 81:2; 122:3,4,4; 123:2,3,4,4; 124:1,1,1,2; 125:1; 164:3; 186:3,3,3; 187:3,3,4,4,4,4,4; 192:2; 221:2; 315:3,3,3,5
capital-investment	(3)	105:2,2,2
capital-profits	(1)	95:1
capital-values	(2)	92:3; 95:4
capitalised	(3)	149:3; 188:1,1
capitalising	(1)	137:3
capitalism	(4)	159:1; 221:2; 317:1; 376:2
capitalist	(2)	33:1; 376:1
capitalistic	(1)	381:2
capitalists	(3)	363:2,2,2
capitals	(1)	363:3
capitaux	(1)	177:1
card	(1)	357:1
cards	(1)	381:1
care	(3)	177:2; 346:1; 361:7
career	(2)	353:5; 365:3
careful	(2)	59:3; 131:2
carefully	(3)	27:1; 148:4; 373:3
carried	(13)	50:4; 67:3; 122:3; 130:2; 137:2; 151:1; 177:2; 178:1; 221:2; 323:1; 330:1; 356:3; 372:2
carries	(1)	194:1
carry	(11)	33:1; 105:1; 108:1,3; 113:1; 121:3; 166:2; 190:3; 248:2; 305:3; 356:3

chaps.	(1)	278:4
chapter	(73)	7:4; 8:4; 11:3; 12:4; 13:4; 15:3; 18:2; 20:1; 21:4; 23:2; 24:4,4; 25:5; 26:2,2; 31:5; 51:2; 53:3; 54:4; 55:4; 74:1; 89:1; 90:2; 91:1; 92:2; 93:4; 111:2; 113:1; 119:5; 124:2; 140:2; 144:1; 147:1,1; 148:1; 165:1,2; 168:2; 175:4; 176:1; 182:5; 184:4; 189:2; 194:1; 195:1,2; 201:3; 208:2,3; 209:4; 213:2; 230:4; 232:5; 243:7; 246:3,4; 253:4; 257:1; 260:4; 280:1,2,3; 281:3; 285:5; 294:3; 297:2; 304:3; 313:2; 314:3; 316:3; 340:1; 364:4; 382:2
chapters	(12)	13:2; 25:3; 27:1; 37:1,1; 177:3; 225:2; 240:2; 247:3; 260:3; 293:1; 313:1
character	(32)	3:1; 4:3; 13:2; 14:3; 27:1; 40:1; 49:1; 63:3; 67:1; 107:2; 109:1; 150:2; 154:1; 159:2; 201:2,4; 203:2; 239:4; 241:2,4; 248:2; 250:2; 257:1; 281:1; 299:2; 313:2; 314:3; 323:1; 338:3; 348:2; 376:1; 383:3
characterise	(2)	229:3; 230:1
characterised	(6)	73:1; 215:2; 241:2; 315:5; 321:2; 329:1
characterises	(1)	9:3
characteristic	(21)	28:5; 72:4; 83:1; 160:1; 161:4; 226:4; 230:2,3; 235:1,3; 236:1; 249:4; 251:3; 294:1; 314:2; 318:1; 320:2; 321:1,3; 327:2; 362:3
characteristics	(22)	3:1; 11:3; 16:1; 32:1; 91:1; 206:2; 229:3; 233:1,2; 234:3; 235:1; 236:4; 237:1; 238:3; 241:3; 249:3; 293:1; 314:3; 318:1; 335:3; 337:3; 341:1
characters	(3)	356:1,1,1
charge	(9)	57:2; 129:2; 163:2; 190:3,3; 208:2,2; 357:1; 368:4
chargeable	(1)	63:1
charged	(1)	69:4
charges	(7)	59:2; 145:1; 160:1; 196:3; 216:2; 355:3; 356:1
charity	(2)	362:2; 366:1
chart	(1)	127:2
cheap	(6)	234:3; 345:2,2,3,4,4
cheaper	(1)	377:1
cheaply	(1)	141:2
cheapness	(4)	196:3; 216:2; 345:2,2

clearly (cont.)		332:2; 340:1; 347:2; 355:3; 357:1
clearness	(2)	64:3; 371:1
cleavage	(1)	350:1
Clement	(1)	347:1
clever	(1)	183:1
climb	(1)	365:3
climber	(1)	365:3
close	(10)	59:3; 130:2; 131:2; 139:1,2; 293:1; 313:2; 331:2; 338:1; 353:5
closed	(10)	11:3,3; 16:1; 121:3; 263:1; 265:1; 269:4; 270:1,2; 301:3
closely	(10)	25:5; 43:3; 60:3; 84:3; 102:2; 151:3; 169:4; 194:1; 241:2; 299:2
closer	(1)	59:2
closes	(2)	353:5,5
closest	(1)	148:4
cloth	(1)	347:2
clothed	(1)	383:3
clothing	(3)	359:1; 363:3,3
clue	(1)	223:4
co-extensive	(1)	167:3
co-operate	(1)	378:1
coaches	(1)	360:3
coal-mines	(1)	129:3
coffers	(1)	345:1
cogency	(1)	297:2
cognisance	(1)	340:2
coin	(2)	342:1,2
coincidence	(1)	218:2
coincides	(2)	75:1; 157:1
coins	(1)	200:2
coke	(1)	346:1
cold	(1)	150:2
Colin	(1)	102:2
collaboration	(1)	365:2
collaborator	(1)	366:2
collapse	(14)	19:3; 104:1; 158:2,2,2; 249:4; 315:4; 316:1,1,1,1,2; 322:1; 331:2
collapses	(1)	329:1
collections	(1)	39:4
collective	(4)	6:2; 8:1; 63:2,2
collectively	(1)	160:2
collisions	(1)	16:2

colour	(1)	345:2
coloured	(1)	249:3
colours	(1)	380:2
combination	(8)	5:6; 6:2; 11:2; 14:2; 232:2; 234:3; 278:4; 322:3
combine	(1)	238:3
combined	(2)	163:2; 379:1
combines	(1)	274:1
combining	(1)	273:5
come	(20)	11:1; 57:1; 77:1; 79:2; 84:3; 85:2; 130:2; 141:2; 157:1; 161:4; 162:1; 174:2; 178:1; 200:2; 228:2,2; 233:2; 234:3; 267:4; 290:3
comes	(22)	59:3; 100:1; 122:4; 141:2; 149:1; 169:2; 175:2; 200:2; 212:1; 218:2; 228:3; 276:2; 278:4,6; 287:2,2; 289:2; 317:3; 321:3; 326:3; 376:1; 378:2
comfort	(3)	80:3; 97:2; 204:3
coming	(4)	114:1; 265:2; 288:1; 300:5
command	(13)	91:3; 158:2; 166:2,3,3,3,3,3; 167:3; 213:4; 215:2,2; 230:2
commanding	(1)	367:1
commencement	(1)	38:1
commended	(1)	33:1
commensurate	(1)	161:3
comment	(3)	19:5; 301:2; 344:5
commentary	(1)	361:4
commented	(1)	19:5
comments	(1)	189:3
commerce	(3)	334:3; 369:1,1
commercial	(5)	163:2; 348:5; 367:1; 368:4; 369:1
commissioners	(1)	59:3
commitment	(1)	160:2
commitments	(1)	151:1
commits	(1)	46:2
committed	(2)	151:1; 366:1
committees	(1)	157:1
commodities	(39)	18:5,5,5; 19:1,2,2,2,2; 102:3,3; 103:1; 223:4,4; 226:4; 228:3; 235:1,1,1; 237:1,2; 286:2,3; 296:2,2; 300:3,3,4; 343:1; 345:2,2; 355:3; 356:2; 359:7; 364:1,1,1,4; 369:1,1
commodity	(31)	45:2; 160:3; 175:2; 222:2; 223:2; 224:3,3; 225:1,1,3,3; 226:3; 228:3; 233:1,3,3; 235:1,1; 236:4; 237:1,2,2; 238:1,1,1,2;

commodity (cont.)		281:2,2; 343:1; 344:1; 356:2
commodity's	(2)	228:3; 236:4
commodity-rates	(4)	224:2; 225:3; 231:5; 235:1
common	(25)	32:2; 54:1; 57:1; 60:3; 63:2; 66:2; 74:3; 108:1; 129:2; 137:4; 188:2; 192:1,3; 262:6; 277:3; 345:4; 347:1; 349:1; 350:1; 351:1; 360:1; 366:4; 373:2; 377:2; 382:3
commonly	(10)	19:2; 37:3; 56:1; 58:2; 106:2; 144:2; 229:3; 373:2,3; 383:3
commons	(2)	347:2; 367:1
commonwealth	(2)	345:2; 374:2
communal	(1)	376:1
communities	(4)	126:2; 219:3; 368:2,4
community	(83)	20:2; 21:1,1; 27:2,2; 28:2,5; 29:1; 31:2,2,2,2,3; 38:1; 54:1,4; 56:1; 74:1; 75:1; 84:2; 90:3; 95:3; 97:2; 100:2; 104:3; 108:3; 110:1; 111:2; 114:3; 116:2; 117:1; 119:2,3; 120:4; 121:1,3; 123:3; 125:2,2; 126:2,2; 128:2; 129:1,3; 150:3; 151:1; 153:1; 155:2; 162:2; 192:1; 217:3; 219:3,3,3; 220:1,1,3,3; 232:1; 250:4; 251:3; 260:2; 262:2,5,5; 263:4; 267:5; 279:2; 321:2,4; 330:1,1; 360:2; 366:3; 367:1; 368:6; 369:1,1,1; 370:1; 374:2; 377:1; 378:1
community's	(12)	27:2; 28:5; 38:1; 121:1; 125:4; 153:4; 165:2; 244:1; 261:2; 265:1; 336:1; 373:2
companies	(1)	154:1
company	(1)	342:1
company's	(1)	151:2
comparable	(4)	19:3; 68:1; 241:2; 331:1
comparably	(1)	233:2
comparative	(3)	71:3; 240:3; 356:1
comparatively	(17)	73:1; 118:2; 122:2; 126:1; 163:2; 172:2; 221:2; 233:3; 247:2; 263:1; 268:1,2; 324:1; 349:1; 357:1; 358:2; 374:2
compare	(5)	41:1; 44:1; 280:1; 335:2; 361:8
compared	(19)	7:1; 17:4; 56:1; 70:2; 76:1; 102:1; 128:1; 159:2; 169:2; 187:1; 192:1; 203:1; 225:2; 263:1; 309:3; 330:1; 343:4; 380:2; 383:3
comparing	(2)	39:1; 91:1
comparison	(8)	38:2; 41:1; 43:2; 44:1; 126:2; 140:3; 151:2; 190:3
comparisons	(1)	39:4

compartments	(2)	195:1; 199:3
compass	(1)	361:7
compatible	(15)	6:2,2; 12:2; 29:4; 31:2; 152:2; 191:1,2; 215:3; 267:3; 269:4; 307:3; 337:2; 357:1; 375:4
compel	(1)	31:2
compelled	(1)	83:1
compelling	(2)	232:2; 326:3
compensate	(2)	124:1; 169:2
compensating	(3)	162:4; 254:1; 370:1
compensation	(1)	355:4
compete	(4)	141:2; 143:2,2; 216:2
competing	(1)	25:3
competition	(16)	5:4; 6:1; 11:2; 26:2; 29:5; 154:3; 191:2; 213:3; 241:2; 245:2; 253:2; 277:4; 338:3; 345:2; 355:2; 379:1
competitions	(1)	156:2
competitive	(4)	349:1,1; 381:4; 382:2
competitor	(2)	156:2,2
competitors	(3)	156:2,2,2
compile	(1)	127:2
compiled	(1)	127:2
compiling	(1)	102:3
complain	(1)	276:1
complained	(1)	342:2
complaint	(1)	379:2
complaints	(1)	358:3
complete	(18)	12:4; 40:1; 115:1; 130:1; 138:4; 165:1; 207:4; 249:4; 264:4; 293:1; 299:1; 313:2; 316:2; 332:2; 335:1; 338:2; 359:7,7
completed	(3)	267:5; 331:2; 332:1
completely	(14)	32:2,2; 48:2; 54:2; 55:1; 66:2; 67:3; 145:4; 166:2; 231:2; 246:1,1; 247:2; 365:1
completeness	(4)	32:3; 95:3; 344:5; 370:1
complex	(23)	12:4; 28:1; 32:3; 38:1; 93:3; 143:2,2; 167:4; 168:2,3; 169:1; 184:1; 205:2,3,3; 206:1; 207:1; 247:2; 249:2; 264:4; 299:2; 313:2; 314:3
complexes	(1)	137:5
complexities	(1)	298:1
complexity	(3)	137:3; 249:2; 305:3
complicated	(8)	24:4; 50:2,2; 51:1; 180:1; 257:2; 297:2; 313:2

complicating	(4)	240:2; 297:1,2; 298:3
complication	(3)	55:1; 75:1; 274:2
complications	(5)	43:3,3; 183:1; 246:3; 296:2
components	(1)	68:1
composing	(1)	91:1
composite	(2)	195:1; 225:1
compound	(1)	163:2
compounded	(2)	295:2; 302:2
comprehensive	(4)	6:2; 7:3; 137:3; 378:1
comprises	(1)	59:2
compromise	(1)	38:4
compromises	(1)	378:1
computing	(1)	140:3
concealed	(2)	112:1; 382:3
concede	(1)	325:3
conceivable	(6)	54:3; 90:2; 191:1; 216:1; 241:2; 322:5
conceivably	(2)	69:7; 169:2
conceive	(5)	49:1; 54:3; 113:1; 116:1; 378:1
concentrate	(3)	155:2; 206:2; 325:2
concept	(18)	39:1,1,2; 57:1; 60:2,2; 67:2; 71:5; 77:2; 81:1; 102:3; 174:2,2; 189:3; 195:3; 243:2; 275:2; 284:2
conception	(9)	65:1; 80:3; 113:1; 114:1; 240:3; 259:1; 287:2; 346:1; 348:5
concepts	(11)	37:3; 39:3; 40:1,2; 43:2; 57:1; 60:1; 68:1; 73:3; 146:2; 292:1
concern	(2)	109:3; 155:2
concerned	(33)	4:1,2; 14:1; 20:2; 40:2; 44:2; 46:2; 47:1; 90:2; 106:2; 119:2; 138:2,2; 154:3,3; 166:2; 226:1; 230:2; 232:3; 266:1; 272:1; 275:2; 281:2; 287:1; 292:1; 293:1; 306:4; 316:1; 330:1; 334:2; 340:1; 341:2; 351:2
concerning	(26)	4:2,3; 26:2; 60:2,2; 65:1; 76:1; 94:2; 141:2; 142:3; 143:2; 161:2; 198:1; 202:2; 208:2; 248:1; 254:4; 263:4; 293:2; 294:1; 317:3; 333:1; 342:1; 343:1; 344:2; 347:2
concerted	(1)	267:3
concession	(1)	334:2
concessions	(1)	334:2
conclude	(5)	39:3; 162:4; 238:2; 254:4; 320:1
concludes	(3)	189:5; 278:2; 361:6
concluding	(1)	192:1
conclusion	(39)	16:1; 20:2; 49:1; 63:2,2,2; 83:2; 89:1; 94:1;

conclusion (cont.) | | 95:4; 98:2; 102:3; 110:2; 125:2,3; 137:3; 160:2; 184:2; 191:2; 192:2; 211:1,2; 212:2; 219:3; 230:2; 236:2; 253:2; 261:2; 266:1; 270:2; 290:1; 294:2; 297:2; 330:1; 338:3; 367:1,1; 368:2; 373:3

word	count	references
conclusion (cont.)		95:4; 98:2; 102:3; 110:2; 125:2,3; 137:3; 160:2; 184:2; 191:2; 192:2; 211:1,2; 212:2; 219:3; 230:2; 236:2; 253:2; 261:2; 266:1; 270:2; 290:1; 294:2; 297:2; 330:1; 338:3; 367:1,1; 368:2; 373:3
conclusions	(21)	3:1; 11:3; 19:3; 20:2; 33:1; 61:1; 129:2; 149:2; 193:1; 231:6; 232:1; 243:5; 260:1; 277:4; 285:3; 320:3; 350:1; 353:3; 366:2; 367:1,1
concoction	(1)	273:3
concoctions	(1)	298:1
concomitant	(1)	83:1
concretely	(1)	379:2
concur	(1)	4:3
condition	(40)	29:4; 48:4; 64:2,2; 158:2,2; 168:2,3; 230:2; 231:2,2; 234:3; 236:3,4,6; 239:1; 249:4; 251:1,2,3; 252:2,2,2,3; 253:3,3; 284:1; 296:2,3; 303:2; 304:2,4,4,4; 316:2; 319:2; 322:1; 324:2; 336:1; 380:3
conditions	(98)	4:1; 16:1,1; 44:2; 48:4; 49:1; 55:2; 63:2; 72:2; 73:2; 80:1; 81:1,1,1; 82:2; 83:1; 89:1; 91:3; 104:2; 113:1; 117:3; 122:3; 124:2; 166:3; 187:4; 189:2,2; 192:5; 200:2,2; 212:1; 215:2,3; 217:2,2,3; 218:2; 219:1,2,2; 220:1,3; 235:1; 238:1; 243:1; 244:1; 246:1; 248:1; 250:3; 253:2; 254:2,3,4; 269:3; 273:3; 275:2; 278:1,1; 279:2; 282:2,2; 289:3; 292:1; 293:1; 296:3,3; 303:2; 309:2; 320:1,3; 321:1,2,3; 322:1,1; 324:4,4; 325:1; 328:1; 329:1; 335:3,3; 337:1; 339:3; 347:2; 350:1; 357:1; 368:1; 373:1,1,2,3; 375:2; 376:1; 379:1,3; 382:3; 383:1
conduces	(1)	344:1
conducive	(2)	338:2; 373:1
conduct	(2)	131:2; 361:8
conducted	(1)	273:5
confessions	(1)	365:5
confidence	·(29)	96:4; 120:2; 147:2; 148:3,3,4; 149:1,1,2,3,3; 158:2,2,2,2; 161:2; 203:1; 237:1; 240:2; 248:1; 264:1,3; 265:2; 267:1,1; 275:1; 307:3; 317:1; 368:1
confident	(2)	79:2; 148:2
confidently	(1)	39:1

48

confined	(2)	197:2; 342:2
confining	(1)	366:1
confirm	(1)	157:1
confirmed	(1)	33:2
confirms	(1)	176:4
confiscatory	(1)	93:2
conflict	(1)	183:1
conflicting	(1)	93:3
conform	(2)	60:3; 276:1
conformable	(1)	63:2
conformably	(1)	190:1
conformity	(4)	11:2; 13:2; 307:1; 320:2
confused	(10)	12:2; 24:3; 49:1; 120:2; 329:1; 334:4; 343:1; 348:3; 352:1; 374:2
confusing	(2)	78:1; 193:1
confusion	(13)	61:1,1; 67:3; 122:4; 138:4; 141:2; 174:1; 193:1,1; 299:2; 328:1; 334:1; 373:2
confutation	(1)	359:7
congenial	(1)	162:3
conjunction	(8)	50:3; 55:2; 127:2; 168:1; 244:1; 248:1; 281:2; 307:3
connected	(1)	194:1
connection	(13)	49:1; 52:3,3; 139:1; 168:2; 170:1; 195:3; 205:2,2; 233:3; 275:3; 287:2; 346:4
connects	(1)	292:1
conquered	(2)	32:2,2
conscious	(1)	347:3
consecutive	(1)	186:1
consent	(2)	14:1; 369:1
consequence	(9)	67:3; 162:3; 193:1,1; 334:4; 343:4; 348:3,5; 350:1
consequences	(9)	20:1; 80:3; 82:2; 122:4; 161:4; 245:2; 257:2; 342:5; 365:3
consequent	(3)	6:2; 50:1; 368:2
consequential	(1)	122:3
consequently	(14)	10:2; 71:5; 77:2; 80:3; 125:2; 143:1; 192:1; 216:2; 284:2; 289:2,3; 345:4; 362:4; 376:1
conservatism	(1)	128:1
conservative	(2)	308:1; 377:3
conserved	(1)	53:1
consider	(29)	17:2; 43:3; 48:3; 51:2; 52:3; 90:1,2; 91:1,1; 120:3; 147:1; 165:2; 168:2; 179:2; 190:4; 195:1; 206:2; 225:3; 231:6; 236:4; 239:4;

consider (cont.)		250:2; 265:1; 274:3; 289:2; 293:2; 296:2,3; 297:2
considerable	(13)	47:3; 57:3; 61:1; 115:2; 118:2; 148:2; 152:2; 186:2; 249:4; 252:2; 301:3; 316:2; 362:4
considerably	(6)	93:3; 95:3; 237:1; 286:3; 372:2; 377:2
consideration	(8)	114:2; 147:2; 160:2; 230:3; 233:2; 234:2; 236:4; 363:3
considerations	(16)	89:1; 99:2; 147:2; 152:1; 158:3; 214:2; 262:5; 267:4; 268:2; 270:2,2; 287:1; 341:3; 342:5; 372:2,2
considered	(16)	95:4; 157:2; 201:3; 203:1; 213:2; 237:2; 253:4; 263:4; 295:2; 298:3; 314:3; 323:1; 345:1; 353:5; 364:1; 366:1
considering	(9)	57:1; 68:3; 119:2; 120:4; 186:2,2; 245:2; 281:3; 325:2
considers	(1)	59:2
consigned	(1)	362:2
consilience	(1)	379:1
consist	(2)	18:5; 188:2
consisted	(4)	210:2; 302:2; 332:1; 378:2
consistency	(4)	192:1,1; 204:3; 371:1
consistent	(15)	12:2; 16:1; 20:5; 28:2; 33:1; 181:1; 203:1; 220:2; 227:2; 243:3; 253:2; 293:2; 308:1; 339:3; 349:3
consistently	(3)	20:1; 61:2; 192:1
consisting	(1)	246:2
consists	(8)	73:3,3; 75:2; 200:2; 239:3; 343:4,4; 361:7
consolidated	(1)	67:1
consommé	(1)	364:1
consonant	(2)	146:3; 281:1
conspicuously	(1)	349:3
constant	(40)	17:3; 27:1; 29:4; 48:4; 50:2; 55:5; 56:2,2,2; 60:1; 120:4; 179:2; 183:1; 187:3; 201:2,2; 209:2,2; 237:2; 243:5; 244:1; 245:2; 270:1; 279:2; 284:1; 293:1; 295:3; 296:2,3; 299:2,3,3; 304:4,5; 306:2,2; 328:1; 329:1; 330:1; 356:1
constantly	(2)	351:2; 369:1
constituent	(2)	358:2,2
constituents	(1)	166:4
constitute	(5)	15:3; 38:4; 48:4; 234:2; 287:2
constituted	(1)	332:1

consumption (cont.)   84:2,2; 89:2; 90:1,2,2,2,3; 91:3;
                             92:1,1,2,2,2,2,3; 93:3,3,3; 96:2,3,4,4;
                             97:2,2,2; 98:1,1,3,3,3; 99:1,2,3; 102:3,3;
                             103:1; 104:2,3,3,3,3,3;
                             105:1,1,1,1,1,2,2,2,2,2; 106:3,3; 107:1,2,2;
                             108:2; 109:2,2; 110:1,2; 111:1; 114:3;
                             115:1,2,2; 116:2; 117:1,1,1,1,2,3; 118:1;
                             120:3; 121:3,3,3,3; 122:3; 123:4;
                             124:1,1,2,2; 125:1; 126:4; 161:2; 166:2,3;
                             167:2; 188:2,2,3,4; 210:1,1,1,2,2;
                             211:1,1,1,1,1,2,2,2,2,2; 214:2; 216:2; 217:1;
                             226:4,4; 248:2,2,2,2; 251:3; 252:1; 260:3;
                             261:2,2; 263:3,3; 277:3,3; 281:3; 287:2;
                             325:1,2,2,3; 326:1,1,1,2,3; 327:2; 329:1;
                             330:1,2; 332:2,2; 348:1; 362:4; 363:2,2,2,3;
                             364:1; 368:2,2,5; 369:1,1,1,1,1; 370:1,1;
                             371:1; 373:2; 377:2
consumption-constituent   (1)   96:2
consumption-demand   (3)   210:1,1,1
consumption-goods   (14) 24:4; 49:1; 116:1; 122:3; 123:4,4; 124:1;
                                192:2; 210:1; 221:1; 252:2; 273:2,2; 287:2

contact   (2)   293:1; 365:3
contain   (3)   12:4; 181:1; 220:1
contains   (3)   176:4; 189:5; 353:3
contemplate   (2)   153:4; 337:3
contemplated   (1)   178:1
contemplating   (1)   300:3
contemporary   (20) 19:3; 20:1; 74:1; 153:2; 160:2; 183:3;
                                250:2; 266:1; 288:1; 308:2; 309:2; 324:2,3;
                                334:2; 338:2; 346:3; 348:3; 373:3; 380:3;
                                383:3

contend   (1)   233:3
contended   (1)   72:5
content   (12) 141:2,2; 143:2,2; 148:4; 191:2; 212:2;
                                213:1; 220:1; 295:3; 345:4; 360:3

contention   (2)   9:3; 13:2
contentions   (3)   176:1; 334:2; 369:1
context   (11) 40:2; 110:1; 178:1; 186:3; 187:3; 225:3;
                                230:2; 233:2; 245:2; 333:1; 353:5

contexts   (6)   114:2,2; 124:2; 138:3; 172:1; 315:6
contingencies   (3)   107:2; 196:2; 216:1
contingency   (3)   229:1; 265:2,2
continually   (2)   278:1; 346:1

continuance	(4)	154:2; 265:2; 327:2; 376:2
continue	(12)	48:1,2; 51:1,1; 152:1,1; 200:2; 217:3; 228:3; 229:2; 233:1; 290:2
continued	(5)	100:2; 251:2; 323:1; 362:4; 363:2
continues	(9)	19:5; 20:5; 25:4; 99:3; 156:3; 229:2; 289:2; 290:3; 352:2
continuing	(1)	317:3
continuity	(2)	152:2; 163:2
continuous	(11)	6:2; 50:4; 68:3; 112:1; 197:1,1,2; 267:2; 326:1; 367:2; 375:2
continuously	(3)	122:4; 164:2; 301:3
contract	(6)	27:2; 77:1; 223:2,3; 241:4; 332:2
contracted	(2)	222:2,2
contraction	(3)	95:2; 105:2; 303:3
contracts	(11)	163:2; 223:2,4; 224:2; 233:4; 236:5; 237:1,1; 347:2; 348:4; 360:5
contractually	(1)	268:2
contradicted	(1)	364:1
contrariwise	(2)	81:2; 105:2
contrary	(24)	5:7; 20:1; 71:5; 106:3; 108:1; 110:3; 111:1; 119:4; 162:4; 167:1; 169:2; 232:3; 265:1; 303:4; 322:1; 323:1; 329:1; 338:2; 341:2; 345:2; 361:6; 368:2; 373:1; 380:3
contrast	(2)	3:1; 79:1
contre	(1)	177:1
contribute	(1)	243:2
contributed	(3)	52:2; 189:5; 347:2
contributes	(1)	240:3
contributing	(2)	42:1; 316:1
contribution	(4)	188:2; 340:1,1; 355:3
contrive	(1)	81:2
control	(16)	56:1; 167:1,2; 172:2,2; 189:2,2; 205:3; 206:2; 207:3; 235:2; 316:2; 317:1; 327:2,2; 336:2
controlled	(4)	203:1; 219:3; 247:2; 325:3
controlling	(2)	270:1; 339:3
controls	(4)	377:3; 378:2; 379:1,3
controversies	(1)	334:2
controversy	(6)	32:2; 334:2; 342:3; 364:2,2; 365:3
controverts	(1)	189:2
conundrums	(2)	39:1,3
convenience	(9)	149:3; 168:2; 172:1; 226:2,2; 233:3; 236:5; 237:1; 367:2

conveniences	(4)	367:2,2,2,2
convenient	(32)	7:1; 15:3; 24:1,4; 38:4; 41:4; 54:4; 59:1; 62:1; 67:3; 68:3; 90:2; 93:3; 114:1,2; 116:1; 128:3; 129:4; 135:1; 167:3,3,4; 171:4; 172:1; 187:2; 195:2; 249:2; 272:3; 315:6; 324:3; 333:1; 353:3
conveniently	(1)	37:2
convention	(12)	109:3; 152:1,1,2,3; 153:1,1,2; 204:1,1,3; 354:2
conventional	(11)	58:2; 152:2; 154:2,3; 155:3,3; 159:1; 203:3; 204:2,3; 325:1
conventionally	(1)	158:1
conventions	(1)	336:1
convert	(1)	166:3
convey	(3)	139:2; 279:1,1
conveyed	(1)	359:2
convicted	(1)	359:2
conviction	(6)	12:2; 19:3; 154:2; 203:1,2,3
convinced	(2)	76:1; 365:3
Conway	(1)	365:5
cook	(1)	216:1
cool	(1)	355:2
cooler	(1)	322:3
coolly	(1)	323:1
copies	(1)	353:3
copper	(9)	70:4,4; 71:1,1,1; 73:2,2,2; 149:4
copper-rate	(2)	223:1,4
corn	(1)	17:4
corollary	(3)	19:1; 178:1; 238:2
corporate	(2)	95:2; 128:1
corporation	(2)	59:2; 75:1
corporations	(2)	100:2; 108:3
corpus	(1)	364:2
correct	(23)	4:3; 127:1; 145:3; 152:1,1; 154:3; 167:2; 188:2; 191:2; 214:2; 218:1; 219:1; 229:1; 254:4; 259:1; 277:1; 322:3; 323:1; 327:2; 344:5; 357:1; 382:3; 383:3
corrected	(2)	59:2; 319:3
correcting	(1)	102:3
correction	(2)	76:1; 142:2
correctly	(4)	4:3; 50:3; 103:1; 183:2
correlated	(3)	17:3; 178:2; 260:3
correlation	(3)	17:3; 238:3; 246:1

54

correlative	(1)	61:1
correspond	(19)	12:2; 24:4; 31:2; 62:1; 73:2; 100:1; 102:3; 117:2; 198:2; 218:1; 243:6; 246:1; 247:2; 268:2; 275:2; 281:3; 282:2; 299:1; 325:3
correspondence	(1)	33:2
corresponding	(70)	6:2; 11:1; 24:2; 26:1; 29:4; 30:1; 45:1; 48:2,2,2; 60:1; 64:1; 68:3,3; 69:5; 82:1; 83:1; 90:2; 92:1,2; 101:1; 108:2; 109:2; 110:3; 124:1; 125:2; 136:3; 137:5; 147:1; 151:2; 177:1; 178:1,1,1; 181:1; 182:1; 191:1,2; 198:1; 199:3,3; 205:2; 214:2; 219:4; 240:2; 246:1; 248:2; 261:2; 269:4; 275:2; 279:2; 280:1; 281:2,3; 282:1,2,2; 286:2; 303:3; 307:1; 314:3; 320:1,1; 330:1,1; 347:2; 357:1; 369:1; 375:2; 378:2
correspondingly	(6)	99:2; 118:2; 206:2; 369:1; 370:1; 373:2
corresponds	(31)	15:4; 16:1; 26:1; 28:2; 55:2; 59:3; 67:1; 68:2; 75:1; 76:1; 80:2; 81:2; 82:2; 102:2; 151:3; 156:2; 173:2; 191:1; 195:2; 200:2; 202:2,2; 218:1; 220:2; 286:2; 299:2,2; 328:2; 329:1; 371:1; 375:1
cost	(294)	12:2,2,2; 13:1; 15:1; 20:2; 23:1,1,1,1,1,1,2; 24:1,2,4,4,4,4,4,4,4,4,4; 25:1; 42:1; 44:2; 45:1; 47:2; 53:1,1,1,1,1,1,2,3; 54:1,3,3,3,3; 55:3,3,3,4,4,5,5; 56:1,1,1,1; 57:1,1,1,1,1,1,1,3; 58:1,1,1,2,2,2,2,2,2; 59:1,1,1,1,2,2; 64:1,1; 66:1,2,2,2; 67:1,1,2,2,2,3,3,3,3,3,3,3; 68:1,1,1,1,1,1,1,1,1,1,1,1,1,1,1,1,1,1,1,1,1,1, 2,3,3,3; 69:2,2,3,3,3,3,3,3,3,4,4,4,5,5,5,5,5,5,5,5,6,7, 7,7,7,7,8; 70:1,1,1,2,2,3,3,3,3,3,3,3,3,4,5,6; 71:1,1,1,1,2,2,3,3,4,4,4,4,5,5; 72:1,2,2,2,2,3,3,4,4,4,4,5; 73:2,2,3,3; 77:2; 99:2,2; 100:1; 101:1; 102:2; 109:1,1; 119:4; 127:1; 135:2,2,2; 136:2; 139:1; 140:3,3,3,3; 141:1,2,2,2; 144:4,4; 146:2; 151:1; 172:1; 196:3,3,3,3; 201:2; 208:3; 213:3,4; 216:2,2,2,2; 225:6,6; 226:2,3,4,4,4; 227:1,1,1,1,1; 228:3,3,3; 234:2; 237:1; 238:1; 249:1; 252:2; 258:3; 261:2; 262:4; 266:2,2; 268:2; 271:1; 272:3,4,4,4,4; 273:3,5,5,5; 276:2; 277:1,2; 283:1,1,3;

cost (cont.)		290:2; 292:1; 294:2,2; 295:2,3; 296:2;
		299:3; 302:2,3,3,3; 309:2; 315:3; 321:1;
		323:1,1; 324:1; 357:1; 360:3; 375:3
cost-price	(1)	238:1
cost-unit	(8)	302:4,4,4,4; 303:2,2; 309:3; 328:1
cost-units	(2)	303:3,3
costs	(45)	5:4; 18:3; 23:1; 25:3; 27:1; 28:4; 46:1;
		47:2; 55:3; 56:2; 58:2; 62:1; 68:1,2; 71:2;
		72:2,3; 73:3,3; 131:1; 140:2,3; 195:4;
		208:2; 216:2; 217:2; 218:3; 219:1; 226:1,4;
		229:1; 237:2; 259:1; 261:2; 271:1; 294:2,2;
		300:1; 315:5; 317:3; 336:3; 337:1,1; 359:1;
		375:3
could	(69)	18:5; 32:2,2; 33:1; 37:2; 64:2; 69:4; 108:2;
		131:2; 143:1; 151:1,2; 168:2,3,3; 179:2;
		180:1; 181:2; 183:1; 192:5; 207:3,4; 208:1;
		211:1; 215:3; 216:1,1; 221:3; 225:1,1;
		227:2; 229:2; 230:3; 238:3,4; 239:1; 243:1;
		253:2; 257:1,2; 261:2; 265:2; 269:3,3;
		275:1,3,4; 298:2; 302:2; 309:1,1; 323:1,1;
		324:1; 345:1; 346:1; 347:2; 350:3; 353:2;
		357:1,1; 360:3; 362:2; 363:2; 366:1,1;
		369:1; 376:1; 377:1
count	(1)	41:2
counted	(1)	216:1
counter	(1)	365:3
countering	(1)	348:4
counterpart	(1)	109:2
countries	(10)	120:3; 231:1; 323:2; 331:1; 333:1; 345:1,3;
		349:1,2; 354:2
country	(42)	11:3; 18:5; 44:1; 120:3,3; 121:3; 122:1,1;
		159:1; 186:2,2; 187:2; 203:1,1; 229:2;
		230:2; 331:1; 333:1; 335:3; 337:1,1,2,2,2;
		338:3,3,3; 342:1; 344:4; 345:2,3;
		347:2,2,3,3; 361:5; 363:1,2; 373:2;
		382:3,3,3
country's	(3)	120:3; 349:1; 360:3
country-houses	(1)	360:3
coupled	(5)	73:1; 163:2; 213:1; 339:3; 365:3
courage	(2)	364:2; 381:1
course	(85)	4:2; 10:3; 11:3; 23:1; 24:4,5; 27:1,1; 33:2;
		39:4; 49:1; 50:2; 54:3; 57:3; 59:1; 64:2;
		71:3; 78:1; 81:1; 83:1; 84:2; 95:1; 119:2;

criterion (cont.)		375:2
critical	(8)	19:5; 269:4; 270:1; 277:3; 301:3; 303:3,3; 336:3
criticise	(1)	348:3
criticised	(2)	260:4; 279:3
criticising	(1)	277:1
criticism	(8)	51:3; 109:1; 157:1; 279:3; 325:2; 339:2; 371:1; 378:2
criticisms	(3)	39:5; 352:2; 366:2
critics	(1)	367:1
crop	(1)	230:3
crowd	(3)	155:2; 157:1,1
crucial	(1)	272:2
crude	(3)	19:3; 261:2; 289:3
crudest	(2)	258:1; 334:2
cruelty	(2)	33:1; 374:2
crusades	(1)	350:2
Crusoe	(2)	20:2; 356:2
culminated	(1)	3:2
cult	(1)	354:2
cultivating	(1)	241:2
cultivation	(1)	33:3
cumulates	(1)	319:3
cumulative	(9)	100:1; 161:2; 238:3; 251:4; 252:1; 289:1; 314:1; 318:3; 376:1
cumulatively	(1)	100:2
cup	(1)	173:1
curb	(1)	351:2
curbed	(2)	351:3; 380:1
cure	(4)	161:2; 334:2,2; 381:2
cured	(1)	278:3
cures	(1)	323:1
curiosity	(2)	32:3; 40:1
curious	(2)	106:2; 129:2
currencies	(1)	364:6
currency	(11)	207:4,4; 230:2,2; 234:2; 306:3; 329:1,1; 342:1; 357:1; 358:1
current	(153)	7:3; 13:1,1,2; 15:3; 23:1; 27:2,2,2; 28:2; 38:1,1; 41:1; 44:1; 47:2; 49:1; 50:4; 51:1,2,2; 52:2; 55:2; 56:1; 57:3,3; 58:1; 59:1,1,1,2,2; 60:2,3; 61:1; 62:3,3; 63:2,2,2; 64:1; 66:2,2,2; 67:1; 68:1; 69:3; 70:3,3,3; 71:1,2,5; 74:1; 77:3,3; 78:2; 82:1,1,1,1,2;

dangerously	(1)	327:2
dangers	(1)	161:3
dark	(1)	155:2
data	(5)	102:3; 181:1; 276:1,2,2
date	(27)	33:2; 44:1; 59:1; 70:2,6; 71:1,1,2,5; 73:2; 100:1; 107:2; 109:2; 169:1; 210:1; 211:1; 212:1; 215:3,3; 216:2,2,2; 221:2; 228:3,3; 262:1; 302:3
dated	(2)	363:5,6
dates	(7)	70:4; 127:2; 168:3; 207:4; 215:3,3; 233:3
Davenant	(1)	345:1
day	(15)	4:3; 15:3; 17:4,4,4; 47:3; 48:1; 51:1; 76:1; 106:1; 141:2; 151:1; 160:3; 220:1; 358:2
day's	(2)	47:2; 50:3
day-to-day	(1)	153:5
days	(5)	49:1; 157:1; 161:4; 167:3; 331:1
dead	(1)	131:2
deal	(21)	5:7; 9:1; 42:3; 72:3; 89:1; 93:3; 116:1; 129:3; 151:1; 162:3; 205:3,3; 207:2,3; 276:1,2; 302:1; 304:5; 331:3; 332:1; 381:1
dealer	(1)	206:2
dealer's	(1)	206:2
dealers	(3)	195:4; 205:2; 224:2
dealing	(22)	41:2; 43:2,3,3; 56:1; 67:3; 75:1; 119:2; 137:5; 169:3; 170:2; 182:4,4; 190:1; 197:3; 198:1; 199:1; 240:2; 262:6; 285:2; 294:2; 350:2
dealings	(1)	160:1
deals	(2)	177:1; 206:2
dealt	(8)	8:4; 42:1; 43:1; 56:1; 81:1; 183:1; 362:3; 379:1
dear	(3)	175:2; 345:3,4
dearer	(1)	345:2
death	(8)	160:2; 162:2; 220:1; 354:2; 372:2; 373:2,2,3
death-duties	(1)	95:1
debates	(1)	347:2
debit	(1)	58:2
débouchés	(1)	364:1
debt	(24)	81:2; 95:2; 101:1; 108:3; 109:1; 167:1,3,4; 169:1,1,2; 200:2; 202:1; 206:1; 207:3; 241:2,4; 264:3,3; 268:3,3; 271:3; 307:2; 342:1

decrease	(30)	7:1; 41:1; 68:3,3; 75:1,1; 76:1,1,1,2; 111:1,1,1,2,2,2,2; 114:2,2,3; 184:2; 185:1; 191:2,2; 248:2,2; 252:1,1; 274:3; 299:1
decreased	(7)	97:1; 110:3; 119:2; 185:1; 193:1; 194:1; 265:1
decreases	(7)	40:2; 114:2,2,3; 196:3; 250:4; 336:1
decreaseth	(1)	342:1
decreasing	(10)	10:1; 17:3; 83:1; 92:1; 114:2; 122:3; 268:3; 289:3; 301:3; 306:1
decree	(3)	265:2; 267:5; 346:3
decreed	(1)	269:3
decreeing	(1)	229:2
decrement	(3)	248:3,4; 251:3
decrements	(1)	75:3
deduce	(2)	137:3; 165:2
deduct	(6)	52:2; 57:1,1; 67:3; 189:5; 226:1
deducted	(2)	67:3; 309:2
deducting	(3)	5:4; 24:4; 135:1
deduction	(7)	38:2,2; 52:2; 60:1; 103:1; 104:1,2
deductions	(4)	59:2; 189:5,5,5
deducts	(1)	38:2
deemed	(7)	5:1; 67:3; 101:2; 265:2; 268:1; 301:3; 315:3
deep	(5)	183:1,1; 189:5; 353:3; 365:3
deep-rooted	(3)	341:3; 350:2; 358:3
deeper	(1)	213:2
deeply	(2)	20:1; 350:4
default	(3)	144:3,3; 168:2
defeat	(2)	155:2; 157:1
defeated	(1)	336:3
defeatist	(1)	327:2
defeats	(1)	84:2
defect	(3)	60:1; 342:1; 356:2
defective	(1)	327:2
defects	(3)	31:2; 353:3; 380:2
defence	(1)	352:3
defend	(1)	380:3
defended	(1)	352:2
defer	(1)	215:3
deferred	(6)	124:1; 137:2; 166:3; 168:3; 169:1; 242:2
deficiency	(1)	80:2
deficient	(8)	30:2; 32:2,2; 289:2; 307:2; 330:1; 340:1; 380:4

deficit	(2)	98:1; 129:4
define	(11)	6:2; 15:2; 23:1; 53:2,4; 90:2; 115:1; 135:2; 176:3; 282:3,4
defined	(53)	16:1; 18:3; 23:1,1; 24:4,4; 27:1; 31:5; 37:4; 41:2; 54:2; 55:3,4; 57:1,1; 60:3; 61:1,2; 62:1,1,2,3; 67:3,3; 70:2; 74:1; 75:2; 76:2,2; 77:2; 78:1,2; 119:2; 136:2; 137:2; 143:1; 146:2; 170:2; 173:2; 201:2; 209:1,3; 242:3,3; 243:4,5; 246:4; 275:3; 280:1,1; 282:2; 328:1; 366:3
defining	(5)	24:4; 52:2; 55:4; 57:1; 92:1
definite	(24)	41:1; 45:2; 48:2; 51:1; 58:2; 64:2,2; 79:2; 108:1; 113:1; 131:2; 148:2; 154:2; 178:2; 201:3; 214:2; 222:2; 223:2; 240:3; 276:2; 303:2; 314:3; 318:1; 362:3
definiteness	(1)	24:5
definition	(62)	15:3,3,3,4; 23:2; 24:4; 26:2; 31:4; 37:2; 38:1; 39:1; 56:1,1; 59:2,3,3,3; 60:1,3; 61:1,2; 62:2,3,3; 63:2; 66:2; 67:2,3; 74:2; 75:1,1,2,3; 77:1,1,1; 78:2; 80:2,2; 89:1; 92:2; 102:2; 137:4; 138:2; 139:2; 140:3,3; 167:1,3; 239:4; 242:4,4; 243:6; 278:4,4; 279:1,1,2; 284:2; 287:3; 304:4,4
definitions	(7)	55:3; 60:3; 63:2; 74:1,1; 174:2; 243:6
deflation	(3)	291:2,2; 292:1
deflationary	(1)	331:2
defunct	(1)	383:3
degree	(33)	14:1; 24:4; 90:2; 128:1; 146:2; 148:2; 156:2; 162:3; 166:3; 171:2; 173:1; 184:1; 198:2,2; 201:3; 205:1; 221:1; 226:4; 239:3; 245:2; 270:1,2,3; 288:1; 303:2; 309:1; 314:1; 331:2; 338:2; 350:2; 357:2; 363:2; 379:1
degrees	(9)	24:5; 156:2; 182:2; 205:3; 225:4; 226:4; 254:2; 286:2; 302:2
delay	(2)	6:2; 211:1
delayed	(1)	262:1
deliberate	(4)	95:1; 206:2; 230:3; 334:4
deliberately	(3)	83:1; 219:3; 247:2
delicate	(1)	162:3
delightful	(1)	354:1
deliver	(2)	241:4,4
delivered	(2)	222:2; 365:5

delivery	(20)	214:2; 215:3,3,3; 216:2; 222:2,2,2; 223:2,2,3,3,3,3,3,3,3,3; 235:1; 241:4,4
delude	(1)	290:2
delusive	(1)	4:3
dem	(1)	354:2
demand	(313)	6:2,3; 7:3; 8:3; 15:3; 16:1; 18:3,5; 20:2; 21:3,4; 22:1; 25:2,3,3,3,4,4; 26:1,1,2,2,2,2; 27:2; 28:2,2,2; 29:1; 30:1,2,3; 31:1,2; 32:2,2,2,2; 33:3; 40:2,2; 42:2; 43:3,3,3,3,3,3; 44:1; 55:2,2,2,2; 69:7,7; 76:1,1; 77:2; 78:1,1,2; 79:1; 85:2,2,2; 89:1,1,1,2; 93:3; 95:2; 96:2; 99:2,2; 100:1,1; 104:3,3; 105:1,1,2,2; 106:2,2,3,3; 115:5; 123:3,4; 124:1; 126:4; 137:2; 146:3; 147:2,2; 165:2; 167:2; 171:2; 175:2,2,2; 176:1,1,1; 177:1; 178:1,1,2; 179:1,2,2,2,2,2; 186:2,2,3,3,3; 187:1,3,4,4; 189:2; 194:1,1,2; 195:1,4; 197:1,1,1; 204:2; 210:1; 211:2,2; 212:1,1; 214:1; 215:3,3; 216:2; 217:1,1; 220:1; 227:2; 231:4,4,4; 234:3; 235:1,1,1,1,2; 238:1; 241:4; 246:1; 248:4; 251:4; 252:1,2; 257:3; 258:1,1,1,1,1,1,1,3; 259:1,1,1,2,2,2,2,2,2,2; 260:3,3; 261:2; 265:2,2; 266:2; 272:1,2; 273:1,1,3; 274:1,3,4; 275:2; 278:1,1,1,2,4,4,4,4,4,4,4; 279:1,1,1,2,2; 280:1,1,1,1,1; 281:2,2,3,3,3; 282:1,2,2; 283:1,1,1; 284:4; 285:1,1,4,4; 286:1,2,2,3,3,3,4,4; 287:1,1,2,2,2; 288:1; 289:2,2; 291:2; 292:1,1,1; 294:2,2,2; 295:1,1,3,3,3; 296:2,3,3; 297:2,2,2; 298:2,2,3; 299:1,1,1,2,2; 300:3,3,5; 301:2,3,3,3,3,3; 302:1,3; 303:2,2,2,3,3; 304:4,4,4; 305:1,3; 307:1,1; 315:4; 358:2; 359:7,7; 362:3; 363:2,2,2; 364:1,4,4; 368:5; 375:3; 380:4; 381:1
demand-price	(1)	228:2
demand-prices	(1)	227:2
demand-schedule	(17)	110:3; 111:2; 136:3; 137:1,3; 142:1; 149:1; 178:1; 180:3; 181:1,1,1,1,1; 182:3,4; 183:1
demanded	(5)	7:3; 165:1; 186:3; 272:1; 342:1
demanding	(2)	9:3; 18:2
demands	(3)	9:3; 116:1; 267:3
demolished	(1)	99:3

demonstrate	(2)	341:3; 356:2
demonstration	(1)	260:1
denied	(2)	350:3; 367:1
denominator	(1)	224:3
denounce	(1)	346:2
denounced	(2)	358:3; 374:2
deny	(9)	16:2; 178:1,1; 259:2; 275:3; 324:1; 369:1; 370:1; 377:2
denying	(2)	63:2; 350:4
déouché	(1)	364:1
departing	(1)	190:4
departure	(4)	17:2; 123:2; 204:3; 289:1
depend	(50)	10:3; 12:2; 21:4; 25:3; 27:2,2; 28:1,5,5; 43:3; 46:2; 47:2,2; 58:2; 70:3; 71:4; 90:2; 96:2,4; 110:2; 111:4; 112:1; 140:3; 148:3; 149:2; 161:4; 162:1; 163:1; 165:2; 184:2; 190:3; 195:3,4; 196:3,3; 201:1,2; 202:2; 257:3; 272:1; 276:1; 286:3; 294:2; 298:3; 302:4; 309:3,3; 336:1; 356:1; 361:7
depended	(7)	113:1; 150:2; 341:2; 343:1,1; 364:2; 370:2
dependence	(4)	105:1; 143:3,3; 144:1
dependent	(13)	11:3; 24:4; 93:3; 162:3; 172:2; 220:1; 245:1,4; 298:3; 331:1; 349:1; 372:2; 373:3
dependents	(1)	107:2
depending	(11)	29:2; 39:4; 53:2; 58:2; 67:1; 109:1; 170:2; 240:3; 266:2; 273:3; 343:1
depends	(82)	7:1; 12:2; 14:2,2; 24:2; 28:4; 29:1,3; 38:1; 50:3; 56:1; 63:2; 68:3; 69:7; 77:2; 80:1; 84:2; 89:1; 90:3; 91:1; 92:2; 94:1,3,3; 96:2,3; 97:2; 112:1; 130:2; 136:2; 137:3; 141:2; 143:1; 145:4; 147:1,1; 148:3; 151:2; 162:2,3,4; 184:1,1,2; 199:3,3; 200:2; 201:1; 205:1; 212:1,1,1; 213:1; 219:3; 220:1; 237:2; 244:1; 246:1,1,2,2; 258:1; 278:4; 279:2; 284:3; 294:2,2; 295:2; 298:3,3; 299:2,3; 300:5; 305:3; 315:3; 335:3; 343:1; 356:1; 358:2; 363:3; 372:2; 373:1
depletion	(7)	38:2; 50:1; 103:1; 104:1; 124:1,1; 288:1
deposit	(1)	196:3
depositor	(1)	81:2
depositor's	(1)	81:2
deposits	(1)	167:3
deprecated	(2)	328:1; 359:1

depreciated	(1)	53:1
depreciating	(1)	155:2
depreciation	(15)	56:1,1,1; 69:3; 94:1; 99:4; 100:2; 102:2; 103:1; 104:1,1; 140:2; 188:1; 227:2; 228:1
depress	(4)	210:1,1,1; 320:1
depresses	(2)	162:3; 210:1
depressing	(7)	142:1; 143:2,2; 211:1; 264:3; 319:2,2
depression	(6)	9:3,3; 338:1; 339:5; 347:2; 367:1
depressions	(4)	108:3; 162:3; 231:1; 265:2
deprived	(1)	358:1
deprives	(1)	67:3
depriving	(1)	377:2
depth	(1)	130:1
depths	(2)	129:3; 130:1
derivatives	(1)	246:1
derive	(3)	19:2; 166:4; 184:2
derived	(5)	20:2; 104:3; 211:2; 231:3; 298:2
derives	(2)	60:1; 355:2
deriving	(1)	357:2
des	(Count: 2 – not included)	
describe	(2)	15:4; 151:2
described	(10)	50:3; 144:1; 155:1; 158:2; 164:3; 243:3; 248:3; 308:1; 347:2; 355:2
describes	(1)	103:1
description	(5)	40:1; 41:1; 46:1; 122:4; 330:2
descriptively	(1)	4:2
deserves	(4)	154:3; 199:1; 234:2; 351:2
design	(1)	28:2
designate	(2)	52:1; 333:1
designated	(4)	28:5; 52:1; 115:4; 303:2
designation	(1)	169:5
designed	(3)	254:4; 324:2; 338:2
desirability	(2)	55:1; 170:2
desire	(22)	101:1; 167:2; 170:2; 171:2; 174:2; 198:2; 211:2,2,2; 212:2; 213:1; 214:2; 218:2; 219:1; 220:1; 235:2; 241:2,3; 336:1; 341:2,5; 348:1
desired	(6)	71:5; 211:1; 212:1; 213:1; 215:3; 240:1
desires	(6)	157:1; 212:1,1,2; 213:1; 360:1
desperate	(2)	250:1; 382:3
destined	(4)	105:2; 320:3; 321:2; 322:3
destroy	(3)	362:4; 363:3; 365:3
destroy'd	(1)	361:1

destroyed	(3)	188:2; 337:2; 347:1
destruction	(5)	56:1; 57:2; 242:1; 351:3; 380:3
destructive	(1)	371:1
detail	(21)	4:2; 7:4; 8:4; 11:3; 38:2; 50:2; 51:2; 56:1; 91:1; 130:1; 147:1; 194:1; 232:5; 240:2; 253:4; 258:2; 260:4; 265:1; 271:3; 367:1; 371:1
detailed	(9)	7:2; 43:3; 96:4; 111:2; 196:4; 249:2; 327:2; 342:1; 347:2
details	(1)	313:2
detected	(1)	331:2
deter	(3)	321:1; 323:1; 327:2
deteriorate	(1)	239:4
deteriorates	(1)	101:1
deterioration	(3)	62:3; 69:4; 216:2
determinant	(2)	191:2; 270:1
determinants	(4)	183:2,2; 184:1; 247:2
determinate	(8)	39:3; 181:1; 194:1; 205:2,2; 281:3; 299:1,1
determinates	(1)	183:2
determination	(3)	69:7; 331:2; 376:3
determine	(43)	4:1,3; 11:1,2; 12:2,2,2; 13:2,3; 21:2,2; 30:2; 64:1; 90:1,1; 107:1; 140:2; 147:1; 166:3; 174:2; 182:3; 185:1; 201:4; 227:2; 245:2; 246:1,1; 247:1,2; 248:1; 273:4; 274:4,4; 282:2; 305:3,3,3; 335:3; 337:3; 356:1; 378:1,1; 379:1
determined	(35)	6:3; 13:2; 30:2; 47:2; 50:4; 68:1; 77:2; 78:1,2; 89:1; 90:2; 110:1; 123:3; 170:1; 174:2; 189:2,2; 217:2; 247:1,1; 248:2; 254:4; 268:2; 270:1; 278:3; 301:3; 317:1; 324:4; 335:3,3; 348:4; 356:1; 368:2; 375:1; 378:2
determinedly	(1)	111:3
determines	(25)	4:2; 13:2; 29:4; 70:1,1; 89:1; 140:2; 165:1; 166:2; 168:1; 189:2; 190:1; 200:1,1,1,1; 247:2; 260:1; 275:2,2,3; 276:1; 293:1; 313:1; 369:1
determining	(12)	51:1; 77:3; 90:2; 91:3; 137:3; 149:1; 164:1; 272:1; 275:1; 296:3; 315:3; 379:2
deterred	(1)	372:2
deterrent	(3)	318:2; 322:3; 327:2
détruit	(1)	364:1
devaluation	(2)	309:1; 340:1

develop	(8)	13:2; 118:2; 172:2; 194:1; 271:3; 280:2; 313:2; 382:3
developed	(3)	153:2; 209:4; 257:2
development	(11)	78:1; 80:3; 94:2; 150:3; 159:1; 242:3; 308:1; 314:1; 331:1; 338:2; 360:1
developments	(3)	78:1; 101:1; 141:2
develops	(1)	235:2
device	(2)	234:2; 294:1
devices	(1)	378:1
devise	(2)	39:1; 215:2
devised	(3)	192:5; 339:3; 349:1
devote	(4)	29:1; 89:1; 156:2; 354:1
devoted	(8)	19:2; 27:2; 89:2; 90:1; 246:1,1; 354:2; 378:1
devotees	(2)	353:3; 355:2
devotion	(1)	355:2
diagnosis	(2)	371:1; 383:3
diagram	(4)	180:2,3,4; 181:1
dialogue	(1)	356:2
dichotomy	(1)	293:1
dicta	(1)	186:1
dictators	(1)	381:4
dictionary	(1)	359:2
did	(22)	20:4; 77:2; 81:2; 100:2; 131:2; 178:1; 240:2,2; 251:4; 333:1; 334:2; 341:3; 344:3; 346:1; 350:2; 357:2; 358:3; 359:2; 362:3; 365:3,3,3
die	(6)	162:1; 354:1,2,2,2; 359:1
differ	(12)	51:3; 59:1; 64:1; 81:2; 123:3; 172:1,2; 221:3; 240:1; 242:1; 258:2; 325:2
differed	(3)	77:1; 355:4; 357:2
difference	(41)	19:3; 57:3,3; 58:2; 71:4; 73:3; 74:2; 79:2,2; 85:2; 92:2,2; 96:1; 97:1; 116:4; 128:1; 154:2; 156:3; 177:3; 178:1,1; 202:1; 223:2; 224:2; 227:1; 228:1; 232:3; 237:1; 240:2,2; 257:2,2; 259:1; 261:2; 267:4; 273:2; 277:4; 327:2; 330:1; 332:2; 381:1
differences	(16)	41:3; 42:1; 72:3,3; 74:2; 75:2; 116:1; 159:2; 172:2; 198:3,3; 199:1; 240:2,2; 277:4; 297:2
different	(120)	4:1; 14:1,1,2,2; 21:2,4; 33:1; 41:1,1,2,3; 42:1; 43:1,3,3; 44:1,1,1; 45:2; 54:3; 60:1; 69:7,7; 74:1; 83:1; 90:2,2,2,2,2; 91:1; 92:2;

different (cont.)   107:2; 114:2; 115:4,5; 116:1; 118:1; 121:1;
                                     136:3; 137:5; 145:4; 147:1; 149:2; 159:1;
                                     164:3; 165:1; 166:3; 167:4,4; 168:3; 169:3;
                                     171:3; 178:1,1; 182:2,2,4; 183:3; 185:1;
                                     187:2; 191:1,1; 195:1; 198:1,3; 201:2;
                                     202:1; 205:2; 206:2; 207:1; 210:2; 215:3;
                                     216:1; 219:3; 223:4,4,4; 224:2,2; 225:3,4,4;
                                     226:2,4; 227:2; 240:1,2,2,3; 242:4; 245:2;
                                     246:1,2,3,3; 251:4; 258:3; 259:1,1; 264:2;
                                     281:2; 282:1; 286:2,2,3; 293:1,2; 295:2;
                                     297:2; 299:1; 302:2,2,3; 323:1; 330:1;
                                     379:2; 382:3; 383:3

differentia   (1)   231:3
differential   (1)   40:1
differentials   (3)   275:4; 297:2; 305:3
differentiated   (1)   239:4
differently   (5)   60:1; 169:3; 198:1,1,3
differing   (5)   43:3; 68:1; 224:2; 226:4; 304:4
differs   (3)   169:3; 170:1; 280:1
difficult   (19)   20:2; 54:3; 105:1,2; 127:2; 137:5; 142:2;
                              157:1; 175:1; 176:3; 203:1; 212:1; 241:2;
                              268:1; 275:3; 279:2; 327:2; 331:1; 375:3
difficulties   (15)   24:4,4; 34:1; 39:3; 43:1; 81:1; 102:3;
                              108:3; 129:3; 138:2; 204:2; 229:2,2; 327:2;
                              357:2
difficulty   (14)   24:4; 38:2; 42:3; 43:1; 102:3,3; 105:2;
                              106:2; 116:1; 196:3; 208:2; 239:1; 274:2;
                              339:1
dig   (2)   129:3; 220:1
digestions   (1)   162:3
digging   (2)   129:2; 130:1
dignity   (1)   366:4
digression   (4)   37:1; 66:1; 104:2; 149:2
digressions   (1)   109:3
dilemma   (5)   142:2,2; 160:2,2; 170:2
dimension   (1)   138:3
diminish   (26)   7:1; 93:3; 100:1; 105:1; 110:3; 120:2,3,3,4;
                              121:1; 130:2; 136:3; 160:1; 185:1; 188:1;
                              213:1,3; 262:5; 263:3,4; 265:2; 291:2;
                              321:1; 341:2; 351:3; 358:3
diminished   (17)   10:1; 31:2; 99:2; 105:2; 127:1; 141:2;
                              167:2; 172:1; 211:1,2; 216:2; 248:2; 251:3;
                              253:1; 289:3; 290:3; 370:1

diminishes	(10)	7:1; 18:1; 42:1; 126:4,4,4,4; 251:3,3,3
diminishing	(26)	42:1,2; 81:1; 101:1; 108:1; 110:3; 120:4;
		121:1; 126:3; 130:2; 176:1; 257:3,3; 268:2;
		269:3,3; 271:3; 289:3; 296:2; 299:3; 302:4;
		326:2; 328:1; 341:2; 349:1; 372:2
diminution	(5)	18:1; 144:4; 210:1; 362:4; 363:2
dimmed	(1)	162:1
dining	(2)	216:1,1
dinner	(7)	210:1,1,1; 215:3,3; 216:1,1
dinners	(2)	216:1,1
direct	(18)	93:3; 139:1; 146:1; 157:2; 159:1; 160:2;
		205:2,3; 260:2; 275:2; 296:3; 335:3;
		336:2,2; 344:1; 366:2; 372:2; 376:3
directed	(20)	5:7; 159:1; 164:3; 227:2; 234:3; 241:2;
		280:1,1; 283:1; 286:3,3; 287:1,2; 339:2;
		346:3; 347:2; 349:2; 352:1; 358:2; 377:2
direction	(36)	10:1,1,1; 49:1; 68:3; 83:1; 93:3; 94:1;
		110:3; 140:3; 152:1; 170:1; 206:2; 207:4;
		248:2; 251:1,2; 252:1,2; 254:2,2; 260:2;
		265:2; 266:2; 279:2; 286:4; 287:1; 288:1;
		301:2; 307:2; 313:3; 314:1,1; 318:3; 332:2;
		379:2
directions	(14)	43:3; 117:1; 119:2,2,4; 254:3; 300:3,3;
		323:1,1; 330:1; 331:2; 332:1; 371:1
directly	(18)	13:2; 18:3; 46:1; 79:2; 99:2; 101:1; 113:1;
		142:3; 164:3; 200:2; 209:2; 316:2,3,3;
		339:1; 349:1; 364:1,1
directness	(1)	206:2
directs	(1)	288:1
dirges	(1)	131:2
dis-saving	(1)	82:1
disabuse	(1)	212:1
disadvantage	(5)	130:2; 214:2; 290:3; 338:3; 342:1
disallowed	(1)	297:2
disappear	(4)	81:2; 221:3; 304:1; 376:2
disappearance	(3)	221:2; 347:2; 376:2
disappeared	(2)	32:2; 364:2
disappoint	(2)	261:2; 320:3
disappointed	(1)	150:2
disappointment	(8)	51:3; 144:3; 169:2; 262:1; 293:2; 294:1;
		321:2; 327:2
disastrous	(6)	3:1; 157:1; 158:2; 161:2; 267:5; 349:1
disbursement	(2)	195:3,3

discard	(1)	61:1
discarded	(1)	71:3
discharge	(4)	75:1; 95:2; 109:1; 241:4
disciples	(2)	193:1; 354:2
disclaimed	(1)	5:7
discontent	(1)	264:1
discontinuities	(1)	68:3
discontinuity	(4)	68:3,3; 198:1; 301:3
discontinuous	(4)	198:1; 204:3; 301:3; 307:1
discontinuously	(1)	301:3
discount	(3)	135:2; 137:5; 224:3
discounted	(6)	58:2; 70:2,6; 71:2; 157:1; 188:1
discounts	(1)	191:2
discouraging	(1)	340:1
discourse	(4)	297:2; 305:3,3; 345:4
discover	(11)	31:2; 32:1; 61:2; 76:2; 89:1; 175:1; 247:2; 274:2; 332:2; 341:3; 353:3
discoverable	(2)	79:2; 362:2
discovered	(4)	102:3; 184:2; 327:1; 365:3
discovering	(2)	16:2; 159:1
discovers	(1)	97:1
discredited	(1)	350:3
discrepancy	(1)	33:2
discriminate	(1)	94:3
discuss	(7)	89:1; 95:5; 148:4; 257:2,3; 275:3; 294:1
discussed	(14)	32:2; 37:1; 49:1; 55:4; 61:2; 90:2; 107:1; 169:5; 170:1; 194:1; 207:3; 208:2; 257:1; 342:1
discussing	(1)	170:2
discussion	(36)	4:2; 5:2,7; 11:3; 24:4; 50:3; 61:1,2; 67:3; 74:1; 79:4; 92:2; 122:3,4; 149:3; 167:4; 176:1,2,3,4,4; 184:3; 186:1; 190:4; 275:2; 276:2,2; 287:4; 299:2; 319:4; 346:4; 347:2; 364:2,4,4; 382:1
discussions	(12)	4:3; 26:2; 74:1; 83:1; 106:3; 138:2,4; 288:1; 292:1; 351:4; 352:1; 364:2
disease	(3)	323:1; 324:2; 381:2
diseconomies	(1)	42:2
disentangle	(1)	32:1
disequilibria	(1)	73:1
disequilibrium	(1)	289:1
disette	(1)	342:2
disharmony	(1)	348:5

dishonest	(1)	208:2
disillusion	(3)	316:1; 317:3; 321:3
disinvestment	(17)	54:4; 67:1,3,3; 72:3,3; 73:2; 75:1; 76:2,2; 105:2; 318:3,3,3; 319:1; 331:2,2
dislike	(1)	280:3
dismay	(1)	316:1
dismiss	(1)	364:2
disobedient	(1)	317:1
disparities	(2)	372:2; 374:2
dispense	(3)	27:1; 29:4; 140:1
displacement	(1)	198:2
display	(2)	332:2; 359:1
disposal	(4)	226:2,2; 336:2; 351:3
dispose	(2)	373:3; 379:3
disposed	(4)	96:4; 100:2; 217:2; 303:3
disposition	(1)	65:1
disproportion	(2)	250:5; 251:1
disproportionate	(3)	220:2; 337:1; 353:3
disproportionately	(1)	148:2
dispute	(3)	178:1; 232:2; 383:3
disputing	(2)	13:2; 17:3
disquisitions	(1)	352:1
disregard	(2)	57:2; 365:3
disrespectfully	(1)	366:4
dissentient	(1)	345:1
dissimilar	(1)	199:1
dissociated	(1)	101:1
dissolution	(1)	340:3
distilling	(1)	383:3
distinct	(13)	4:3; 90:1; 97:1; 120:3; 164:2; 166:2; 167:4; 222:1; 230:2; 281:1; 301:1; 341:3; 351:2
distinction	(10)	20:5; 75:2; 78:2; 125:3; 138:4,4; 142:2; 168:2; 287:2; 299:3
distinctly	(2)	72:1; 362:4
distinguish	(8)	20:2; 32:1; 77:2; 144:2; 197:3; 209:2; 231:2; 240:2
distinguished	(7)	53:4; 75:1; 109:1; 144:2; 148:1; 170:2; 344:2
distinguishes	(1)	355:3
distinguishing	(2)	80:1; 351:4
distress	(2)	359:1; 382:2
distributed	(5)	45:2; 286:3; 299:1; 355:1; 379:1
distribution	(30)	4:1,3; 14:2; 16:1; 43:3; 79:3; 83:1; 91:3;

distribution (cont.)		92:1; 95:1; 109:3; 110:1; 117:2; 139:1; 176:1; 201:2; 245:2; 265:1; 281:3; 282:1; 286:2; 293:1,1,2; 294:1; 321:4; 324:3; 340:1; 362:4; 372:1
distributions	(1)	90:2
distributors	(1)	47:2
districts	(1)	186:2
disturbance	(4)	122:3; 125:2; 167:3; 250:1
disturbed	(2)	5:4,6
disturbing	(2)	219:3; 267:1
disturbs	(1)	264:1
disused	(1)	129:3
disutility	(30)	5:5; 6:1,3; 7:1; 8:3; 10:2; 11:1,2,2; 13:2; 14:3; 15:1,4; 21:4; 26:1; 28:2; 29:4; 30:2,2; 31:1; 128:2,2; 129:2; 176:1; 245:2; 278:3; 284:2,2; 291:2,2
dive	(1)	183:1
dived	(1)	183:1
divergence	(2)	201:3; 333:1
divergences	(1)	77:1
divergent	(2)	61:2; 116:1
diversification	(1)	380:2
diversion	(2)	220:1; 231:1
divert	(2)	300:3; 339:1
diverted	(5)	12:2; 231:1,4; 241:3; 354:2
diverting	(1)	232:1
divide	(1)	82:2
divided	(7)	91:1; 115:2; 195:1; 272:1; 281:3; 297:2; 298:3
dividend	(13)	4:3; 5:7,7; 37:3,4; 38:2,4; 59:2,3; 188:2; 220:1; 245:4; 247:1
divides	(1)	272:3
division	(16)	4:3; 73:2; 91:1; 201:1; 247:2,2; 293:1,1,2,2; 333:1,2; 338:3; 362:4; 382:3,3
divisions	(1)	170:2
divorces	(1)	67:3
do	(Count: 71 − not included)	
doctrinaire	(1)	350:3
doctrine	(27)	17:1; 18:4; 19:1,3,3; 25:4; 32:2,3; 33:2; 80:3; 155:2; 190:4,4; 213:4; 333:1; 335:2; 339:2; 351:2,2; 359:3,7; 362:2,3; 364:1,4; 367:1,1
doctrines	(1)	354:2

does	(90)	5:7; 8:3,3; 10:2; 13:1,1; 14:1; 15:2,3; 19:2; 24:5,5; 31:3; 34:1; 37:1; 56:1; 58:1,1; 65:1; 69:5,5; 73:2; 76:2; 83:1; 97:1; 110:3; 111:1; 123:2; 124:1,2; 125:4; 130:2; 131:2; 136:3; 138:2; 140:3; 148:3; 150:1; 151:3; 152:1,1,1; 155:3; 158:3; 160:2; 163:1; 166:3; 181:1; 188:4; 191:2; 192:5; 208:2,2; 209:2; 210:1; 211:1; 212:1,1; 220:2; 225:6; 228:3; 233:2; 238:1; 243:6; 245:2; 252:1; 257:3; 260:2,2; 272:3; 273:5; 276:2,3; 277:3; 281:1; 284:2; 288:1,1; 289:1,3; 301:3; 305:3; 316:1; 317:2; 334:2; 338:2; 366:3; 372:2; 373:3; 376:1
dog	(1)	183:1
dogmatic	(1)	242:1
doing	(6)	7:3; 64:1; 67:3; 234:3; 297:2; 301:2
dollars	(1)	224:2
domestic	(24)	19:1; 120:3; 203:1,1; 334:2; 335:3,3; 336:2,2,3,3,3; 337:2; 339:3,3; 340:1; 343:4; 348:4,4; 349:1,2,2; 382:2,3
dominant	(4)	33:1; 247:2; 315:3; 382:1
dominated	(1)	163:2
dominates	(1)	3:1
domination	(1)	335:1
done	(6)	53:1; 139:3; 177:2; 266:2; 273:5; 376:2
doomed	(1)	350:3
doth	(1)	345:2
double	(10)	18:5,5,5,5; 41:2; 126:3,3; 269:2,2; 293:1
doubly	(1)	131:2
doubt	(13)	9:2; 59:2; 60:1; 92:2; 93:3; 208:2; 262:5; 305:3; 317:3; 322:4; 333:1; 334:2; 375:2
doubted	(1)	353:2
doubtful	(8)	20:4; 127:1,1; 169:2; 221:3,3; 309:2; 345:1
doubtless	(3)	131:2; 355:2; 356:3
doubts	(7)	61:2,2; 144:2; 161:2,2; 182:3; 317:3
Douglas	(4)	32:2; 370:2; 371:1,1
Douglas's	(1)	370:2
down	(35)	4:3,3; 8:3; 68:3; 113:1; 118:2; 123:3; 165:2; 177:2; 179:2; 183:1,1; 197:2; 220:3; 235:1,1,1; 258:1,2; 275:1,4; 277:1; 279:3; 297:2; 305:3; 307:2; 323:1; 337:2; 340:1; 352:1; 353:3; 360:2; 362:2; 367:1; 379:2
downward	(15)	68:3; 252:2; 264:2; 265:2; 303:3; 307:2;

downward (cont.)		314:1,1,2,2; 317:2; 318:3,3; 319:3; 330:1
downwards	(1)	265:2
drag	(4)	33:3; 99:3; 104:2; 269:2
dragged	(1)	203:1
drain	(2)	330:1; 340:1
drama	(1)	362:2
drastic	(3)	118:2; 192:2; 321:1
draw	(5)	62:1; 108:2; 167:3; 226:1; 303:2
drawing	(5)	140:2; 331:1; 342:1; 344:4; 354:2
drawn	(8)	20:1; 161:4; 186:2; 204:3; 281:2,2; 330:1; 373:2
draws	(1)	176:1
dreaded	(2)	342:1; 346:1
dream	(1)	15:1
dreaming	(1)	292:1
dreary	(1)	366:4
dresses	(2)	20:4,4
drew	(1)	344:4
drink	(2)	173:1; 347:1
driven	(1)	16:1
drives	(1)	367:1
droop	(1)	382:3
dropping	(1)	332:2
dropt	(1)	344:5
dubious	(2)	140:2; 281:1
duck	(1)	183:1
due	(100)	6:2,2; 8:1,1,3; 9:3,3; 11:3; 12:3; 14:1; 16:1; 18:2; 27:1; 32:3; 38:1; 42:2; 43:3,3; 47:3; 49:1; 50:2; 55:1; 56:1; 57:2; 67:3; 69:5; 70:2; 71:3,4,4; 72:3; 73:2,2; 75:2; 77:1; 80:1; 81:2; 82:1; 98:1; 101:1; 109:1,1; 112:1; 120:3; 126:2; 138:2,2; 142:3; 144:3,3; 149:3; 154:2; 158:2; 159:2; 161:4,4; 169:3; 170:2; 171:1,2,2,4; 172:2; 173:2; 174:1,1; 187:3,4; 189:3; 197:3,3; 198:1; 200:2; 207:4; 208:2; 214:2; 233:3; 237:1; 251:2; 252:2; 264:1; 265:1; 271:1; 275:1; 278:1,2; 288:1; 300:1; 303:3; 308:1; 313:2; 318:2; 328:1,1; 329:2,3; 341:2; 366:1; 367:1; 370:1
dues	(1)	186:1
duly	(2)	6:3; 82:1
duplication	(3)	24:4; 145:1,2

durability	(1)	318:1
durable	(21)	51:2; 73:3; 102:3; 103:1,1; 131:1; 144:3; 146:3,3; 203:3,3; 222:2; 294:1; 315:3; 317:2,3; 318:1; 319:1; 324:1; 348:1; 375:3
duration	(4)	313:2; 314:1; 317:2; 318:1
durch	(1)	354:2
during	(43)	17:3; 38:2; 49:1; 52:1; 53:1,2; 54:3; 58:2; 61:2,2; 62:1,3; 97:1; 100:1; 128:1; 135:1,2; 136:3; 142:2; 143:2; 145:2; 147:2,2; 150:2; 213:3; 218:2; 226:2; 227:2; 262:1; 276:1; 279:2; 307:3; 319:3; 322:4,5; 323:1; 329:1; 334:2; 341:3; 346:1,4; 354:2,2
dutch	(1)	342:1
duties	(5)	372:2; 373:2,2,2,3
duty	(2)	234:3; 320:1
dwelling-houses	(1)	106:2
dynamic	(2)	348:5,5
each	(55)	5:6; 10:1; 18:5; 24:2; 45:2; 47:2,2; 52:3; 55:5; 56:2; 63:2; 64:1; 99:4; 105:2; 127:2; 130:1; 136:3; 156:2; 160:2; 166:2; 171:2; 177:1,2; 184:1; 188:1; 195:1; 198:2,2; 204:3; 224:3; 225:3,3; 229:1; 242:4; 248:1; 253:1; 265:2,2; 281:2,3; 282:2,2,2,2; 286:2,2; 297:2; 301:2; 305:3; 307:3; 333:1; 349:1; 353:5; 357:1; 364:1
eager	(2)	343:1; 383:3
eagerness	(1)	221:3
ear	(1)	366:4
earlier	(15)	20:4; 43:3; 49:1; 79:2; 216:1; 240:2; 241:2; 257:1; 288:1; 301:3; 329:2; 331:3; 334:2; 338:2; 346:4
earliest	(2)	318:3; 346:3
early	(10)	19:5; 100:2; 106:2; 214:2; 326:4; 340:1,2; 342:1; 365:3; 366:2
earn	(4)	47:1; 309:2; 321:1; 354:1
earned	(6)	17:3; 73:3; 110:2,3; 196:3; 221:2
earning	(2)	77:1; 144:2
earnings	(1)	202:1
earns	(1)	167:1
earth	(4)	347:2; 361:7,7; 366:1
earthquake	(1)	56:1
earthquakes	(1)	129:1
ease	(1)	271:3

easier	(3)	106:2; 271:3; 342:1
easily	(21)	44:2; 93:3; 106:2; 115:1; 118:2,2; 149:3; 152:1; 161:1; 203:1,2,2; 232:4; 241:3,3; 281:1; 285:4; 309:2; 344:2; 360:1; 377:2
east	(2)	342:1,1
eastern	(1)	345:1
easy	(15)	19:3; 49:1; 116:1; 126:2; 131:2; 137:4; 221:2; 227:2; 266:1; 268:1; 317:1; 341:1; 371:1; 377:2; 381:4
eccentric	(1)	157:1
echo	(1)	364:2
econ	(1)	369:1
economic	(130)	3:1,1; 9:3; 14:2; 19:2; 25:4; 26:2; 30:1; 31:2; 32:2; 33:3; 37:2,2; 38:1,5; 39:1,3; 43:2; 44:2; 47:4; 50:2; 59:4; 72:3; 79:4,4; 85:2; 96:2; 97:2; 103:2; 104:3; 109:3; 113:1,1; 120:3; 138:4; 143:4; 146:2,3; 149:1; 161:2,4; 162:3,4; 168:1; 172:2; 173:1; 176:1; 180:4; 185:1,1; 191:2; 193:2; 196:5,5; 197:1; 200:2; 205:2; 211:2; 214:1; 220:1,1; 223:5; 241:1; 245:1; 246:1; 247:2,2; 249:3,4; 257:1; 266:2; 267:2,5; 269:3; 293:2; 297:2,2; 313:2; 327:2; 333:1,1; 335:3; 337:2; 340:1,1,1,2,3; 341:1,1; 346:4; 348:1,5; 349:2; 350:1; 351:1,3,3; 354:2; 355:2; 356:2,4; 358:2; 359:3; 364:5; 365:1,3,3,5; 366:1,1,3; 367:1,1,1; 368:2; 369:1,1; 371:1; 372:1; 378:1,2; 379:1,3; 380:1,3; 381:4; 382:2,3; 383:3
economica	(4)	39:5; 60:4; 72:5; 176:4
economical	(1)	272:4
economically	(1)	369:1
economics	(28)	3:2,2; 5:7; 16:2; 19:5; 20:4; 32:2; 38:3,5; 72:3; 80:4; 129:1; 137:4; 186:1; 188:2; 189:3; 190:1,1; 242:1; 247:2; 293:1; 298:1; 334:3; 364:2; 365:3; 366:1,2; 378:2
economies	(1)	241:2
economist	(6)	16:1; 158:3; 177:2; 344:5; 359:7; 383:3
economists	(44)	3:2; 14:3; 17:3; 18:3; 19:3; 20:1; 33:2,2,2,3; 37:3; 55:3; 63:2; 76:2; 112:1; 138:1; 148:4; 183:3; 185:1; 193:1; 258:1,2; 279:3; 292:1; 317:1; 333:2; 334:2,2; 339:2;

effective (cont.)		283:1,1,1; 284:4; 285:1,1,4,4; 286:1,2,2,3; 287:2; 289:2,2; 291:2; 295:3,3,3; 296:2,3,3; 297:2,2,2; 298:2,2,3; 299:1,1,1,2,2; 300:5; 301:2,3,3,3,3,3; 302:1,3; 303:2,2,2,3,3; 304:4,4,4; 305:1; 307:1,1,2; 316:2; 320:2; 358:2; 362:3; 366:3; 375:1; 380:4; 381:1
effects	(25)	8:1; 11:3,3,3; 51:1; 94:1; 109:3; 125:3; 162:4; 163:2; 196:4; 230:3; 239:2; 245:2; 253:4; 257:1; 262:2; 264:2,2,3; 266:3; 319:1; 331:1; 337:1; 377:2
effectual	(1)	369:1
efficacy	(3)	263:1; 266:3; 349:1
efficiencies	(14)	43:3; 135:2; 136:1; 224:3,3; 232:3; 236:2,3; 238:3; 261:2,2; 262:2; 298:2,3
efficiency	(203)	28:1; 31:4; 42:1,2,2; 43:3,3,3,3; 70:3; 71:3; 109:1; 111:2,3; 112:1; 120:1,2; 135:2,2; 136:1,2,3,3,3,3,4; 137:1,3,4,4; 138:3,4; 139:1,1,2; 140:2,3; 141:1,2,2,2; 142:1,1,3,3; 143:1,1,1,2,3; 144:1,1; 145:3,3; 146:1,2; 147:1,1; 149:1,1; 151:2,2; 158:2; 164:3,3; 165:1,1,1,2; 170:1,1,2; 173:1; 174:1; 178:1; 184:1,2,2,2,2,2; 187:3,4,4; 190:1; 192:1,1,2; 193:1,1,1,1; 204:2; 207:4; 210:1; 211:1; 214:2,2,2,2; 216:2,2; 217:2,2; 218:1,1,1,2,2; 219:2,4; 220:1,3; 221:2; 222:1; 223:4; 224:3,3,3,3,3; 225:1,1; 228:2,2,2,2; 229:1; 232:3,4; 234:3; 245:3; 246:1,2; 248:1; 249:3; 250:5; 251:2; 253:3,3; 257:3; 260:2,3; 263:3,3; 264:2; 265:1,2; 266:1; 269:2; 270:1; 274:4; 278:3; 295:3; 299:3,3,3; 307:3; 308:1,1,2; 309:2,3; 313:2,2,2; 314:3,3; 315:3,4,6,6; 316:1,1,1,1,2; 317:1,2,3,3; 318:1; 319:2,2,3; 320:1; 323:1; 324:4; 325:3; 344:2; 351:3; 352:1,1; 355:3; 356:1; 357:1; 375:1,2,3; 380:2,2; 381:2,2
efficient	(11)	42:1; 43:3; 147:2; 214:2,2; 215:3,3; 216:2,2; 300:4; 369:1
efflux	(3)	333:1; 337:1,1
effort	(7)	42:2; 117:2; 246:1,1; 325:2; 336:3; 352:1
efforts	(3)	104:3; 123:4; 346:1
Egypt	(1)	131:2
eight	(2)	107:2; 108:2

eight-hour	(1)	15:3
eighteenth	(2)	353:2; 359:7
eighties	(2)	354:1; 365:3
either	(58)	9:3,3; 16:1; 27:2; 61:2; 64:1,1; 70:3; 74:2; 76:2; 79:3; 81:2; 93:3; 121:1; 137:3; 144:3; 152:1; 153:4; 158:2,2; 162:3; 179:2; 182:4; 188:3; 189:5; 191:2,2; 193:1; 200:2; 204:1; 207:4; 215:1; 228:3; 243:5; 249:4; 252:1; 258:1; 262:2; 265:1; 271:3; 275:1; 276:1; 279:2; 291:1; 304:1,4; 306:2; 314:3,3; 326:2; 327:2; 328:1; 330:2; 335:3; 347:2; 352:2; 369:1; 370:1
elaborate	(1)	365:3
elapse	(9)	46:1; 48:1; 71:4; 124:2; 137:5; 300:5; 316:2; 317:2; 318:1
elapses	(1)	46:1
elastic	(7)	26:2; 234:4; 246:1; 295:3; 300:3,3; 339:5
elasticities	(10)	116:3; 234:3; 236:3; 238:3; 241:2; 285:1,2; 292:1; 300:5; 302:2
elasticity	(44)	42:1; 44:2; 230:2,2,3; 231:3; 235:1,1; 236:6; 237:1; 238:2; 243:4; 258:1; 259:1; 273:1,3; 275:2; 282:3,3,3,4; 283:1; 284:2,3,4; 285:4,4; 286:3,3,4; 287:1,1,2,2,2; 288:1,1,1; 292:1,1; 296:3; 300:5; 305:1,1
electric	(1)	106:2
element	(13)	12:4; 39:2,4; 146:2; 153:4; 216:2; 270:1; 273:5; 302:3; 309:2; 313:2; 318:3; 335:2
éléments	(12)	12:2; 20:2; 177:1; 231:2; 245:1; 246:1; 247:1; 266:2; 283:1; 298:2,3; 334:2
elenchi	(1)	259:2
eliminated	(3)	51:2; 95:4; 358:1
eliminating	(1)	188:2
Elizabeth	(1)	40:1
else	(11)	21:1,3; 81:2; 82:1; 84:1; 273:5; 274:1,1; 369:1; 376:2; 383:3
else's	(1)	84:1
elsewhere	(5)	37:1; 203:1; 277:3; 301:3; 337:1
elucidate	(3)	13:2; 116:1; 295:3
elucidated	(1)	18:2
elucidation	(1)	352:1
embarked	(1)	150:2
embarrassment	(1)	264:3
embodied	(7)	50:3,3; 213:4; 214:2; 221:1; 240:1; 377:2

embodies	(1)	179:1
embodiment	(1)	32:2
embody	(3)	246:1; 287:3; 380:2
embrace	(1)	378:1
emerge	(3)	43:3; 104:1; 143:2
emergence	(1)	235:1
emergencies	(1)	108:3
emerges	(3)	63:3; 102:2; 380:2
eminent	(1)	354:2
emotional	(1)	355:2
emphasis	(9)	3:1; 51:3; 60:2; 76:1; 178:1; 190:4; 325:2; 338:2; 370:1
emphasise	(4)	76:1; 104:2; 277:2; 381:3
emphasised	(2)	145:2; 161:3
emphasising	(3)	17:2; 239:3; 317:1
emphatic	(1)	341:2
emphatically	(1)	342:1
employ	(9)	29:1; 42:1; 139:3; 140:1; 141:1; 160:2; 168:2; 214:2; 327:3
employ'd	(1)	361:1
employable	(2)	4:2; 5:6
employed	(72)	4:1; 5:4,5,6,6,6; 6:3; 8:1,3; 10:2,2; 13:1; 17:4; 27:1; 28:2; 42:1,1,2,2; 43:3,3,3; 56:2; 61:1,1; 72:3; 77:1; 79:2; 80:3,3; 81:1; 113:1; 114:2,2; 116:3; 123:4; 125:4,4,4; 126:1,1,3; 127:1; 140:3; 206:2; 214:2,2,2; 230:2; 234:3; 235:2; 247:1; 252:1; 263:2; 272:3; 273:1,5; 274:1,2; 277:3; 278:1,1,4,4; 280:1; 282:3; 283:2; 293:1; 344:4; 361:7; 379:2,2
employers	(10)	11:2,2; 12:2; 27:2,2; 247:1; 264:2,2; 301:3; 308:1
employing	(7)	23:1; 25:2; 125:4; 176:1; 319:2; 348:1; 363:1
employment	(615)	3:1; 4:1,2,2; 5:2,4,5,7; 6:2,2,3,3,3; 7:1,2; 8:1,3; 9:3; 10:1,1; 11:1,2,3; 12:2,2; 13:2; 14:1,2,3,3; 15:1,1,3,4; 16:1,1,1,1,2; 17:3,3,3,3,4,4; 18:1,1,2,2; 19:3; 20:4; 21:4; 22:1; 23:1,1,1,1,1; 24:1,1,1,1,1,2,2; 25:1,2,3,3,3,5; 26:1,1,2,2,2,2,2,2; 27:1,2,2,2,2,2,2,2; 28:2,2,2,2,2,4,5; 29:3,3,5,6; 30:1,1,1,1,2,2,2,2,2,2,3,3; 31:1,1,2,2; 33:3; 40:2,2;

employment (cont.)

41:1,1,2,2,2,2,2,2,2; 42:1,2; 43:3; 44:2,2,2;
45:1,2; 47:2,2,3,3,4; 48:1,1,1,2,2,2,2,2,2,2,4;
49:1,1,1,1,1,1,1,1,1; 50:3,3,4; 51:1,3;
54:2,2; 55:2,2,2; 60:1; 67:1; 77:2,2;
78:1,1,1; 79:3; 80:2,2; 81:1,1,1,1,1,1; 82:2;
83:1,1,1; 89:1,1,1,2,2,2; 90:1,2,2,2,2,2;
92:1; 96:2; 97:1,2,2; 98:1,1,1,2,2,2,3;
99:1,2,2,3; 100:2; 101:1; 104:3; 106:2;
112:1; 113:1,1,1,1,1,1,1; 114:1,2,2;
115:4,4,4,4,4,5; 116:2,3; 117:1,1,1,1,1,1,1,2;
118:1,1,1,2,2,2,2,2,2,3; 119:2,4;
120:3,3,3,4,4; 121:1; 122:1,1,2,4; 123:4;
124:2,2,2,2; 125:1,2,4; 126:1,1,1,2,3,3;
127:1,1,1,1,1,1,1,1,1,1; 130:2,2; 138:2,2;
141:3; 171:2; 172:1; 173:1,1; 182:1;
185:1,1; 187:3; 190:1,3,3;
191:1,1,1,1,1,2,2,2,2; 192:1; 202:2,2; 203:1;
204:1,1,2; 209:2; 211:1,1,1,1; 214:2;
217:2,3,3,3,3; 218:1,2,2; 219:2; 220:1,1,2;
222:1; 225:2; 235:1,1; 236:3,3; 239:1;
242:4,4,4,4; 243:1,3,4,4,5; 244:1; 245:4;
246:1,1,1,1,3,3; 247:1,2; 248:3,3,4;
249:1,1,4; 250:1,4; 251:1,1,1,1,3,3; 252:1,1;
253:1,1,2,2; 254:3,3,3; 257:3; 258:1,1;
259:1,1,2; 260:1,1,2,2,3; 261:1,2,2,2; 262:2;
263:1; 265:1; 266:3; 267:2,3,3,3;
269:3,4,4,4; 270:1; 271:1,2,3,3,3; 272:1;
273:1,2,4; 274:2,2,3,3; 275:1,1,1,2,2,2,2,2,3;
276:1,1,1,2,2; 277:1,3,3,3,3,3,3,3; 278:3;
279:2,2,2; 280:1,1,1,1,1,1,1,2,2;
281:2,2,2,2,3,3; 282:2,2,2,2,2,2,2,3,3,3;
284:1,2,2,2,2,2,2; 286:2,3,3,3,3,3,3,4,4;
287:1,1,2,2,2; 288:1,1,1; 289:2,3;
290:2,3,3,3; 291:1,2,2,2,2; 293:1,1; 294:2;
295:2,2,3,3,3; 296:1,1,2,2,3,3,3; 298:3;
299:3; 300:3,3,5; 301:1,2,3; 302:1,2,3;
303:1; 304:1,1; 305:3; 306:1,2; 307:3;
308:1,1,1,2; 309:1,2,2; 313:1; 314:3; 318:2;
320:1; 321:1,3; 322:1,1,3,4,4; 323:1,2;
324:2; 325:1,1,3; 326:1,1,1,1,2,2,2;
327:1,1,3; 328:1; 334:2; 336:3; 337:2;
339:3; 340:1,1; 349:2,2; 357:1; 368:1,1;
372:1,2; 373:1,2; 375:1,1,2; 376:1;

employment (cont.)		377:2,2,2; 378:1,2; 379:2,3; 382:3,3
employments	(1)	90:2
employs	(1)	119:2
empty	(1)	360:3
enable	(6)	41:1; 68:1; 235:1; 296:2; 322:2; 382:3
enables	(4)	67:2; 137:3; 234:3; 282:2
enabling	(1)	131:2
enchained	(1)	350:3
encourage	(3)	152:3; 308:1; 361:7
encouragement	(4)	271:3; 319:1; 334:2; 363:3
encouraging	(2)	94:1; 204:3
encroachment	(2)	380:3; 383:3
encumbrances	(1)	241:2
end	(17)	52:1; 53:1,1; 56:1; 62:3; 66:2,2; 71:4; 89:1; 99:4; 104:3; 143:2,2; 226:2; 322:3; 372:2; 376:1
endanger	(1)	254:3
endeavour	(4)	13:2; 25:1; 166:4; 352:2
endeavoured	(1)	364:4
endeavours	(3)	23:1; 53:2; 54:2
ending	(2)	101:3,3
endless	(1)	348:5
endorsed	(1)	58:2
endow	(1)	220:1
ends	(1)	348:5
endure	(1)	321:2
endured	(1)	332:1
energies	(1)	154:3
energy	(1)	381:1
engaged	(2)	272:3; 277:3
engineered	(1)	328:2
England	(11)	32:2; 172:2; 334:4; 342:1,1,2; 344:1; 346:4; 347:1; 353:2; 354:2
England's	(1)	344:2
English	(7)	343:3; 346:1,3; 347:2; 354:2; 359:7; 361:5
Englishman	(1)	159:2
Englishmen	(1)	159:1
enhances	(2)	237:1; 238:3
enhancing	(1)	344:3
enjoy	(8)	41:2; 93:2; 107:2; 108:1,1; 188:2; 219:3; 326:3
enjoyed	(1)	124:1
enjoying	(1)	94:1

enjoyment	(7)	19:2,2; 108:1,2; 131:2; 156:1; 361:7
enlarged	(1)	252:2
enlargement	(1)	380:3
enlarging	(1)	107:1
enlightened	(2)	327:2; 351:2
enormous	(5)	100:2; 159:1; 221:2; 323:1; 337:2
enormously	(3)	109:3; 252:1; 320:1
enough	(26)	70:6; 97:1; 100:1; 127:2; 157:1; 158:2; 181:1; 201:2; 204:2; 206:2; 214:2; 217:2,3; 299:1; 307:3; 308:1,1; 316:2; 323:1,1; 327:2; 342:2; 343:4; 356:3; 369:2; 381:1
enquire	(1)	222:1
enquiries	(1)	347:2
enquiry	(8)	4:3,3,3; 9:4; 37:1; 91:1; 272:2; 298:3
enrich	(5)	21:1; 128:2; 131:2; 345:4; 366:3
enriches	(2)	21:1; 366:3
ensconced	(1)	244:1
ensue	(4)	187:3; 204:2; 229:2; 337:1
ensued	(1)	141:2
ensues	(1)	302:1
ensuing	(4)	13:2; 149:2; 172:1; 320:2
ensure	(4)	220:2; 308:1; 337:2; 379:3
ensures	(2)	218:1; 288:1
ensuring	(1)	58:2
entangled	(1)	365:3
enter	(17)	39:3; 56:1; 58:1; 69:7; 70:3; 119:2; 148:2; 152:1; 221:1; 240:2; 265:2; 273:5; 294:1,2,2; 295:2; 358:3
entered	(3)	150:3; 160:3; 163:2
entering	(8)	262:4; 283:1; 295:3; 296:2; 302:2,4,4; 305:3
enterprise	(18)	108:2,3; 111:4; 129:3; 151:1,1,3; 158:3,3; 159:1,1; 160:1; 161:4; 162:1,2,3; 221:3; 230:2
enterpriser	(1)	381:1
enterprises	(1)	150:2
enters	(5)	58:1; 139:1; 168:1; 191:2; 220:2
entertain	(1)	24:5
entertained	(3)	51:3; 237:1; 334:2
entertainments	(2)	359:1; 362:2
entire	(2)	340:1; 342:1
entirely	(14)	8:3; 11:3; 100:2; 101:1; 123:4; 157:1; 199:2; 247:2; 303:2,2; 342:1; 344:5; 353:3;

entirely (cont.)		365:4
entirety	(1)	380:3
entitled	(6)	96:4; 164:2; 276:1; 280:1; 365:3; 371:1
entity	(1)	106:3
entrepreneur	(45)	23:1,1,1,1; 24:5; 40:2; 46:1; 47:1; 50:3; 52:1; 53:1,1,2; 54:3; 56:1,2; 57:1,1; 59:2; 62:1,1,1,1; 64:1; 66:2; 68:1; 69:5,5; 70:1,1; 77:2; 82:2,2; 151:1; 192:5; 213:4; 261:2; 264:2; 283:1; 288:1; 290:3,3,3; 348:1; 376:3
entrepreneur's	(19)	23:1,1; 24:1; 53:2; 54:1,2,4; 55:2; 58:1; 64:1; 66:2,2,2,2; 68:2; 72:2; 141:2; 144:2; 145:1
entrepreneurs	(74)	10:3; 11:2; 13:2; 17:4; 23:1,1; 24:1,2,2,4,4; 25:1,2,3,3; 26:2; 27:2; 29:1,5; 30:1; 42:2; 44:1; 52:1,1; 53:1; 54:3; 55:1,2; 56:2; 60:3; 62:1,3,3; 63:2; 64:1; 66:2,2,2; 70:2; 71:4; 76:1; 77:1,1; 78:1,1; 82:2; 92:1; 100:1; 104:1; 121:1; 189:5,5; 217:3; 230:2; 261:1,2,2,2,2,2; 262:4,5; 264:2,3,3; 287:2,2; 288:1,1,1; 290:2; 301:2; 316:3; 371:1
entrepreneurship	(1)	273:5
enunciate	(1)	296:2
enunciated	(1)	296:1
envelop	(1)	155:2
environment	(13)	32:3; 45:2; 198:3; 214:1; 250:2; 278:4; 281:1; 290:2; 314:3; 335:3; 374:2; 377:2; 379:3
environments	(1)	241:2
envisages	(1)	176:1
ephemeral	(1)	154:1
epoch	(6)	317:2; 318:1,1,1; 356:1; 365:1
epoch-making	(1)	252:2
equal	(145)	5:3,4,5; 18:2; 20:2; 21:1,4; 22:1; 25:3; 26:1,1,2; 28:2,2; 43:3; 53:2; 54:1,1,4,4; 55:1,5; 57:1; 58:1; 62:2,2,2,2,3; 63:2,2,2,2,2; 64:1,2,2; 66:2,2; 68:1,1,1,1,2; 69:3,3; 70:2,6; 71:1; 74:1,1; 75:1; 78:2,2,2,2; 81:2; 82:1,1; 83:2; 84:2,3; 95:1; 97:2; 98:3; 115:2; 121:1; 123:2,3; 135:2,2; 137:1,2; 139:1; 140:3; 142:2; 152:1; 157:1; 163:2; 165:1; 169:2; 171:2; 174:2,2; 175:2,2; 176:1; 177:1,2,4; 178:1; 184:1,2,2;

establish	(9)	58:2; 68:1; 136:3; 180:1; 207:1; 270:1; 307:1,3; 377:2
established	(18)	58:2; 80:2; 89:1; 109:3; 113:1,1; 115:1; 118:1; 154:2; 192:3; 204:1; 230:1; 251:3; 254:4; 309:1; 324:2; 341:2; 371:1
establishes	(1)	113:1
establishing	(2)	377:3; 378:2
establishment	(2)	268:2; 355:2
estate	(1)	361:5
esteem	(1)	360:3
estimate	(8)	104:1; 113:1; 122:5; 150:1; 169:3; 187:2; 240:2; 316:1
estimated	(5)	57:1; 71:1,1,2; 188:1
estimates	(10)	78:1; 102:2; 119:2; 127:2,2; 128:1; 148:1; 149:4; 240:2; 264:2
estimating	(4)	58:2; 149:4; 162:3; 240:3
estimation	(10)	5:6; 58:2; 145:2; 164:3; 208:2; 221:3; 234:2; 240:2,2; 320:1
et	(7)	60:4; 192:4; 292:1; 356:4; 358:3; 364:4; 376:3
etc	(16)	8:1; 17:3; 27:1; 38:2; 70:3; 100:1; 101:3; 102:2; 104:1; 181:1,1; 221:1; 233:3; 263:1; 359:1; 362:2
ethical	(2)	365:5; 366:4
Euclidean	(1)	16:2
Europe	(2)	207:4; 338:2
European	(1)	329:1
euthanasia	(3)	376:1,1,2
evaluate	(2)	39:1; 45:2
evasions	(1)	372:2
evasive	(1)	20:4
even	(130)	10:2,3; 13:1; 14:3; 24:4; 27:1; 32:2; 38:2; 42:1,2; 43:1; 47:2; 48:1; 49:1; 51:2; 57:2; 67:3,3; 68:2; 94:1; 98:1; 101:1; 104:1,2; 108:1; 110:3; 111:2,2; 127:1; 128:1; 129:1; 141:2; 145:3; 148:2; 150:1,2,2; 151:1; 154:1,2; 155:3; 156:2; 159:1; 161:2,4; 162:3,4; 167:3; 172:2; 177:2,2; 180:1; 186:2; 188:2; 191:1; 195:1; 199:1; 205:3; 207:4; 208:2; 211:1; 214:2; 215:3; 217:1; 218:2; 220:1; 223:1; 224:2; 232:1; 233:2,3; 237:1; 242:1; 249:1; 250:1; 254:2; 258:1; 263:3; 267:1; 269:3; 273:5; 276:1; 290:3;

exact	(12)	14:1; 39:2; 40:1; 69:3; 162:1; 223:2; 259:1; 289:3; 295:3,3; 296:2; 373:2
exactly	(16)	20:2; 21:1; 68:2; 72:3; 75:1; 78:2; 79:2; 84:2,3; 99:4; 171:2; 187:3; 193:1,1; 200:2; 226:1
exaggerated	(2)	162:3; 383:3
examination	(4)	111:2; 196:4; 200:2; 313:2
examine	(7)	11:3; 37:1; 66:1; 249:2; 313:2; 334:2; 340:2
examined	(9)	4:2,2; 7:4; 121:3; 148:1; 219:1; 232:5; 319:1; 358:2
examining	(2)	25:3; 281:2
example	(63)	3:2; 5:7; 6:2; 19:3; 38:1; 42:2; 48:4; 54:3; 55:5; 57:3; 60:1; 75:1,3; 76:2; 77:1; 98:1; 100:2; 102:2; 107:2; 109:2; 116:1; 119:2; 121:3; 125:3; 126:2; 127:1; 129:2; 154:1; 167:3; 168:3; 175:3; 177:4; 187:4; 188:2; 192:1; 193:1; 202:1; 203:1; 204:3; 207:3; 215:2; 229:2; 239:4; 246:1,1; 265:2; 276:1; 277:1; 286:3; 297:2; 306:5; 318:1; 331:3; 334:2,2,2; 337:2,2,2; 342:2; 344:2; 347:1; 361:5
examples	(8)	105:1; 106:3; 207:4; 219:2; 332:2; 338:2; 341:3; 358:3
exceed	(16)	29:4; 54:3; 68:1,3,3; 69:3; 78:2; 82:2; 98:1; 125:4; 141:1; 167:2; 171:2; 226:4,4; 368:2
exceeded	(4)	61:1; 150:2; 176:1; 277:1
exceeding	(4)	82:1; 128:1; 241:2; 252:1
exceeds	(9)	14:3; 31:1; 99:2; 136:4; 216:2; 227:1,1; 238:1; 306:5
excellence	(1)	234:2
excellent	(1)	356:2
excellently	(1)	332:2
except	(65)	5:7; 16:2; 19:3; 26:1; 28:5; 30:1,2; 38:1; 40:2; 51:1; 82:2,2; 91:1; 93:3; 94:1; 105:1; 109:3; 124:2; 138:4; 139:1; 145:1; 152:1; 159:1; 160:2; 161:1; 171:2; 196:3; 197:1; 215:3; 225:6; 229:1; 230:2; 231:3; 253:2; 258:1; 259:1; 262:2,2; 263:2; 267:5; 272:4; 275:4; 277:1,3; 279:2; 294:1; 299:2; 316:1; 322:4,4; 323:1,1; 325:1; 329:1; 331:1; 333:1; 348:4; 362:2; 364:1; 368:1; 369:2; 373:2; 376:1; 382:2,2

exception	(3)	151:3; 243:5; 350:2
exceptional	(6)	57:2; 92:2; 145:1; 238:3; 299:1; 381:1
exceptionally	(2)	71:4; 329:3
exceptions	(1)	16:1
excess	(67)	23:1; 25:1; 27:2; 28:2; 53:1,2; 54:2; 56:1; 58:1,2; 61:1,1,2; 62:2,2,3; 63:2,2; 64:1,1,1; 68:1,1; 72:2,2; 74:2; 76:1; 77:1,1,1,2,2; 78:1,2,2,2,2; 80:2,2; 82:1; 99:2; 101:1; 105:2; 109:1,2; 167:3; 176:1; 183:1; 213:3,3; 222:2; 238:2,2; 239:4,4; 288:1; 306:5; 324:1; 332:2; 357:1; 359:1; 363:3; 367:2,2,3; 369:1,1
excessive	(15)	32:2; 71:4; 154:1; 268:3; 321:3; 322:3; 329:1; 337:2,2; 344:3; 345:2; 351:3; 365:3; 367:3; 375:2
excessively	(1)	162:3
exchange	(26)	18:5; 75:1; 93:2; 151:1,1,1,1; 159:2; 160:1; 167:1; 197:2; 200:2; 206:1; 222:2; 224:2; 231:3,3; 319:2,2; 343:1,1,1; 346:1; 358:3; 369:1; 383:1
exchange-value	(1)	231:3
exchanges	(7)	20:1; 75:1; 159:2; 160:3; 170:2; 270:2; 339:3
exchequer	(1)	160:1
excitement	(4)	323:1,1; 381:2,4
exciting	(1)	354:2
exclude	(4)	15:3; 150:2; 167:3; 378:1
excluded	(1)	76:1
excluding	(2)	76:1; 306:3
exclusion	(3)	55:4; 75:2; 82:2
exclusive	(4)	23:1; 37:1; 54:4; 226:2
exclusively	(3)	20:2; 226:1; 367:1
executive	(1)	376:3
exempt	(2)	157:1; 383:3
exercise	(13)	70:1; 82:2; 131:2; 194:1; 247:2; 351:1; 367:1,1,2; 375:3; 378:1; 380:1,2
exercised	(3)	33:3; 100:2; 369:1
exercises	(2)	124:2; 206:2
exercising	(1)	164:2
exert	(6)	95:3; 151:1; 162:4; 172:2; 266:3; 361:7
exerts	(3)	318:3; 319:2; 368:2
Exeter	(1)	365:3
exhausted	(1)	53:1

exhaustion	(1)	375:3
exhibit	(1)	305:3
exhibited	(1)	70:4
exist	(17)	6:2; 13:2; 28:2; 68:3; 106:1; 144:4; 152:3; 163:1; 168:2; 202:1; 229:2; 238:3; 326:4; 367:2; 369:1; 374:2; 376:1
existed	(4)	48:2; 50:3; 270:1; 324:4
existence	(19)	15:3; 30:3; 50:2; 72:2; 146:3; 168:2,3; 169:3; 170:2; 172:2; 178:1; 288:1; 323:1; 350:1,3; 356:2; 363:3; 368:5; 374:2
existing	(92)	7:3; 8:1,3,3,3,3; 10:2,2,2; 14:3,3; 15:1,3; 21:4; 30:2; 31:4; 38:1; 44:1; 48:2,4; 49:1; 50:3; 82:2; 99:2; 100:1; 102:3; 103:1; 106:3; 111:2,2; 124:2; 125:4; 138:4; 142:2,3; 146:1; 147:2,2,2; 148:1,2,2; 151:1,1,2; 152:1,1,1,1,1; 153:5; 154:2; 169:2; 187:1; 192:5; 208:2; 210:1; 213:1; 217:3; 245:2,2,2; 246:1; 252:2; 268:2; 272:4; 274:1,2; 277:1,2; 289:2,2,2; 306:1; 315:3; 324:1,4; 325:3,3; 326:1,2; 327:2,2; 328:1; 348:1; 357:1; 367:2; 373:1,2; 379:2,2; 380:3
exists	(13)	7:2; 60:1; 104:2; 107:2; 128:2; 144:3; 154:2; 168:2; 236:3; 238:1; 239:4; 278:1; 294:1
exorcise	(1)	351:1
expand	(3)	27:2; 64:1; 325:2
expanded	(1)	251:3
expanding	(2)	270:2; 290:2
expansion	(17)	26:2; 95:2; 100:2; 105:2; 106:2; 122:4; 123:2,3,3,4; 124:2,2,2; 193:1; 303:2,3; 322:4
expect	(21)	10:1; 11:2; 24:2; 25:1,2; 30:1; 33:1; 46:2; 55:2; 68:1; 71:4; 116:4; 148:3; 152:1; 164:3; 261:2; 279:2; 299:2; 309:2; 320:1; 340:3
expectant	(1)	383:3
expectation	(120)	24:1,5,5,5,5; 25:3; 37:2; 40:2; 44:2; 46:2; 47:1,1; 48:1,1,1,2,2,2,2,2,2,4; 49:1,1,1,1,1; 50:2,2,2,3,3,4,4; 51:3,3; 54:2; 55:2; 56:1; 58:2,2; 59:1; 70:1; 77:3; 78:1; 95:1; 136:2; 138:4; 141:2,3,3; 142:1,3,3,3; 143:1,1,2,2,3; 144:3; 145:1,3; 146:3; 147:2; 148:1,1,3;

expenses	(3)	135:1; 208:2; 221:2
expensive	(4)	159:2,2; 215:2; 360:5
experience	(45)	3:1; 9:2,2,3; 16:2; 20:1; 59:3; 64:2; 93:3; 94:1; 96:4; 109:3; 130:1; 152:1; 155:2; 157:1; 162:2; 164:2; 192:1,1; 197:1,2; 202:1,1; 203:1; 210:1; 219:1; 239:2; 247:2; 249:3; 250:2; 251:4; 252:1,3; 253:2; 254:3; 301:3; 322:4; 332:2; 338:2; 340:3; 364:1; 366:1; 373:1; 377:2
experienced	(3)	9:3; 207:4; 318:2
experiences	(2)	219:2; 347:4
experiment	(1)	380:2
experimental	(2)	203:2; 354:1
expert	(1)	154:3
expiry	(1)	169:2
explain	(9)	32:2; 33:1; 72:3; 187:3; 254:3; 343:1; 356:2; 362:4; 364:4
explained	(10)	76:2; 77:1; 79:2; 81:2; 176:1; 242:1; 335:3; 342:1; 345:1; 367:1
explaining	(5)	250:3; 313:1; 315:4; 329:1; 370:1
explains	(4)	140:3; 214:1; 299:2; 343:1
explanation	(26)	30:3; 81:1; 98:1; 122:2; 123:4; 144:1; 167:2; 168:2; 174:2; 201:3; 209:2; 257:3; 301:2; 313:2; 314:2; 315:4; 317:2; 329:2; 330:2; 348:1; 350:4; 356:2,3; 358:2; 362:3; 366:1
explanations	(2)	189:2; 314:3
explicit	(2)	175:1; 368:5
exploded	(1)	367:1
exploit	(1)	376:1
exploitation	(1)	150:2
export	(6)	344:1; 345:1; 347:2,2,2; 348:4
exports	(1)	272:3
exposition	(4)	5:7; 27:1; 78:1; 149:3
expound	(1)	25:3
express	(12)	37:2; 50:4,4; 61:1; 66:2; 154:2; 155:2; 240:3; 304:3; 305:3; 342:3; 382:3
expressed	(11)	7:1; 25:4; 27:2; 39:3; 44:2; 78:1; 137:2; 169:3; 242:1; 366:1,2
expresses	(3)	56:1; 281:1; 350:1
expression	(5)	129:4; 205:3; 273:2; 305:3; 366:2
expressions	(1)	39:3
expressly	(13)	4:3; 5:7,7; 18:4; 72:3; 80:3; 167:4; 177:1;

expressly (cont.)		178:1; 191:2; 254:4; 276:2; 297:2
extend	(4)	81:1,1; 260:1; 285:3
extended	(1)	380:2
extension	(5)	81:1; 365:3,3; 366:1; 379:3
extensive	(7)	59:3; 151:3; 152:1; 187:1,3,4,4
extent	(29)	4:2; 24:4; 69:2; 104:2,3; 105:2,2; 124:1;
		140:3; 143:1; 144:3; 148:2; 177:2; 186:2;
		200:2; 206:2; 211:2; 230:1; 231:3; 233:2;
		270:3; 284:3,3; 301:1; 305:3; 348:1;
		363:3,3; 375:1
extinct	(1)	359:3
extra	(10)	72:3; 117:2; 118:1; 139:3,3; 186:2;
		187:1,3,3,3
extracts	(1)	361:4
extraordinarily	(1)	183:1
extraordinary	(2)	326:4; 350:1
extravagance	(1)	108:2
extravagant	(1)	151:1
extreme	(12)	14:1; 69:2; 73:2; 94:2; 98:1; 123:4; 128:1;
		149:4; 191:2; 249:2; 305:3; 345:1
extremely	(5)	93:1; 251:4; 329:2; 338:1; 352:2
extremes	(5)	118:2; 250:1,1; 254:3; 363:3
exuberance	(1)	353:2
eye	(1)	365:3
eyes	(4)	157:1; 325:2; 350:3; 359:2
fable	(3)	106:1; 359:2; 360:2
fabled	(1)	131:2
fabric	(1)	59:3
face	(7)	43:3; 101:1; 191:2; 219:2; 350:4; 357:2;
		360:7
faced	(3)	24:4; 43:3; 327:2
faces	(2)	156:2,2
facet	(1)	158:2
facie	(2)	9:3; 230:3
facilitate	(2)	27:1; 151:1
facilitates	(2)	150:3; 160:2
facilitating	(1)	381:4
facilities	(3)	136:3; 215:2; 337:2
facility	(1)	224:3
fact	(121)	5:7; 6:2; 7:3; 9:2; 14:1,1; 17:3; 19:5; 31:1;
		39:4; 41:3; 43:3; 50:4; 56:1; 59:1; 64:1,2;
		68:3; 73:2,3; 79:2; 80:3; 81:1,1; 84:3;
		85:2,2; 96:2; 98:3; 99:2; 102:3; 106:3;

fact (cont.)		114:2,2; 118:2; 122:4; 124:2; 146:2; 149:4; 150:1; 152:1; 154:3; 159:1,2; 160:2; 174:2; 179:1; 180:1; 184:1; 187:5; 189:1; 191:1; 192:1,2; 197:2; 198:3; 205:2; 211:1; 212:1,2; 214:2; 218:3; 220:1; 224:2; 230:2; 232:1,4; 236:5; 237:1; 238:3; 239:2; 241:4,4; 242:4; 250:1; 252:1; 254:4; 261:2; 264:2; 271:3; 272:1,1; 274:2; 275:4,4; 276:2,3; 278:1; 288:1; 290:2; 291:2; 296:2,3; 302:2; 304:1; 314:2; 316:1; 317:1,2; 321:3; 322:1,1,3; 323:1; 325:2; 328:1,1; 337:1; 338:2,3; 343:4; 345:1,4; 355:3; 356:1; 358:3; 364:2; 367:3; 368:5; 370:1; 374:2
facto	(1)	288:1
factor	(76)	23:1,1,1,1; 24:1,2; 25:1; 27:1; 42:1; 51:2; 53:1,1; 54:1; 55:3,3,3,5; 56:2; 57:3; 67:1,2,3; 69:3,3,3,5,5,7,7; 70:1,4; 72:2,2; 76:1,1; 90:2; 92:2; 93:3,3; 95:3; 100:2; 101:1; 110:1; 128:1; 136:3; 139:2; 141:1,3; 145:3; 150:3; 165:2; 168:1; 175:2; 176:1; 179:1; 185:1,1; 187:3; 196:3; 205:2; 214:1; 218:3; 220:2; 231:3,3; 234:3; 264:2; 275:4; 278:4; 279:1,2; 304:1; 315:4; 329:2; 341:3; 381:4
factor-cost	(1)	55:5
factories	(1)	106:2
factors	(128)	16:1; 23:1,1; 24:4; 25:3,3; 53:1; 54:2,2; 55:2; 60:2; 66:2; 76:1; 80:1; 89:1; 90:1,1,1; 91:1,1,1,1,1,1,2; 93:1; 96:1,2,2; 97:2; 99:4; 107:1,1,1; 110:2; 119:2,3; 120:5,5; 121:3; 122:1; 136:3; 137:3; 147:1; 149:1,1,4; 153:3; 154:2; 157:1; 162:4; 163:2; 165:2; 187:3,4; 201:2; 218:3; 219:2; 245:2,5; 246:1,1,1,1,2; 247:1,1,2,2,2,2,3; 248:3; 249:2,2; 253:3; 254:1,2; 258:1; 260:2; 261:1; 262:2,3,4,5; 268:2,2; 270:1; 272:1,4; 273:5,5; 276:2; 278:4; 281:3; 287:2; 288:1; 294:2,2; 295:2,3; 296:2; 297:1,2,2,2,2; 298:3; 299:2; 302:2,2,2,4,4; 303:1,1,3,3; 304:2; 305:3,3,3,3; 319:1; 350:3; 368:1; 379:1,2
factory	(6)	71:2; 139:3,3; 149:4; 150:2; 235:2

falling (cont.)		337:1,1; 370:1,1; 377:2
falls	(27)	31:3; 32:1; 42:1; 94:1; 98:1; 103:1; 105:1; 126:1,1,1; 127:1; 137:2; 171:4; 182:3; 216:2; 228:2; 229:1; 233:2; 253:3,3; 260:2; 316:1; 319:2; 325:1; 336:3; 337:1; 352:2
false	(3)	20:2; 91:1; 293:1
falters	(1)	162:1
fam'd	(1)	361:1
familiar	(9)	17:3; 19:2; 61:1; 89:1; 137:4; 182:3; 224:2; 241:2; 279:1
families	(2)	281:2; 361:5
family	(5)	97:2; 107:2,2; 109:2; 361:8
famous	(4)	346:3; 357:1; 365:3; 370:2
fancy	(3)	156:2; 380:2,2
fanning	(1)	381:4
fans	(1)	360:7
fantastically	(1)	277:1
far	(77)	9:2,3; 10:1; 12:2; 14:3; 26:1; 30:2; 31:2; 41:2; 43:3; 47:2; 48:4; 49:1; 50:3; 51:1; 56:1; 61:2; 69:4; 74:2; 89:1; 93:2; 94:3; 98:1; 99:2; 104:3; 110:1; 112:1; 118:2; 119:2; 121:3; 122:3; 124:1,1; 141:2; 142:3; 145:2; 152:1; 158:2; 164:2; 178:1; 183:1; 187:4; 198:1; 205:2; 215:3; 218:3; 220:1; 225:2; 230:2; 236:4; 242:2; 264:3; 266:1; 273:2,2,5; 277:1; 284:2; 288:1; 303:2; 306:4; 329:2; 331:1; 337:1; 341:3; 342:1; 346:3; 351:1; 356:3; 362:2; 368:2; 370:1; 373:3; 375:2; 377:2,2; 380:2
far-reaching	(4)	20:1; 109:3; 161:2; 320:1
fare	(1)	360:5
farm	(1)	150:2
farmer	(2)	151:1; 347:2
farmers	(2)	330:1,1
farming	(2)	151:1; 354:1
fashion	(4)	115:1; 184:1; 238:3; 292:1
fashionable	(1)	240:1
fast	(3)	114:3; 183:1; 219:4
faster	(6)	82:2; 202:1; 204:1; 273:5; 289:2; 308:1
fatal	(2)	275:3; 277:3
fate	(1)	219:3
father	(2)	221:2; 353:6
fault	(2)	209:2; 297:2

faults	(1)	372:1
faulty	(3)	183:2; 339:3; 349:1
favour	(11)	109:2; 116:1; 117:1; 123:4; 194:1; 216:1; 238:4; 239:1; 286:4; 366:4; 382:3
favourable	(45)	99:1; 111:2; 112:1; 120:3,3; 145:1; 151:2; 159:1; 192:2,2; 211:1; 218:2; 232:3; 261:2; 262:5,6; 263:2,3,3,4,4; 264:2; 265:1,2,2; 287:2; 319:1; 330:2; 333:1; 335:3; 336:1,2,2,2; 337:1; 338:1,2,2,2,2,3,3; 343:4; 373:1; 381:3
favourably	(1)	251:2
favoured	(1)	352:2
fear	(7)	162:3; 202:1,1; 346:2; 350:2,3; 372:2
feared	(1)	202:1
fears	(1)	162:1
feasible	(1)	357:1
feature	(2)	154:3; 241:2
features	(2)	221:2; 254:3
federal	(1)	327:2
feed	(1)	155:3
feeds	(1)	319:3
feel	(5)	60:1; 79:2; 148:2; 171:2; 375:3
feelings	(2)	240:3; 365:3
feels	(1)	208:4
felicity	(1)	361:7
fell	(2)	124:1; 359:3
fellow	(1)	155:2
fellow-citizens	(1)	374:2
fellows	(1)	11:3
felt	(5)	150:2; 198:2; 271:3; 347:2; 362:2
fermé	(1)	364:1
fervour	(2)	354:2,2
fetish	(1)	155:2
few	(8)	23:1; 89:1; 155:3; 186:1; 276:2; 322:4; 353:3; 383:3
fickle	(1)	204:2
field	(11)	11:3; 40:1; 159:1; 176:4; 206:2; 284:2; 380:1,1,2,2; 383:3
fields	(2)	193:1; 378:1
fifteenth	(1)	337:2
fifth	(2)	156:2; 346:1
fifty	(3)	307:3; 364:2; 369:1
fight	(1)	360:3

figure	(33)	13:2; 58:2,2; 84:2; 101:1; 104:1,1; 120:3; 124:1; 125:1; 127:2,2; 128:1; 136:3; 141:2; 181:2; 203:2; 206:2; 208:2,2; 221:3; 233:2; 248:1; 253:3; 261:2; 266:3; 270:1; 303:1; 307:1; 323:1; 357:1,1; 375:3
figures	(5)	101:1,2,3; 127:2; 325:4
fill	(7)	30:1,1; 31:4; 98:2; 105:2; 129:3; 229:2
filled	(1)	129:3
filling	(2)	262:1; 379:3
final	(4)	119:2; 247:2; 301:3; 379:1
finally	(18)	138:4; 140:1; 157:1; 163:2; 173:1; 183:1; 201:3; 208:2; 226:2; 229:1; 246:1; 248:3; 278:4; 298:3; 319:1; 339:1; 367:2; 368:3
finance	(8)	101:1; 111:3; 128:1; 130:1; 155:2; 159:1; 354:2; 362:2
financed	(7)	109:2; 121:1; 122:1; 128:3; 129:2,4; 330:1
financial	(23)	98:1,3; 99:2,2,2; 100:1,1,1,2,2; 104:3,3; 105:1; 109:1,1; 128:1,1; 131:2; 207:4; 208:2; 253:1; 307:3; 371:1
financially	(1)	316:3
financier	(2)	376:3; 380:3
financiers	(1)	131:2
financing	(2)	119:4; 129:2
find	(45)	16:1; 30:1; 32:1,2; 37:1; 38:2; 43:3; 64:2; 66:2; 100:2; 105:1,2; 138:1; 139:2; 156:1; 165:2; 166:4; 175:1,4; 189:3; 202:2; 205:3; 215:3; 220:1; 223:4,4; 241:4; 249:2; 250:1; 279:1; 282:4; 287:2; 309:1,1; 313:2,2; 316:3; 327:2; 330:1; 345:1; 351:4; 352:2; 369:1; 374:2; 381:4
finding	(4)	292:1; 352:2; 365:3; 378:2
finds	(7)	47:2; 156:2; 159:1; 213:1; 217:2; 326:2,4
finest	(1)	353:5
finish	(1)	334:1
finished	(16)	46:2,2; 47:1; 49:1; 52:1,1,1; 53:2; 54:3; 62:3,3; 75:1; 103:1; 148:1; 257:3; 332:2
firm	(23)	24:2; 40:2; 42:1; 44:2,2; 47:2,2,4; 55:4,5; 67:1,3,3,3; 72:3; 268:2; 280:1,1,1; 281:1; 293:1,1; 339:4
firm's	(4)	67:2,3,3,3
firms	(11)	40:2,2; 43:2; 46:2; 47:2; 54:3; 67:3,3; 103:1,1; 293:1
first	(106)	6:1,3; 8:2; 9:2; 12:3; 17:2; 20:2; 23:1;

foreseen	(18)	38:2; 48:4; 56:1; 83:1; 93:2; 122:3,4; 123:2,3; 141:2; 142:2,2,2,2,2; 168:3; 287:1; 293:2
foresight	(9)	7:1; 108:2; 111:4; 144:4; 218:1; 323:1; 367:3; 368:1; 379:2
forfeit	(1)	333:1
forget	(2)	51:2; 298:3
forgetful	(1)	278:4
forgets	(1)	155:2
forgoing	(2)	196:3; 377:2
forgot	(1)	340:1
forgotten	(2)	96:2; 365:1
form	(38)	19:3; 46:1; 70:4; 82:1; 83:1; 89:1; 116:1; 129:2,4; 130:1,2; 148:3; 153:1; 166:2,3,3,3; 167:2; 168:2,2; 180:1; 188:2,2; 189:4; 196:3; 209:1; 213:1,1; 218:2; 236:2; 240:1; 258:1; 272:2; 282:2; 304:3; 334:2; 357:1; 367:2
formal	(5)	95:3; 179:1; 278:3; 297:2; 305:3
formalising	(1)	297:2
formally	(3)	83:2; 115:1; 234:3
formation	(11)	4:3; 76:2,2; 102:3,3; 104:1,1,1; 128:1; 148:2; 193:1
formed	(1)	109:3
former	(41)	4:3; 20:1; 21:2; 47:1; 57:3; 58:2,2; 59:2; 60:3; 61:1; 78:1,1; 90:1,2; 104:3; 118:2; 126:1; 138:2; 142:2; 149:1; 150:2; 195:2; 197:1; 210:1; 222:2; 239:3; 250:5; 268:1,2; 269:1; 272:3,4; 273:5; 290:3; 292:1; 321:2; 349:1; 352:2; 370:1; 374:2; 380:2
formerly	(8)	82:1; 151:3; 242:1; 251:2; 253:3; 348:1; 349:1; 354:2
formidable	(1)	279:3
forming	(3)	148:2; 192:5; 346:3
forms	(14)	42:2; 129:2,2; 131:1; 195:1; 213:1; 233:2; 234:3; 240:3; 355:3; 357:1; 370:1; 374:2; 380:3
formula	(3)	39:1; 117:2; 352:1
formulate	(1)	72:1
formulated	(1)	345:3
formulates	(1)	347:1
forth	(17)	18:4; 43:3; 78:1; 94:2; 106:2; 124:2; 140:2; 166:2; 170:2; 245:2; 257:2; 280:1; 297:1;

Freiland	(1)	354:2
Freiland-Freigeld	(1)	354:2
French	(5)	342:2; 346:3; 353:6; 359:1,1
frenzy	(1)	383:3
frequency	(1)	307:3
frequent	(2)	83:1; 151:1
frequently	(8)	48:2; 61:1,2; 137:4; 151:1; 157:2; 163:2; 337:2
fresh	(2)	44:1; 213:1
friction	(1)	307:2
frictional	(8)	6:2,2,2; 7:1; 10:2; 15:3; 16:1; 278:1
frictionally	(1)	19:3
friend	(1)	344:2
friends	(2)	121:1; 150:2
from	(Count: 496 – not included)	
frontier	(1)	353:6
fronts	(1)	325:3
frugal	(2)	361:5; 363:3
frugality	(4)	80:3,3; 81:1; 361:7
fruitful	(2)	81:1; 361:5
fruition	(1)	374:2
fruits	(6)	130:2; 131:2; 220:1; 347:2; 361:7; 382:3
fulfilled	(1)	72:2
fulfilment	(2)	144:3; 383:2
full	(154)	5:7; 6:2; 12:2; 16:1,1,1,2; 26:2,2,2; 28:2,2,2,2; 29:4; 30:1,3; 31:2; 47:3; 68:3,3; 80:2,2; 81:1,1; 82:2; 100:1,2; 101:1; 112:1; 118:2,2,2,3; 120:3; 122:4; 124:1,2; 125:4; 127:1,1,1; 161:4; 164:2; 168:2; 182:1; 191:1,1,1,2,2; 202:2,2; 203:1; 204:1,2; 209:2; 214:2; 215:3; 217:2,3; 218:1,2,2,2; 220:1,2; 222:1; 235:1,1; 236:3,3; 243:1,3; 250:1,1; 251:3,3,4; 252:1; 253:2,2; 254:3; 260:1; 266:3; 267:2,3,3,3; 271:3; 275:1,2,2; 277:1; 284:2; 290:3,3,3; 291:1,2; 295:3,3; 296:1,2,3; 300:3; 301:2,3; 302:1; 303:1; 304:1,1; 306:2; 308:1; 321:1,3; 322:1,1,3,4; 323:1,2; 324:1,1,2; 325:3; 326:1,1,1,1; 327:1; 337:2; 339:3; 357:1; 368:1,1; 372:1,2; 373:1,2; 374:2; 375:1,1,2; 376:1; 377:2,2,2,2; 378:1,2; 379:3,3; 382:3
Fullarton's	(1)	364:6
fuller	(2)	24:4; 92:2

fully	(13)	18:2; 27:1; 28:2; 50:2; 119:3; 122:4; 257:2; 289:3; 301:3,3; 303:2; 338:3; 362:3
function	(112)	8:3; 9:1; 25:2,2,3,3,3,3,5,5; 29:2,2,3; 30:1,1; 32:2; 40:2; 43:1,3; 44:1,2,2; 45:2; 55:2,2,5,5; 56:2; 77:2; 89:1,1,1,1,1,1,1,2; 90:2,2,2,2; 91:3; 92:2; 95:4; 96:2,2,3,3; 98:3,3; 113:1; 117:2,3; 168:1; 180:1; 197:3,3; 198:1; 199:3; 200:1; 204:3; 205:1; 207:4; 208:4; 209:2,2; 246:1,1,2; 266:2; 269:3; 272:1,1,2; 273:1,1,2,2,3,3; 274:1,1,1,1,3; 275:1,2,2,4,4,4; 278:1,2,4,4; 280:1,1,1,1,1,1,1,1,2,2; 281:2,2; 282:2,2; 283:2; 286:2; 318:1
functional	(5)	90:2; 168:1; 173:2; 275:2; 279:2
functioning	(3)	33:3; 269:3; 380:3
functionless	(2)	376:2,3
functions	(18)	25:3,4; 26:2; 90:2; 115:5; 116:1,4; 173:1; 181:2; 199:3; 246:1,3; 279:2; 282:2,2; 334:4; 379:3; 380:3
fund	(2)	186:2; 366:1
fundamental	(25)	4:2; 5:2; 8:2,2; 10:3; 13:2,2; 20:1; 32:2; 41:2; 85:1; 96:4; 97:2; 113:1; 145:3; 184:3; 233:2; 246:2; 272:1; 277:1; 346:1; 348:5; 354:1; 374:3; 383:3
fundamentally	(2)	189:3; 258:2
funds	(16)	95:2,2,2; 100:1,2; 101:1,1,1,1,1,3; 157:1; 165:1,1; 251:3; 319:2; 373:1
furnish	(6)	32:2; 181:2; 246:1; 275:1; 297:2; 369:1
furnished	(2)	362:4; 381:1
furnishes	(1)	135:2
furnishing	(4)	9:3; 219:2; 259:1; 382:3
further	(72)	26:2; 31:3; 45:2; 48:1; 49:1; 53:3; 55:4; 66:1; 78:1; 105:1; 108:3,3; 113:1,1; 118:3; 127:1,1; 130:2,2; 157:1; 166:3; 169:3; 176:2; 177:2; 195:2; 196:2; 199:2; 204:3; 209:4; 213:2; 219:1; 220:2; 228:2; 232:3,4; 236:2; 245:3; 247:1; 259:1; 263:3; 265:1,2,2; 272:3; 282:1; 287:2,4; 289:3; 290:3; 293:2; 295:3; 301:3; 303:2,2; 304:1,4,5; 305:3; 317:3; 318:2,3; 319:1,2; 321:1,1; 322:4; 323:1,1; 324:1; 330:1; 335:3; 372:2
furthermore	(19)	15:3; 38:1; 55:2; 68:1; 100:2; 120:4; 127:1;

furthermore (cont.)		157:1; 233:1; 246:1; 252:1; 273:2; 298:3; 324:2; 326:1; 336:2; 352:2; 378:1; 379:3
furtively	(1)	32:2
futile	(4)	26:2; 191:2; 269:3; 333:1
future	(130)	19:2; 21:2; 47:1; 69:6,7; 70:1,4; 71:1; 93:2,2,2; 94:2,3; 95:3; 104:3,3,3,3,3; 105:1,2; 106:2,2; 107:2; 110:3; 143:1,2,2; 145:3,3,4; 146:1,3,3; 147:2,2; 148:2; 153:1; 155:2; 157:1; 159:1; 161:2; 162:2,4; 163:2,2; 166:2,3,3; 168:3,3,3,3,3; 169:2,3; 170:1,1,2,2,3; 171:2; 172:1,2,2,2; 188:1; 198:1; 201:3; 202:1,2; 203:1,1; 204:3; 207:3; 208:4; 210:1,1,1,2,2; 211:1; 212:1,1; 218:1,2; 219:1; 223:2,2,3,4; 224:2; 228:3,3; 231:5; 233:3; 237:1,1,1; 241:3,4; 247:1; 263:3,4; 271:3,3; 293:2,2,2; 294:1,1,1; 298:3; 301:3; 308:2; 309:2; 315:3,3,5; 316:1,1; 355:2; 362:4; 369:1,1,1,1,1; 375:1; 380:2
gain	(15)	12:2; 56:1; 57:3; 58:1,2,2; 139:3; 142:2; 169:2; 214:2; 288:1,1; 301:2; 309:2; 333:2
gained	(1)	156:3
gains	(2)	157:1; 338:3
gambling	(2)	130:2; 157:1
game	(7)	150:2; 155:3; 156:1; 157:1; 374:2,2; 381:1
game-players	(1)	156:3
games	(1)	156:1
gap	(11)	30:1,1,1; 31:2; 97:2; 98:2; 105:2; 248:2; 261:2,2; 262:1
gaps	(2)	31:4; 379:3
gardens	(1)	33:3
gather	(3)	245:1; 314:1,1
gathered	(2)	329:3; 358:2
gave	(7)	33:1; 79:2; 195:1; 340:2; 359:3; 362:2; 369:1
gay	(1)	106:1
general	(103)	3:1,1,1; 9:1; 10:1; 12:1,2,2; 13:2,2,2; 14:1,2; 17:3,3; 25:3; 28:2; 29:3; 32:1; 37:3; 39:2; 40:1; 41:1; 43:2,3; 44:1; 47:3; 71:4; 72:3,3; 89:1; 90:2; 91:1; 96:2; 107:2; 113:1; 114:2,2; 115:5; 117:2; 120:5,5; 122:2,4; 136:1,3; 137:1; 147:2; 149:1;

gilt-edged	(2)	206:1; 308:1
gist	(2)	139:2; 186:1
give	(18)	24:1; 48:1; 54:2; 55:2; 67:2,3; 70:6; 107:1; 145:1; 151:1; 198:1,1; 239:4; 299:1; 304:1; 314:1; 344:2; 353:3
given	(263)	4:1; 5:5; 9:2; 10:1; 12:2; 13:2; 15:3; 17:3,3; 23:1,1,1,2; 24:1,1,2,4,4,5; 25:3,3; 26:2; 27:2,2,2,2; 28:2,4; 30:1,2,2; 40:2,2; 41:1; 42:1,2; 43:3,3; 44:1,2,2,2; 45:2,2; 50:2; 53:3; 56:2; 58:1; 63:2; 67:1; 69:5; 71:1,3; 72:3,4; 74:1; 77:2; 78:1; 80:1,1; 81:1; 84:2; 89:2,2; 90:1,2,2,2; 91:1,3; 92:1,1,2; 93:3; 94:1,1,1; 95:2,4,5; 96:2; 97:1; 99:1,2; 107:1,1,1; 109:3; 110:1,2; 111:2,3; 113:1,1,1; 114:2,2; 115:4; 119:2; 122:1; 125:2,3; 127:1,1; 135:2; 136:3,3; 138:2; 139:2; 140:2,3; 142:3; 143:1,1,3; 157:1,1; 165:2,2; 166:3; 168:1,1,2; 169:1; 171:3; 173:1; 176:4; 178:1,1,1,2,2; 179:1,1,2,2,2,2,2,2,2; 181:2,2,2; 182:3,3,3,4,4; 184:2; 186:1; 188:2,2; 189:2; 191:2; 192:1; 193:1; 195:1,3; 196:3; 197:1; 201:1,1,3,3; 202:1; 205:1; 207:1; 212:2; 214:1,2; 215:3; 216:2,2; 218:2; 226:2; 228:2; 234:3; 236:2; 240:3; 242:4; 243:3,6; 245:1,2,5; 246:1,1,1,1,1,1,1,1,2; 247:1,2,2; 248:2,2,2; 250:4; 252:1; 257:3; 258:3; 269:2; 271:3; 272:2; 273:3,3; 274:3; 275:2,2,2,4,4; 276:3,3; 277:1,3; 278:4,4; 279:2; 280:1,1,1; 281:1,3,3,3; 282:1,2,2,3; 287:1,2; 288:1,1; 289:3; 293:1; 294:2; 295:2; 298:2,2; 299:3; 300:2; 302:4; 305:3; 317:2,2; 318:1,1; 320:2; 324:2; 334:4; 335:3; 340:1; 343:1; 356:1,2; 365:3; 368:1; 378:2
gives	(17)	6:3,3; 33:2; 99:2; 122:4; 135:2; 170:2; 224:3; 225:2; 230:3; 243:5; 259:1; 273:1; 282:2; 305:2,3; 367:1
giving	(8)	20:4; 103:2; 164:2; 184:2; 294:1; 342:1; 346:3; 361:7
Gladstonian	(1)	362:2
glimpse	(1)	173:1
gloom	(1)	367:1

glorious	(1)	360:7
glory	(1)	360:3
go	(6)	140:1; 163:1; 258:1; 279:1; 287:2; 297:2
goal	(1)	212:1
God	(1)	347:2
goes	(7)	98:1; 124:1; 264:3; 273:2; 279:1; 345:1; 346:3
going	(4)	48:2; 49:1; 59:2; 265:2
gold	(22)	130:1,1,2,2,2; 200:2,2; 203:1; 204:3; 229:2,2; 236:1; 237:1; 294:1; 343:4; 345:1; 348:3; 349:1,1; 361:7; 362:1; 382:2
gold-digging	(1)	130:1
gold-miners	(1)	200:2
gold-mines	(2)	130:1,1
gold-mining	(6)	129:2; 130:1,2,2; 230:2; 231:1
gold-standard	(1)	230:2
golden	(1)	361:3
gone	(4)	229:2; 258:1; 360:7; 380:2
good	(52)	5:7; 10:2; 16:1; 20:4; 33:1; 43:3; 56:2; 69:3,4; 72:3; 80:2; 90:2; 93:3; 99:2,3; 122:4; 123:3; 129:3; 131:2; 139:3,3; 153:1; 169:3; 193:1; 211:2; 230:1; 252:1,2; 270:2; 275:4; 277:3; 284:2; 302:1; 330:1,2,2; 331:1; 332:2; 343:4; 344:5; 345:2,4,4; 349:2; 352:2; 356:2; 359:2; 366:3; 380:1; 381:1,1; 384:1
goods	(57)	7:1; 38:1,4; 49:1; 51:2; 52:1,1; 60:1; 61:2; 67:1; 75:1,3; 76:1,1,1; 93:2,2; 103:1; 119:4; 142:2,2; 147:2; 166:3,3; 192:2,2,2,2,3,5,5; 193:1,1,1,1; 207:4; 220:1; 226:4; 248:1; 273:2; 317:3; 318:2; 319:1; 320:3; 324:1; 332:2; 343:1; 346:2,3; 347:3; 350:2,3; 357:1; 359:1; 375:3,3; 383:1
goodwill	(1)	149:4
got	(5)	184:2; 193:1; 260:1; 347:2; 360:3
govern	(12)	12:2; 90:1; 129:4; 139:3; 149:4; 150:1; 165:1; 221:1; 244:1; 272:2; 317:2; 383:2
governed	(15)	12:2; 50:3; 70:4; 110:3; 112:1,1; 150:2; 151:1; 173:1; 203:3; 292:1,1; 335:3; 336:1; 356:2
governing	(3)	3:1; 78:1; 235:1
government	(16)	94:3; 95:2,2; 98:1; 108:3; 119:2; 120:2; 160:1; 162:3; 198:1; 200:2; 335:3; 351:2;

government (cont.)		379:3; 380:3; 382:2
government's	(1)	361:7
governments	(3)	98:1; 251:3; 268:1
governs	(3)	17:3; 165:1; 206:2
grade	(2)	130:1; 299:3
grades	(1)	41:2
gradual	(15)	49:1; 50:4; 122:4; 123:2,2; 153:4; 197:1; 218:2; 221:2; 264:2; 265:2; 267:5; 290:3; 376:2; 383:3
gradually	(25)	49:1; 51:1; 70:4; 72:2,2; 73:3; 108:1,1; 109:1; 120:4,4; 121:1; 187:1; 221:2; 269:3,3; 271:3; 279:2; 296:2,3; 314:1; 339:3; 340:3; 378:1; 383:3
grand	(1)	359:2
grandmotherly	(1)	177:2
grant	(2)	82:2; 83:1
granted	(2)	21:3; 96:3
granting	(1)	144:3
grasp	(1)	19:5
gratifications	(1)	242:2
gratifies	(1)	108:1
grave	(5)	38:1; 106:1; 160:2; 333:1; 369:1
gravest	(1)	254:3
great	(81)	4:2; 20:2; 32:2; 41:3; 43:1; 63:2; 73:1; 75:3; 96:4; 100:2; 101:1; 102:2; 108:3; 118:2; 122:1; 139:3; 143:2; 148:2; 150:3; 164:2,3; 204:3; 206:2; 209:2; 214:2; 217:1,1; 218:2,2; 219:2; 242:2; 250:1,5,5; 251:1,1,3; 252:1,2,2; 253:1,2; 263:1; 269:3,3; 276:1; 277:1; 288:1; 297:2; 316:2; 323:2; 324:1; 325:2; 326:3; 333:1; 337:2; 338:2,2,3; 339:3; 341:1; 342:3; 345:1; 346:4; 347:1,1; 348:4; 353:5; 356:2; 359:3; 361:7,7,8; 363:3; 365:3; 367:1; 372:2,2; 373:3; 376:2,2
greater	(79)	15:3; 25:3,3; 28:2; 30:1,1,2; 31:2; 38:2; 40:1,2; 49:1; 95:1,1; 97:1,2,2,2; 102:2; 105:1,1,1; 111:1; 114:2; 121:2; 122:2; 124:1,1; 125:2,2,2; 126:2,4; 127:1; 129:3; 151:1; 157:1,1; 164:3; 192:1; 193:1; 197:2; 202:1; 207:4; 213:3; 216:2,2; 228:2; 232:5; 234:1; 238:1,2; 239:4; 250:4; 251:3; 253:1; 260:1; 263:1; 264:3; 270:3; 271:3; 274:3;

gun	(2)	155:2; 157:1
habit	(5)	106:3; 174:2; 317:2; 367:1,2
habitable	(1)	99:3
habits	(7)	64:2; 91:1; 93:3; 97:1; 109:3; 201:2; 245:2
habitual	(4)	97:1,1; 98:1; 373:2
habitually	(1)	67:3
had	(84)	6:1; 20:4; 32:2,2; 37:2; 48:1,2,2; 52:2; 53:1,1,1; 60:1; 66:2,2,2; 80:3; 81:1; 82:1,1; 100:2; 101:1; 123:3; 140:1,1,1; 145:3; 150:2; 158:2,2; 161:3; 162:1; 182:4,4; 184:2; 189:5; 191:2,2; 209:3; 235:1; 241:2,2; 242:4,4; 243:6; 252:1; 257:2; 261:2; 314:3; 323:1,1,1; 332:1,1; 334:2,2; 336:2; 338:2; 340:1,2,3; 343:4; 346:1,1,1; 347:2,2; 349:1; 353:3; 354:2; 356:2,3; 363:2; 364:2; 365:3,3; 366:1,1,1,1,2,4; 371:1; 375:3
hales	(1)	345:4
half	(11)	71:5; 101:1; 160:3; 187:3; 333:1; 342:1; 343:4; 345:3; 356:2; 368:1; 382:2
half-crown	(1)	155:2
half-finished	(1)	47:2
half-way	(2)	184:2; 190:4
half-year	(1)	364:1
hall	(1)	365:5
halls	(1)	106:2
hand	(38)	14:1; 24:1; 25:4; 47:2; 53:1,1; 55:2; 63:3,3; 68:1; 98:1; 103:1; 117:1; 118:2; 120:3; 126:1; 128:1; 137:2; 150:2; 203:2; 247:2,2; 263:3; 264:2,3; 265:2; 267:5; 271:3; 288:1; 290:3; 293:1,1,1,1; 328:1; 345:4; 347:3; 371:1
handed	(1)	189:5
handicrafts	(2)	347:1; 361:7
handle	(1)	76:1
handled	(2)	44:2; 118:2
handling	(3)	77:2; 167:3; 367:2
handmaid	(1)	380:2
hands	(6)	32:2; 80:3; 103:1; 196:1; 320:1; 356:3
Hansen	(1)	193:1
happen	(10)	3:1; 37:1; 54:3; 153:1; 173:1,1,1; 222:1; 288:1; 289:2
happened	(3)	181:1; 276:2; 366:1

heads	(3)	91:1; 297:2; 360:2
health	(2)	101:1; 349:2
healthy	(1)	162:2
hear	(2)	292:1; 383:3
hearing	(2)	215:3; 353:2
heavily	(2)	128:1; 264:3
heavy	(10)	72:2,2; 73:1; 101:1; 104:2; 160:1; 208:2; 316:1; 323:1; 373:2
Heckscher	(17)	341:2,5; 342:4; 344:5; 345:2,5,6; 346:5; 347:3,5,6,7; 348:5; 350:1,5; 358:3,4
Heckscher's	(1)	341:1
hedonistic	(1)	161:4
height	(1)	341:3
held	(25)	11:1; 24:5,5; 143:2; 178:1; 187:4; 195:1,1,4,4; 198:3; 199:3,3; 221:3; 242:2; 259:1; 329:1; 330:2; 333:1; 343:1,1; 351:2; 354:2; 357:1; 373:1
help	(8)	27:1; 64:1; 83:1; 101:1; 129:3; 192:1; 261:2; 272:4
helped	(1)	366:1
helpful	(1)	382:2
helps	(3)	318:3; 349:2; 370:1
hemispheres	(1)	331:1
hence	(50)	17:3; 18:1; 27:2; 29:3; 30:1; 54:1; 57:1; 64:1; 77:1; 84:1; 97:2; 110:3; 117:1; 120:4,5; 125:2; 141:3; 149:4,4; 150:1; 153:1,1; 155:1,1,3; 169:1; 193:1,1; 195:4; 209:1; 210:1,1; 217:3; 222:2,2; 223:3; 228:3; 234:1; 249:2; 261:2; 264:3; 270:1; 277:3; 278:1; 283:3; 295:2; 300:2; 316:1; 369:1,1
Henry	(4)	346:4; 354:2; 355:2; 365:3
her	(Count: 6 – not included)	
here	(24)	6:1; 18:2; 37:1; 43:3; 47:4; 54:4; 78:1; 90:2; 118:1; 136:2; 174:1; 176:1; 184:3; 188:3; 195:1; 206:2; 224:2; 253:2; 274:2; 315:1; 330:1; 344:1; 362:3; 365:5
heresy	(1)	365:4
heretic	(1)	365:5
heretical	(2)	365:3; 370:2
heretics	(1)	371:1
heretofore	(1)	17:2
hesitate	(2)	19:3,3

heterodoxy	(1)	365:3
hibernated	(1)	364:2
high	(52)	69:5; 104:1; 123:4; 125:3,3; 139:3; 151:2,2; 154:1; 157:1; 159:2; 200:2; 204:1,2; 207:4; 219:1; 235:1; 236:5; 237:1,1,1; 239:1,3; 241:2,2,2,2,2,2; 242:1; 252:3; 286:3; 307:3; 320:2,2; 321:1; 322:3; 323:1,1,1; 327:2,3; 332:1; 341:2; 342:2; 344:2; 351:2,3; 352:1; 357:1; 374:2; 375:1
higher	(41)	42:1; 43:3; 48:1; 49:1; 97:2; 102:1; 110:3; 111:3,3; 123:4; 124:1; 142:3; 154:1; 156:2; 157:1; 170:3; 187:3; 193:1,1; 203:1; 208:2; 215:2,2; 219:3; 228:3; 230:3; 232:1; 238:1; 251:2; 253:3; 271:3; 317:3; 322:2; 324:2; 325:1,3; 326:4; 327:1,2; 328:1; 377:2
highest	(3)	203:1,1; 308:1
highly	(21)	16:1; 42:1; 80:1; 127:2; 130:2; 148:3; 151:1; 170:2; 202:2; 203:3,3; 204:2; 251:3; 269:3; 276:1; 299:1; 313:2; 314:3,3; 322:4; 369:1
him	(Count: 36 – not included)	
Himalayan	(1)	365:3
himself	(Count: 25 – not included)	
hint	(2)	180:1; 278:6
his	(Count: 286 – not included)	
historic	(1)	241:2
historical	(7)	40:1,1; 43:2; 91:1; 136:2; 302:1; 306:5
history	(7)	241:2; 337:2,2; 349:1; 359:2,7; 364:5
hit	(1)	340:2
hitherto	(10)	145:2; 165:2; 207:3; 286:3; 309:2; 368:4; 373:3; 375:1,2; 381:1
hive	(2)	360:2,7
hoard	(5)	174:2,2,2; 208:4; 209:2
hoarding	(16)	79:4; 160:2; 161:3,3; 174:2,2,2,2,2,2,2,2,2; 292:1; 345:1,1
hoards	(2)	167:1; 344:3
Hobson	(14)	19:5,5; 364:2,2; 365:2,4; 366:2,4; 367:4; 368:7; 369:2; 370:1,5; 371:1
Hobson's	(3)	364:4; 365:5; 367:3
hoc	(2)	292:1; 376:3
hold	(51)	5:7; 10:2; 16:1; 43:3; 56:2; 83:1,1; 84:3,3; 154:2; 160:2; 166:3,3; 167:2,2,2; 168:1,2; 169:1; 171:2; 172:1,2; 180:1; 183:1; 191:2;

hold (cont.)		194:1; 195:3; 196:2,3; 199:2; 200:2; 211:2,2; 213:1,1; 220:1; 230:1; 240:2; 241:2; 251:4; 252:1,2; 253:2; 270:2; 284:2; 290:3; 306:2; 320:2; 329:1; 350:3; 380:1
holder	(2)	195:1; 355:3
holders	(2)	142:2; 298:2
holding	(26)	84:3; 142:2,2; 155:2; 168:2,2; 169:2; 170:3,3,3; 174:2; 195:3; 196:2,3,3,3,3; 198:2; 199:2; 201:2,3; 205:1; 207:3; 234:1; 237:1; 240:3
holdings	(6)	194:1; 198:2,2,3; 207:4; 208:1
holds	(11)	18:1; 84:3; 122:4; 123:3; 153:1; 209:3; 215:2; 235:1; 290:3,3; 349:2
holes	(3)	129:2; 130:1; 220:1
holy	(1)	32:2
home	(15)	113:1; 205:3; 272:3; 333:1; 335:3,3; 336:2,2; 337:1,2; 339:3; 348:4; 366:1; 382:2,3
homely	(1)	292:1
homogeneity	(1)	41:3
homogeneous	(9)	40:2; 41:2; 42:1,1; 43:1; 45:2; 295:3; 296:2; 380:2
honest	(2)	352:1; 360:2
honesty	(3)	208:2; 360:7; 361:3
honour	(2)	351:2; 360:3
hope	(14)	39:3; 47:1; 145:1; 159:1; 174:1; 202:1; 204:3; 238:1; 247:2; 266:2; 327:1; 339:3; 381:1; 383:2
hoped	(1)	265:1
hopeless	(1)	100:2
hopes	(8)	109:3; 140:2; 144:2; 150:2; 159:1; 162:1,2; 265:1
horizontally	(1)	180:3
horror	(1)	366:1
horses	(1)	360:3
hospitals	(1)	362:2
hour	(4)	41:2; 215:3; 216:1,1
hour's	(2)	41:2,2
hourly	(1)	151:1
hours	(6)	15:3; 44:1,1; 167:3; 216:1; 289:2
house	(13)	61:2; 75:1; 99:3,3,3; 101:1,1; 130:2,2; 226:4; 323:1; 347:2; 367:1
house-building	(3)	101:1; 106:2; 130:2

hung	(1)	360:3
hurt	(1)	345:2
hypotheses	(3)	77:2; 355:2; 371:1
hypothesis	(13)	154:2; 228:3,3; 234:4; 235:1; 261:2; 290:3,3,3,3; 297:2; 367:1; 383:3
hypothetical	(7)	24:5; 55:2; 113:1; 121:3; 192:1; 242:4; 250:2
hysteria	(1)	162:3
I	(Count: 409 – not included)	
ice	(2)	154:1,1
idea	(18)	10:3; 12:2; 32:2; 56:1; 81:1,1,2; 93:3; 108:1; 153:1; 174:2; 177:2; 183:1; 211:2; 243:2; 287:3; 351:1; 357:2
ideal	(4)	327:1; 348:5,5; 374:2
ideas	(19)	20:4; 43:3; 61:1; 79:2; 112:2; 116:1; 198:2,3; 294:2; 295:3; 316:3; 350:2; 354:1; 383:2,3,3,3; 384:1,1
identical	(7)	39:1; 42:2; 71:3; 76:2; 108:3; 140:3; 287:3
identically	(1)	71:3
identification	(2)	72:5; 273:2
identified	(2)	192:2,2
identifies	(1)	278:4
identify	(2)	93:2; 273:2
identity	(1)	84:2
ideology	(1)	350:3
idle	(7)	23:1; 72:4; 73:1; 196:3; 201:2; 306:5; 347:2
idly	(1)	347:1
if	(Count: 566 – not included)	
ignorance	(5)	152:1,1; 155:2; 157:1; 163:2
ignorant	(4)	154:2,3; 316:1; 324:4
ignoratio	(1)	259:2
ignore	(4)	43:3; 56:1; 157:1; 189:4
ignored	(7)	5:7; 55:4; 72:3; 188:2; 272:1; 305:3; 350:1
ignoring	(2)	55:3; 246:3
ill-conceived	(1)	338:2
ill-done	(1)	159:1
illegitimate	(1)	67:3
illicit	(1)	13:2
illiquid	(2)	160:2; 213:1
illiquidity	(3)	194:1; 202:1,1
illogical	(3)	9:2,2,2
illusion	(2)	21:2; 81:2

illusions	(2)	321:3; 348:2
illustrate	(3)	171:2; 224:3; 341:5
illustrated	(7)	37:3; 125:3; 141:2; 180:2; 275:4; 344:2; 373:2
illustrates	(2)	19:1; 344:5
illustration	(3)	227:1; 325:4; 326:1
illustrations	(1)	139:3
im	(1)	354:1
imagine	(3)	54:3; 269:3; 361:5
imagined	(1)	339:3
imbecility	(1)	368:4
immediate	(11)	27:2; 43:3; 97:2; 107:2; 151:1; 166:3,3,3; 211:1,2; 309:3
immediately	(6)	71:5; 100:1; 187:4; 188:2; 369:1; 383:3
immoderate	(3)	267:1,1; 338:3
impair	(1)	105:1
impaired	(1)	33:2
impairing	(1)	362:4
impairment	(1)	63:1
impede	(1)	160:2
impeded	(2)	37:2; 373:3
impedes	(1)	160:2
impediment	(1)	351:3
impediments	(1)	338:2
impending	(1)	155:2
imperative	(2)	325:2; 340:3
imperfect	(5)	5:4; 14:1; 206:2; 301:3; 379:1
imperfections	(1)	5:6
imperfectly	(5)	97:1; 123:2; 300:3; 353:3; 371:1
impious	(1)	367:1
implication	(1)	278:1
implications	(1)	377:3
implicitly	(2)	62:1; 72:1
implied	(2)	176:1; 360:1
implies	(5)	139:3; 167:2; 211:2; 328:1; 362:4
imply	(1)	188:4
import	(1)	349:1
importance	(25)	19:5; 66:1; 68:2; 72:3,3; 75:3; 92:2,3; 98:3; 110:2,3; 115:2; 130:1; 145:3; 150:3; 151:3; 164:2; 185:1; 225:2; 278:4; 293:2; 302:1; 343:4; 357:2; 377:3
important	(58)	17:2; 26:2; 68:3; 74:2; 76:1,1; 94:1,1; 95:5; 96:1; 104:2; 107:1; 119:2,3; 122:1; 124:2;

important (cont.)		136:3; 141:2; 143:3; 144:2; 145:2; 149:1; 163:2,2,2; 172:2; 178:1; 179:1; 186:1; 196:4; 197:2,3; 206:1,2; 207:3; 208:2,2,2; 262:3; 264:4; 268:2; 270:1; 277:2,4; 287:1; 302:3; 324:3; 329:3; 331:1,2; 337:1; 348:5; 355:2; 364:4; 372:1; 373:3; 378:1; 382:3
imports	(3)	146:2; 338:2; 346:3
imposed	(1)	368:2
impossible	(20)	32:2; 39:1; 82:2; 84:2,2; 165:2; 174:2; 231:4; 238:1; 252:1; 284:2,2; 287:1; 288:1; 320:1; 339:3; 340:1; 347:4; 349:1; 368:4
impoverish	(2)	333:1; 346:1
impoverished	(2)	217:3; 337:2
impoverishes	(2)	366:3; 367:1
impoverishment	(1)	290:3
impracticable	(7)	14:1; 197:2; 235:1; 268:1; 325:1; 327:1; 342:3
imprecise	(1)	298:1
impressed	(1)	325:2
impresses	(1)	161:2
impression	(1)	365:3
improbable	(4)	148:5; 233:1; 314:3; 334:2
improbably	(1)	128:1
improve	(4)	212:1; 302:3; 338:2; 382:2
improved	(5)	53:1; 141:2; 210:2; 253:1,1
improvement	(13)	7:1; 53:1; 62:3; 66:2; 108:2; 109:1; 111:4; 206:1; 265:1; 323:1; 334:2; 344:2; 352:2
improvements	(2)	70:2; 129:2
improves	(3)	158:3; 249:1; 253:1
improvident	(2)	242:1; 362:2
improving	(4)	53:1; 83:1; 108:1; 188:1
imprudently	(1)	145:2
impugned	(1)	340:1
impulse	(2)	287:2,2
impulses	(1)	150:2
in	(Count: 3323 – not included)	
inability	(2)	6:2; 367:1
inaccessible	(2)	159:2,2
inaccurate	(1)	232:1
inaction	(1)	161:4
inadequacy	(1)	339:2
inadequate	(5)	106:3; 266:3; 267:1; 331:2; 369:1
inapplicable	(1)	124:2

increase (cont.)

183:1; 184:2; 185:1,1; 187:1,1,1,3,3,3,4,4,4;
188:2; 189:5; 191:2,2; 200:2,2; 201:1;
202:1; 203:2; 212:1; 214:2; 220:1,1;
230:3,3; 231:5; 233:2,2,3; 234:3; 236:2;
248:2,2,4; 249:1; 251:3,4,4; 257:3; 259:2;
260:2; 261:1,2,2; 262:2,6; 263:2,3; 264:1;
265:2,2; 266:2,3; 267:1; 271:3; 274:3,3;
277:3; 284:2,2,2,2,2; 286:2,3,3,3;
287:1,2,2,2; 288:1; 289:2; 290:3,3,3;
295:3,3,3,3,3,3; 296:3; 297:2; 298:2,2,2,3,3;
299:1,1,1; 300:1,2; 301:2,3; 302:1,3,4;
303:2,2,2,2,2,3; 304:2,4; 307:1,2; 309:3;
316:1,1; 318:1; 323:1; 324:2; 325:1,2;
328:1,2; 334:2,4,4; 336:2,3,3; 342:1; 344:1;
345:2,2; 346:1; 351:3; 361:5; 363:2,3,3;
366:1; 368:6; 369:1,1; 370:1; 373:2,2;
375:3; 376:3

increased

(140) 18:1; 27:2,2,2,2,2; 40:2; 43:3,3,3,3; 54:3;
77:1; 78:1; 80:3; 82:2,2,2; 91:1; 97:1,2;
98:2,2; 105:2; 106:1; 114:2; 116:2;
117:1,2,2,2; 118:1; 119:2,4,4,4; 120:3,3;
123:4,4; 130:2,2; 136:3,3,3; 141:2; 144:4;
170:2; 171:3; 172:1,1; 173:1; 178:1,1;
182:3; 186:2,2; 187:3; 189:5; 192:3,3,3;
193:1; 194:1; 198:1; 200:2; 211:2,2;
212:1,2; 215:3; 216:2,2,2; 228:2; 231:5;
232:1; 233:2; 234:3; 241:3; 248:2; 251:3;
257:3; 258:1,1; 261:2,2; 262:1; 265:1;
266:2,2; 268:2; 271:1; 277:3,3,3; 283:1,1;
284:1,2,3; 286:3; 287:2; 288:1; 289:3;
299:1; 300:2,4; 315:4; 325:2,2,3;
326:3,3,3,3; 327:2; 328:1,1,1,1,1,1,1,1,1,1,2,2;
329:1; 330:1; 337:1; 347:3; 359:3; 363:2,3;
368:6; 369:1,1,1; 371:1

increases

(77) 14:3; 17:3; 26:1; 27:2; 29:6,6,6; 30:1; 40:2;
42:1,1,1; 71:5; 83:2; 84:1; 96:4; 97:2;
105:2; 114:2,2,3; 120:4,4; 124:1;
126:3,4,4,4; 130:1,1; 171:4; 173:1; 182:3;
189:5; 196:3; 202:1; 216:2; 228:3;
229:1,1,2,3; 231:4; 236:3; 249:1; 250:4;
251:3,3; 253:1; 263:2; 266:3; 268:3; 283:1;
284:2,2; 286:2; 288:1,1,1; 289:2,2; 296:2,3;
298:3; 299:3; 300:3,4; 302:4; 303:2; 305:3;

increases (cont.)   317:3; 328:1,1; 336:1; 343:4,4; 367:2

increasing   (93)   7:1; 10:1; 18:1; 30:1,1; 42:2,2; 43:3;
54:3,3; 81:1; 83:1; 95:1; 108:1; 109:1,1,1;
117:2; 119:1,4; 120:3; 127:1; 129:4,4;
130:2; 173:1; 187:3; 189:2; 204:1; 211:2;
214:2; 219:1; 220:3; 230:2; 249:1; 252:2;
261:2,2; 263:1; 266:3,3,3; 268:3,3; 269:3;
284:2,2; 290:2,3; 296:3; 297:2; 300:1,1,2,5;
301:3,3; 302:3,4; 303:2,2,3; 307:1,2; 308:1;
316:1; 318:1,3; 325:1,2,2,3; 326:2,2,3;
328:1; 336:2,2; 340:3,3; 341:2,2; 342:2;
343:4,4,4; 344:2,4; 352:2; 363:1; 373:2;
375:2; 377:2

increasingly   (2)   105:2; 349:1

increment   (59)   21:1; 66:2; 69:5,5; 75:2; 76:1; 94:1; 113:1;
114:1,1; 115:2,3,3,4,4,4,4,4,5,5; 116:2;
117:1,2; 118:2,2,2; 119:2; 121:2,2,3;
123:3,3; 124:1,1,1,1,1; 138:2,2,4; 177:2;
187:3; 189:4; 201:1; 248:2,2,2,2,3,3,4;
251:3; 261:2,2,2,2; 287:2; 324:1; 381:1

increments   (5)   21:1; 75:3; 115:2; 123:3; 138:4

incumbent   (1)   279:3

incur   (3)   226:4,4; 357:1

incurred   (3)   169:2; 272:4; 332:1

incurring   (3)   46:1; 108:3; 195:4

incurs   (1)   23:1

incursion   (1)   189:3

indebted   (1)   264:3

indeed   (67)   10:2; 12:2,4; 18:1; 19:2; 20:1; 32:2; 39:3,3;
47:2; 72:3; 75:1; 79:3; 85:1; 94:1; 98:2;
100:1; 111:1; 114:3; 116:1; 128:2; 129:3;
143:1; 156:3; 174:2; 178:1; 184:1; 187:3;
191:2; 197:2,3; 198:1; 202:1,2; 207:3;
210:2; 212:1; 219:2; 226:4; 230:2; 239:1;
241:4; 249:4; 252:2; 261:2; 264:3; 266:2;
267:3; 275:1; 277:3; 288:1; 304:1; 316:2;
320:2; 321:3; 323:1,2; 331:2; 338:2; 345:1;
351:2; 357:1,2; 371:1; 375:2; 383:3,3

indefeasible   (1)   17:3

indefinite   (4)   154:2; 166:3; 265:2; 363:3

indefinitely   (8)   104:3; 152:1,1; 214:2; 252:2,2; 266:2;
290:3

independence (4)   108:1,2; 111:4; 297:2

independent	(24)	10:1; 11:1; 24:4; 56:2; 65:1; 69:8; 84:3; 179:2; 183:2; 184:1; 190:3; 199:2,2; 241:3; 245:1,3; 246:1,2; 247:1,2; 297:2; 305:3; 341:3; 370:1
independently	(3)	99:2; 179:2; 358:1
indeterminacy	(1)	39:3
indeterminate	(2)	8:3; 26:1
index	(3)	41:1; 114:2; 308:1
India	(3)	337:2; 342:1,1
indicate	(8)	51:3; 139:3; 208:3; 313:2; 320:3; 355:2; 379:3; 383:3
indicated	(4)	198:1; 206:1; 304:4; 308:1
indicates	(6)	197:1,2; 249:4; 340:3; 368:5; 377:3
indicating	(1)	321:2
indication	(1)	10:2
indicator	(1)	124:2
indifference	(1)	348:3
indifferently	(1)	276:1
indirect	(3)	11:3; 94:1; 336:2
indirectly	(5)	18:3; 46:1; 70:3; 79:3; 94:1
indispensable	(1)	106:1
indissoluble	(1)	160:2
individual	(111)	5:6; 11:3; 14:1; 19:1; 21:1,1; 24:2,4; 33:1; 40:2; 41:3; 43:2,3; 47:2; 54:4; 55:4; 56:2; 59:2; 60:1,1; 63:2,2; 65:1; 67:1,3; 72:3; 75:1; 81:2; 82:1; 83:2,2; 84:1,2,3,3; 85:2,2; 90:2; 94:1,3; 101:1; 107:2; 117:1; 121:1; 131:2; 150:3; 151:1,1; 153:1,1; 154:3; 156:3; 160:2,2,2,2; 161:2; 162:2; 163:2; 166:2,2; 170:1,1,3; 177:2; 178:1; 192:3,3; 194:1; 198:1,2,3; 199:1,2; 210:1; 211:1,2,2,2; 212:1,1,1; 221:3; 242:1; 253:1; 261:2; 264:2; 281:2; 282:2; 286:2,2; 290:2; 293:1,1; 308:1; 326:3; 329:2; 331:1; 339:4; 348:1; 352:2; 362:2; 366:3; 367:1; 372:2; 376:1; 378:1; 380:2,3; 381:1,1
individual's	(4)	85:2; 95:3; 166:3; 195:1
individualism	(5)	375:4; 380:1,2,3; 381:2
individualistic	(1)	317:1
individually	(1)	106:2
individuals	(44)	13:3; 14:1; 20:2; 21:1; 42:1; 46:2; 64:2,2,2; 65:1; 84:2,2,3; 91:1; 98:1,1; 101:1; 103:1; 107:2; 108:3,3; 109:2; 128:3; 150:2; 154:2;

inherited	(2)	52:2; 66:2
inhibit	(1)	31:1
inhibitions	(1)	108:1
inimical	(1)	212:1
iniquity	(1)	366:1
initial	(11)	49:1; 59:1; 100:1; 101:1; 152:1; 213:3; 226:2; 287:2; 288:1,1; 298:1
initially	(1)	288:1
initiated	(1)	83:1
initiating	(2)	250:1; 315:4
initiative	(8)	122:4,4; 162:2; 378:1,1; 380:1,3; 381:1
injures	(1)	338:3
injury	(1)	192:1
injustice	(1)	33:1
inland	(1)	58:2
innate	(1)	163:1
innumerable	(1)	345:1
inoperative	(1)	369:1
input	(11)	49:1; 51:1,3,3; 54:3; 216:2,2,2,2,2; 217:1
inquisition	(1)	32:2
insensitive	(1)	233:2
insight	(1)	353:3
insignificant	(1)	221:1
insist	(2)	101:1; 291:2
insistent	(1)	108:1
insoluble	(2)	66:2; 138:2
insolvency	(1)	264:3
inspired	(1)	374:2
instability	(10)	43:1; 151:1; 161:4,4; 252:1,2,2; 253:2; 269:3; 309:3
instalment	(1)	176:1
instalments	(1)	176:1
instance	(14)	20:2; 76:1; 80:3; 117:1; 123:4; 182:4; 187:2; 200:2,2,2; 245:3; 313:2; 344:4; 347:2
instances	(1)	346:3
instantaneous	(1)	123:2
instantaneously	(1)	278:1
instead	(17)	23:1; 26:1; 42:1; 81:2; 128:2; 142:3; 182:2; 185:1; 229:2; 267:3; 285:3; 296:3; 328:1; 339:3; 355:2,2; 370:1
instinct	(2)	108:1; 157:1
instinctively	(1)	14:3

institution	(2)	159:1; 268:2
institutional	(4)	217:2; 218:3,3; 219:2
institutions	(12)	91:1; 98:1; 108:3; 109:3; 155:2; 158:2; 221:1; 240:3; 265:3; 266:1; 268:1; 373:1
instructed	(1)	316:3
instructive	(1)	78:1
instrument	(6)	95:1; 151:3; 339:1; 351:3; 372:2; 380:2
instrumental	(2)	226:4,4
instruments	(6)	167:3; 188:2; 294:1; 375:3; 378:1,1
insufficiency	(9)	30:3; 31:1; 33:3; 144:3; 335:3; 353:2; 358:2,2; 362:3
insufficient	(7)	216:2; 237:1; 276:1; 337:2; 349:1; 369:1; 383:2
insuperable	(1)	14:1
insurable	(1)	56:1
insurance	(3)	157:2; 202:1; 357:1
insusceptible	(1)	317:1
intact	(1)	38:5
integral	(1)	113:1
integrated	(5)	54:3; 55:1; 66:2; 67:1,3
integration	(2)	24:4,4
integrity	(1)	16:1
intellectual	(7)	33:1; 192:1; 334:1; 350:2; 352:1; 365:3; 383:3
intellectually	(1)	348:3
intelligence	(4)	157:1,1,1; 376:3
intelligences	(1)	156:2
intelligible	(7)	27:1; 70:4; 119:3; 138:2; 201:3; 292:1; 335:1
intend	(2)	131:2; 208:2
intended	(8)	11:3; 60:3; 79:2; 109:2; 138:1; 139:2; 339:1; 353:2
intense	(2)	99:2; 340:1
intensified	(1)	253:1
intensities	(1)	245:2
intensive	(1)	124:2
intent	(1)	162:3
intention	(4)	82:2; 108:1; 160:3; 370:1
inter	(1)	246:1
interact	(2)	91:1; 238:3
interaction	(1)	165:2
interactions	(2)	297:2; 299:1
interchangeable	(3)	114:2; 295:3; 296:2

intercourse   (1)   365:3
interdependencies   (1)   298:1
interest   (712)   3:1; 4:3; 21:3; 28:1; 31:3,3,4; 32:1; 40:1;
68:1,1,1,1,1; 69:3; 70:3,3; 71:1,2; 79:3;
93:2,2,3,3,3,3,3,3,3,3,3; 94:1,1,1,1,1,3;
95:1,1,5; 96:1; 101:2; 107:2;
110:2,3,3,3,3,3,3,3,3; 111:1,2,2,2,2,3,3,3,3;
112:1,1,1; 119:4; 120:1; 129:2; 130:2,2,2;
136:4; 137:1,2,3,3,3,5; 138:3; 139:3,3,3;
140:1,2,2,2,3,3; 141:1,1; 142:2,2,2,2,3,3,3;
143:1,1,1,1,2,2,2,2,4; 144:1; 145:1,1,1,3,3,4;
147:1; 149:3,3,3; 150:2; 151:2,2,2; 157:1;
158:2; 159:2; 163:2,2; 164:2,2,3,3;
165:1,1,1,1,2,2,2,2,2; 166:4,4,5;
167:1,1,1,1,2,2,2,2,4,4;
168:1,1,1,2,2,2,2,3,3,3,3,3; 169:1,1,2,3;
170:1,1,3; 171:2,2,2,3,3,4,4; 172:1,1,1,1,2,2;
173:1,1,1,1,2; 174:1,2,2,2; 175:1,2,2,2,2,3;
176:1,1,1,1,1,1,3,4,4,4; 177:1,1,1,2,2,2;
178:1,1,1,1,1,2,2; 179:1,1,2,2,2,2,2,2,2,2;
180:1,3; 181:1,1,1,1,1,1,2,2,2,2;
182:2,2,3,3,3,3,3,4,4; 183:1,1,3;
184:1,2,2,2,2,2,2,2,2,2; 185:1,1;
186:1,1,2,2,2,3,3,3;
187:1,1,1,2,2,3,3,3,4,4,5; 188:1,1,4;
189:2,2,2,2,2,3,3; 190:1,1,2,3,3,3;
191:1,1,2,2,2; 192:2,2,2,2; 193:1,1,1,1,1,1;
194:1; 196:3; 197:1,1,2,2,2,3,3; 198:1,1,2,2;
199:1,1,1,3; 200:1; 201:1,3,3;
202:1,1,1,1,1,1,2,2; 203:1,1,1,2,2,3,3;
204:1,1,1,2,3,3; 205:2,2,2,3,3; 206:1,2;
207:1,3,3,3,3,4,4; 208:2,2,2,2,2,2,4; 209:1;
211:1; 212:1; 213:1,1,1,3; 215:1;
216:2,2,2,2; 217:1,1,1,2,2; 218:2,2,2,3,3;
219:1,1,1,1,2,3,4; 220:1,2; 221:3,3;
222:1,1,2,2,2,2;
223:1,1,1,1,2,2,3,3,3,4,4,4,4,4; 224:1,2,2;
225:1,1,2,2,2,2,2,2,3; 226:3;
227:1,1,1,2,2,2,2; 228:2,2,2,2,3,3;
229:1,1,1,1,2,2,3,3,3; 230:1,1,3,3;
232:2,2,3,3; 233:2; 234:3,3,4;
235:1,1,1,1,1,1,1; 236:3,4,4,4; 237:1,1,1,1;
238:3,3,3; 240:2; 241:2,2,2,2,2,4;

investment (cont.)		181:1,1,1,1,1,2; 182:3,4; 183:1,1,1,2; 184:1,1,1,2,2,2,2; 185:1,1; 187:3,4,5; 188:3; 189:4,5; 190:1; 192:2,2,3; 193:1,1,1,1; 201:1,1; 210:2; 211:2; 212:1,1,1,2; 213:1; 214:2; 217:2; 219:3; 220:2; 221:3; 235:1,1; 236:2; 241:2; 242:3; 248:1,1,2,2,2,3,3; 250:5,5; 251:2,4; 252:1,1,2,2; 253:3,3,3; 260:3; 261:2,2,2; 262:1,6; 263:3,3,4; 264:3; 265:1; 266:3; 269:2,4,4; 270:1,1,1,1,1; 275:1; 279:2; 281:3,3; 287:2; 288:1,1; 298:2,2,2; 308:1; 314:3,3,3; 315:3; 316:1,1,1,3; 317:3; 318:2,2,3; 319:1,1,1,1,3; 320:1,1,3; 321:1,2,3,4; 322:1; 323:1,1,1,1,1; 324:1,1,1,2,2,4; 325:1,2,3,3,3,3; 326:1,1,1,1,2; 327:2,2,2,2,2; 328:1,1,1,1,1,1,2; 329:1,2; 330:1,1,1,1,1; 331:1,2,2; 332:2; 335:3,3,3,3,3,3,3,3; 336:2,2,2,3; 339:2; 349:2; 351:4; 352:2,2; 353:2; 357:1; 364:5; 370:1,1; 371:1; 375:1,1; 377:2; 378:1,1
investment-demand	(1)	210:1
investment-goods	(2)	116:1; 273:2
investment-income	(1)	60:1
investments	(32)	75:1; 101:1; 149:3; 150:2; 151:1,1,1; 153:1,4; 154:1; 156:3; 160:2,3; 163:2,2,2,2; 170:3; 182:2; 187:2; 188:1,1; 211:2,2; 221:3; 319:2,2; 320:3; 321:1,3; 322:1,1
investor	(17)	46:1; 51:2; 120:1; 152:3; 153:1; 154:3,3; 155:2; 157:1,1; 158:2; 160:2,2; 163:2; 316:3; 376:2,3
investor-purchase	(1)	61:2
investor-purchasers	(1)	61:2
investors	(2)	139:3; 160:2
invitation	(1)	366:1
invited	(1)	366:1
invoking	(1)	351:2
involuntarily	(1)	15:3
involuntary	(25)	5:7; 6:2; 8:1; 10:2; 15:2,3,3,3,4; 16:1,2; 17:1; 21:4; 56:1,1,1; 57:2; 118:2; 128:2; 144:3; 190:1; 191:2; 274:2; 275:2,3
involve	(21)	8:3; 17:4; 79:3; 139:3; 211:1; 214:2; 217:1,2; 225:6,6; 238:1; 239:4; 252:1,2,2; 262:4; 305:3; 320:3; 338:3; 356:1; 379:3

involved	(18)	24:4; 27:1; 38:2; 53:1; 67:1,3,3; 70:1; 116:1; 140:2; 174:1; 215:2; 271:3; 272:4; 295:3; 297:2; 350:1; 380:3
involves	(29)	17:2; 23:1; 25:4; 42:1; 43:1; 67:3; 80:3; 81:1,1; 83:2; 89:1; 125:3; 129:2; 138:2,4; 144:4; 151:2; 179:1; 184:2; 212:1; 217:2; 274:3; 275:1; 299:3; 319:2; 330:1,1; 334:2; 355:3
involving	(5)	22:2; 128:2; 182:2; 291:2,2
irrational	(1)	162:4
irrefutable	(1)	344:5
irregular	(1)	267:5
irregularity	(1)	83:1
irrelevant	(1)	344:5
irrespective	(14)	43:3; 56:1,1; 58:2; 65:1; 84:2; 118:3; 216:1; 224:3; 225:6; 242:4; 262:1; 299:3,3
irresponsive	(1)	197:1
irrevocable	(1)	150:3
Irving	(4)	140:3; 142:2; 355:1; 357:1
is	(Count: 2411 – not included)	
isolate	(2)	183:2; 249:2
isolating	(2)	82:2; 297:2
isolation	(3)	43:2; 128:1; 295:1
issue	(2)	148:2; 259:2
issued	(2)	190:3; 200:2
issues	(1)	366:1
issuing	(1)	151:2
it	(Count: 1277 – not included)	
italics	(1)	5:7
Italy	(1)	269:3
item	(3)	59:2; 72:3; 366:1
items	(7)	38:1,2,2; 39:1,1; 100:1; 329:2
its	(Count: 344 – not included)	
itself	(66)	11:1; 26:1; 30:1; 33:2; 43:3; 47:2; 48:2; 49:1; 50:2; 64:1; 84:2; 95:1; 96:3; 97:1; 118:1; 124:1; 130:1; 162:1; 165:1; 167:1; 187:1; 197:3; 198:1; 202:1; 205:1; 207:3; 215:3; 217:2; 222:2; 225:3; 226:2,3,4; 229:3; 237:1,2; 241:2,3,4; 249:1; 251:2; 266:2; 270:1; 274:4; 278:2; 281:1; 285:1; 296:3,3; 298:3; 299:2; 300:5,5; 301:1; 303:2,2; 314:3; 316:2; 319:3; 327:2; 332:2; 336:3; 338:3; 361:7; 378:1; 379:3

jam	(2)	117:2; 118:1
James	(1)	3:2
jeopardise	(1)	157:1
jesuitical	(1)	351:4
Jevons	(2)	329:2,2
Jevons's	(1)	329:3
jewellery	(1)	358:1
job	(2)	43:3; 159:1
jobber's	(1)	159:2
jobs	(2)	6:2; 16:1
John	(2)	309:4; 364:2
Johnson	(1)	359:2
join	(1)	171:2
joined	(2)	354:2; 361:7
journal	(9)	38:5; 59:4; 79:4,4; 80:4; 113:1; 143:4; 180:4; 223:5
journey	(1)	292:1
judged	(1)	129:2
judgment	(11)	39:4; 128:1; 153:1,1; 154:3; 156:2; 198:1; 324:4; 325:2; 327:2; 375:3
July	(3)	363:5,6; 365:5
jumps	(1)	204:3
June	(3)	38:5; 59:4; 113:1
jury	(1)	359:2
just	(54)	5:6; 19:2; 21:1; 24:1; 28:2; 58:1; 62:3; 67:3; 75:1; 83:1,1; 84:2; 111:2; 120:5; 130:1; 135:2,2; 139:3; 140:1; 167:1; 170:1; 172:1; 175:2; 177:2; 180:1,1; 182:2; 184:1; 189:5; 211:2,2; 218:2,2; 221:1; 224:2; 229:1; 243:5; 257:3; 263:4; 266:3; 270:1; 274:3; 276:1,2; 288:1; 305:3; 320:1; 353:2,3; 357:1; 364:1; 365:3; 375:3; 376:1
justice	(5)	80:3; 176:1; 267:5; 268:2; 355:2
justifiable	(4)	130:1; 187:2; 203:1; 267:5
justification	(6)	14:1; 33:1; 96:2; 326:4; 374:2; 375:1
justifications	(2)	373:3,3
justified	(6)	192:5; 229:3; 338:3; 357:1; 359:1,1
justifies	(1)	313:2
justify	(3)	27:2; 70:6; 155:1
justifying	(2)	230:1; 373:3
Kahn	(4)	113:1; 119:2,3; 121:3
Kahn's	(1)	115:4
Karl	(1)	32:2

keep	(15)	105:1; 155:3; 165:1; 172:1; 187:4; 207:4; 213:1; 217:2; 271:3; 297:2,2; 306:5; 352:1,1; 358:1
keeping	(11)	16:2; 60:1; 169:3; 170:1; 241:2; 271:3,3; 322:2,2; 340:1; 343:4
keeps	(2)	155:1; 343:4
kept	(8)	183:1; 213:3; 214:2; 215:2,2; 217:2; 239:4; 360:3
key	(2)	29:6; 348:1
killed	(2)	347:3; 365:3
killing	(1)	323:1
kind	(25)	6:1; 20:2,2; 49:1,1; 51:3; 75:1; 100:2; 119:2; 129:4; 139:3; 155:2; 178:1; 182:2; 207:4; 222:2; 229:3; 247:2; 288:1,1; 305:3; 320:3; 323:1; 347:2; 356:2
kinds	(11)	23:1; 41:2; 62:1; 75:1; 93:2; 203:3; 215:2; 226:2; 246:2; 331:3; 348:1
kingdom	(3)	343:1,1; 361:8
knaves	(1)	360:2
knew	(1)	369:2
Knight	(2)	176:4,4
knocks	(1)	229:1
know	(24)	44:1; 61:2; 74:2; 138:2; 150:2; 152:1; 156:1; 165:1; 172:2; 174:2; 181:1; 183:1; 184:2; 207:3; 227:2; 230:1; 236:4; 237:1; 259:2; 276:1,1,1,1; 297:2
knowing	(3)	170:2; 181:1; 292:1
knowledge	(22)	31:4; 40:1; 96:4; 137:3,3; 148:2; 149:4,4,4; 152:1,1,1; 153:4,4; 154:3; 165:2; 168:3; 198:3; 204:3; 250:2; 340:3; 347:2
known	(6)	129:2; 147:2; 150:2; 169:1; 365:3; 367:1
knows	(1)	161:1
Kuznets	(5)	102:3,3; 103:2; 104:1; 127:2
l'échange	(1)	177:1
l'estat	(1)	358:3
laborious	(1)	157:1
labour	(234)	5:3,5,6,6; 6:1,2; 7:1,1,1,3,3; 8:1,3,3,3,3,3,3,3; 9:1,1,2,2,2,2,2,3,3,3,3; 10:1,2,2,2,3,3,3; 11:1,1,1,1,2,3; 12:2,2,2,2,2,3; 13:1,1,2,2; 14:1; 15:3,3; 16:1,1; 17:3,3; 18:2; 19:1,2,2; 20:4; 23:1; 26:1,2; 27:1; 28:2; 29:1,4,4; 30:2,2,2; 31:1; 40:2; 41:2,2,2,2,3; 42:1,1,1,1,1,1,1,1,1,1,1,2,2,2,3;

Law's	(1)	350:4
lawful	(1)	144:3
laws	(9)	4:3; 241:2; 244:1; 254:4; 274:4; 340:1; 352:2,2,2
lay	(4)	257:1; 315:4; 325:2; 382:3
laying	(3)	70:2; 106:2; 113:1
lays	(1)	76:1
lead	(47)	6:1; 8:3,3; 18:1; 24:5; 26:2; 28:2; 40:2; 49:1,1; 72:2; 90:2; 97:2; 104:1; 107:2; 109:2; 118:1,2,2,2; 125:2; 145:1; 157:1; 179:1; 187:3,3; 200:3; 223:4; 229:3; 250:2; 259:1; 263:3; 271:3; 277:3,4; 288:1; 297:2,2; 304:2; 318:2; 324:1; 327:2; 338:3; 340:3; 356:3; 375:2; 377:2
leader	(2)	342:1; 354:2
leading	(10)	18:2; 42:1; 140:2; 153:2; 171:3; 175:1; 218:1; 307:3; 342:1; 370:1
leads	(21)	19:1; 21:1; 50:3; 62:3; 63:2; 98:2; 115:4; 152:1; 172:1; 183:1; 190:1; 201:3; 224:3; 231:5; 263:3; 321:3; 322:1; 331:1; 338:3; 344:1; 373:3
leakage	(1)	120:3
learn	(2)	355:2; 382:3
learned	(1)	366:1
learnt	(1)	339:3
leases	(1)	129:3
least	(35)	38:2; 42:2; 56:1; 69:5; 70:2; 76:1; 95:1; 138:2; 160:3; 161:3; 163:2,2; 213:3; 217:2; 228:2; 237:1; 238:2,2; 262:5; 266:3; 270:3; 290:2; 304:1; 309:2; 324:4; 327:2; 340:3; 342:1; 346:3; 357:1; 365:3; 371:1; 374:2; 377:2; 381:4
leave	(7)	14:3; 129:3; 180:1; 206:2; 210:1; 258:1; 352:2
leaves	(3)	8:3; 202:1; 259:1
leaving	(7)	12:2; 23:1; 162:1; 166:3; 266:3,3; 268:3
lecture	(2)	366:1,1
lecturer	(1)	365:3
lecturing	(1)	366:1
led	(13)	33:3; 47:2; 100:2; 101:1; 183:1; 253:2; 299:2; 322:4; 344:3; 347:2,4; 354:1; 357:1
left	(13)	12:2; 33:3; 67:1; 95:4; 110:2; 154:3; 188:4; 219:3; 235:1; 271:3; 289:3; 320:1; 377:3

legal	(4)	167:3; 270:1; 294:1; 342:1
legal-tender	(1)	234:2
legislation	(4)	6:2; 269:4; 270:1; 346:3
legitimate	(6)	67:3; 139:1; 154:2; 328:1; 352:2,2
legitimately	(4)	6:2; 40:2; 152:3; 163:2
lehre	(1)	354:2
leisure	(3)	326:3,3,3
lend	(6)	145:1; 190:3,3,3; 302:1; 329:1
lender	(8)	144:4; 145:1,1; 208:2,2,2,2; 309:2
lender's	(2)	144:3; 145:2
lenders	(3)	79:3; 219:1; 309:2
lending	(9)	144:3; 158:2; 160:2; 337:1,2; 342:1; 348:3; 356:2; 382:3
lends	(1)	281:1
length	(12)	48:2; 68:3; 107:1; 170:1; 195:3; 216:2; 217:1; 254:2; 279:3; 317:2; 318:1; 365:3
lengthened	(1)	318:1
lengthening	(1)	76:2
lengths	(2)	98:1; 137:5
lengthy	(6)	46:1; 214:2,2,2,2,2
lent	(4)	33:1; 142:2; 188:2; 190:3
les	(2)	354:2; 358:3
Leslie	(1)	359:2
less	(104)	4:3; 8:1; 9:3; 15:3; 27:2; 28:2; 29:5; 31:3; 41:2; 42:1,1,1,1,1,1,1,1; 49:1; 72:2; 77:1; 81:1,1; 84:2; 92:1; 96:4; 98:2; 99:1; 104:1,1; 110:1; 118:2; 121:1,3,3; 122:1,1; 124:1; 126:3; 128:1,2,2; 131:1; 140:2; 144:3; 147:2,2; 148:2,2; 154:2; 159:2; 161:2; 171:2; 172:1; 188:2; 190:3; 191:2; 196:4; 213:3,3; 215:2; 216:2,2; 219:1; 228:2; 239:4; 243:1; 249:2; 250:4; 251:3,3; 258:1; 263:4; 267:3; 271:2; 279:1; 287:2; 289:2,2; 290:3,3; 291:2; 304:1; 306:3; 307:2; 316:2; 318:2; 322:1,1; 324:1; 331:1,1; 341:5; 343:4; 345:3; 346:3; 348:4; 354:2; 356:1; 362:2; 363:2; 364:2; 370:1,1; 375:2; 382:3
lessens	(1)	130:2
lesser	(2)	322:5; 344:2
let	(52)	8:3; 25:2,2; 33:3; 40:2; 48:3; 52:3; 53:1,1; 55:5; 56:1,1; 70:4; 74:3; 115:1,3; 125:4; 168:2; 177:3; 181:1; 199:2,3; 213:1;

lies	(19)	40:1; 43:3; 57:3; 65:1; 66:2; 73:3; 78:1; 83:2; 142:2,3,3; 152:1; 166:4; 174:2; 189:2; 222:1; 225:2; 355:3; 359:7
life	(51)	44:1; 58:2,2,2; 68:1; 70:3; 71:4; 77:2; 97:1; 99:3; 108:1; 109:3; 135:1,2; 136:2; 138:4; 141:2; 143:2,2,2; 147:2,2; 150:2; 154:3; 157:1; 158:3; 161:2; 213:3,3; 217:2; 218:1; 219:2,3; 220:2; 251:3; 254:3; 262:5; 293:1; 317:2; 318:1; 321:1; 323:1; 351:3; 354:1,2; 359:2; 366:1; 375:3; 378:1; 379:1; 380:2
lifetime	(1)	354:2
light	(12)	19:5; 47:2; 48:1; 50:4; 51:1,2; 78:1; 93:3; 185:1; 270:2; 322:3; 329:2
like	(19)	7:3; 20:1; 34:1; 84:2; 92:1; 95:1; 106:2; 129:3; 160:2; 183:1; 221:3; 230:3; 231:1; 345:1; 353:3; 357:1,1; 359:1; 361:1
likeliest	(1)	156:2
likelihood	(5)	148:3; 153:1; 163:2; 219:1; 287:2
likely	(51)	10:1; 33:1; 49:1; 51:3; 72:2; 81:1; 93:3; 95:3; 96:1; 99:2; 119:2,3; 120:5; 121:1,2; 130:2; 139:3; 158:1; 159:1; 164:3; 171:4; 196:3; 203:3; 210:1; 225:3; 251:3; 252:2; 253:1; 254:2,4; 258:1; 262:3,5,5; 263:2; 264:3; 271:3; 279:1,2; 300:4; 301:2; 302:3; 303:2; 319:1; 321:3; 339:3; 353:3; 373:1,3; 375:2; 384:1
likened	(1)	156:2
limit	(23)	19:5; 26:1; 43:2; 117:1; 118:3; 126:1; 191:2; 203:2; 214:2; 217:1; 218:3; 219:1; 222:1; 229:1; 232:4; 252:2; 253:2; 266:2,3; 293:1; 304:1; 355:3; 366:1
limitation	(1)	244:1
limitations	(7)	207:1,2; 254:2; 266:3; 336:3; 337:1; 374:2
limited	(7)	38:4; 104:3; 187:2; 197:2; 252:1; 371:1; 375:3
limiting	(6)	3:1; 42:1; 207:2,3; 258:1; 273:3
limits	(10)	9:2; 40:1; 43:2; 253:1; 275:4; 276:1; 302:3; 341:3; 368:2,2
limner	(1)	361:1
line	(20)	12:2; 58:2; 60:2; 61:2; 62:1; 70:5; 111:2; 113:1; 167:3; 182:2; 226:1; 277:3; 285:2; 293:2; 303:2; 313:2; 326:4; 352:2; 365:3; 368:5

liv'ries	(1)	360:3
live	(16)	3:1; 13:2; 20:2; 32:2; 131:2; 247:2; 249:4; 250:2; 269:3; 322:1; 347:1; 359:1; 360:3; 361:3; 369:1; 372:1
lived	(1)	360:7
livelihood	(1)	359:1
lively	(1)	100:1
lives	(2)	99:4; 292:1
living	(12)	13:1; 15:1; 93:2; 94:1; 121:1; 192:1; 237:1; 277:1,2; 354:1; 360:2; 377:2
loaded	(1)	381:1
loan	(11)	128:2,3; 129:2,4,4; 130:1; 142:2; 144:3; 331:3; 332:1; 344:5
loanable	(1)	165:1
loans	(17)	28:1; 68:1; 121:1,3; 129:2; 144:3; 182:2; 186:3,3,3; 189:2,2; 208:2,2; 263:4,4; 336:1
loc.	(Count: 1 – not included)	
local	(5)	101:1,1,1,3; 108:3
located	(1)	336:1
Locke	(4)	342:3; 343:1,1; 344:2
Locke's	(2)	344:5,5
lodging	(1)	363:3
logic	(3)	239:2; 349:1; 371:1
logical	(8)	9:2; 16:1; 33:1; 122:4; 192:1; 250:2; 344:4; 378:2
logically	(4)	22:2; 238:1; 249:3; 367:1
London	(10)	131:2; 150:1; 159:2; 160:1; 339:3,3; 365:3,3,5; 366:1
long	(64)	16:1; 18:1; 50:2; 70:6; 71:4; 72:4; 93:3,3; 100:1; 110:1; 125:4; 128:2; 152:1,2; 155:3; 156:3; 157:1; 160:2,2; 164:3; 174:2; 176:1; 189:2,2; 191:1,1,2; 207:3; 214:2; 218:1; 219:1; 230:2; 234:3; 238:1; 271:1,3; 278:3; 279:2; 288:1; 292:1; 293:1; 294:1; 295:3,3,3,3; 296:1; 300:4; 306:4,5; 307:2; 309:1; 317:3; 318:2; 322:3; 331:2; 332:1; 335:3; 338:2; 340:3; 358:1; 365:3; 374:2; 376:1
long-lived	(2)	100:1; 253:3
long-period	(36)	48:2,2,2,4,4; 49:1,1,1,1,1,1,1,1; 50:2; 68:1,1,1,1,1,1,1,1,3,3; 69:3; 80:2; 180:1,1; 190:4; 191:1,1,1,2,2; 192:5; 217:2
long-run	(5)	306:5; 307:2,3; 309:3,3

long-term	(42)	47:1,2,3; 48:1,1; 50:4; 51:2,2,2,2; 148:1,2,3; 154:3; 155:3; 156:3; 157:1,1; 160:2; 162:4; 163:2,2,2; 164:2; 169:2; 197:2; 202:1,1,1,2; 203:1,2; 204:2,3; 206:2; 241:2,2; 246:1; 263:4; 266:3; 323:1; 325:1
longer	(21)	11:2; 26:2; 61:1; 64:2; 79:2; 136:3,4; 167:3; 170:1; 206:2; 216:2; 228:2; 243:2; 295:1; 304:4; 324:1; 350:3; 368:4; 376:3; 381:2; 382:3
longest	(1)	287:2
look	(6)	105:2; 108:1; 122:2; 128:1; 136:2; 234:2
looked	(3)	23:1; 33:3; 185:1
looking	(2)	24:1; 156:2
looks	(1)	360:7
looms	(1)	347:2
lose	(7)	153:1; 280:3; 297:2; 298:1; 314:1; 353:2; 381:1
losers	(2)	345:4; 346:1
loses	(2)	241:3; 279:1
loss	(34)	12:2; 16:1; 27:2; 51:3; 56:1,1; 57:2,2,3,3; 58:1,1,2,2,2; 69:1,4; 72:2,2; 81:1; 82:1,1,1; 162:1,2; 169:2; 172:1; 202:1; 203:1; 234:1; 238:1; 261:2; 327:2; 380:2
losses	(9)	56:1,1,1; 58:2,2; 94:1; 217:3; 380:2; 381:1
lost	(6)	5:4; 81:2; 207:3; 292:1; 297:2; 344:3
lot	(1)	250:1
lottery	(1)	150:2
love	(1)	366:3
low	(48)	69:5,5; 72:2,4; 94:1; 98:1; 100:1,1; 104:1; 118:2; 122:1; 128:1; 145:2; 151:2; 193:1; 202:1,1; 207:3; 208:2; 217:3; 233:3; 237:1; 238:3,3; 241:2; 265:2; 286:3,4; 287:1,2; 307:1; 308:1; 319:3; 320:2,2; 323:1,1; 324:3; 328:1,1; 336:3; 337:1; 344:2; 352:2; 373:1,1; 375:1,3
lower	(33)	8:3; 11:3; 18:2; 40:1; 127:2; 141:2,2,2; 143:2,2,2; 167:2; 171:2; 185:1; 187:3; 193:1,1,1,1; 203:1; 219:1; 248:4; 251:2; 264:3; 271:3; 277:1; 308:2; 322:2; 329:1,1; 342:2; 374:2; 375:2
lowering	(6)	143:2; 193:1,1,1; 264:2; 342:5
lowers	(2)	130:1; 142:1
lowest	(4)	187:1; 308:1,1; 319:1

lucky	(1)	288:1
lump	(1)	99:3
lurid	(1)	344:4
Luxembourg	(1)	353:6
luxurious	(1)	360:2
luxury	(2)	358:3; 359:1
lying	(1)	355:1
Lyons	(1)	346:3
machine	(9)	9:3; 50:2; 69:3; 71:2; 75:1; 140:2; 188:1; 226:4; 297:2
machinery	(6)	139:3,3; 140:1,1,1; 188:2
machines	(2)	138:2; 214:2
made	(71)	10:3; 12:2; 20:4; 21:4; 38:1; 41:2; 42:3; 47:2; 62:1,1; 69:3,4; 78:1; 81:1; 89:2; 90:2; 99:2,2,3; 100:1,1; 101:1; 104:2; 127:1; 128:1; 138:3; 139:3; 149:1,4; 151:1; 153:1; 166:3; 177:3; 179:2; 183:1,1; 188:2,2; 189:3,5,5; 190:3,3; 201:2; 206:1,2,2; 239:1; 240:2; 241:4; 247:2; 267:2; 269:4; 278:1; 292:1; 294:1; 321:2,3; 330:1; 340:1; 341:1,1,2; 349:1; 353:2; 359:3,7; 365:3; 371:1; 378:1; 381:1
madmen	(1)	383:3
magistrate	(1)	343:4
magnanimity	(1)	362:2
magnificent	(2)	359:1; 362:2
magnitude	(11)	57:3; 72:4; 104:2; 141:1; 145:2; 200:2; 224:3; 317:2,2; 331:1; 336:1
maid	(3)	156:1,1,1
main	(20)	13:2; 31:4; 37:1; 42:2; 89:1,1,1; 94:1; 96:2; 107:2; 109:3; 110:2; 138:4; 199:1; 332:2; 341:2; 355:1,2; 367:1; 378:1
mainly	(30)	43:3; 96:3; 108:3; 109:1; 119:2; 138:2; 145:3; 149:2; 150:2; 154:3; 162:1; 190:1,1; 196:5; 197:2; 199:3,3; 219:2,3; 247:2; 265:1; 268:2; 300:5; 313:2; 331:1,2; 341:1; 352:2; 359:2; 372:2
maintain	(16)	17:2; 20:5; 58:2; 112:1; 173:1; 243:5; 252:3; 258:1; 270:1,1; 278:3; 324:3; 362:4; 371:1; 375:2; 382:3
maintained	(9)	12:2; 53:1; 181:2; 268:2; 270:2; 325:3; 333:2; 368:4; 376:1
maintaining	(10)	20:1; 38:5; 53:1; 72:4; 117:1; 204:2; 267:2;

managers	(1)	150:2
managing	(1)	374:2
Manchester	(1)	379:3
Mandeville	(5)	359:3,7; 361:6,8; 371:1
Mandeville's	(1)	359:2
manifest	(1)	318:2
manifestations	(1)	316:1
manifested	(1)	345:4
manifold	(1)	338:2
manipulating	(3)	297:2; 309:1,2
manipulation	(1)	297:2
manipulations	(1)	305:3
mankind	(1)	242:1
manner	(11)	34:1; 80:3; 91:1; 215:3; 269:3; 276:3; 305:3; 319:3; 343:4; 378:1,2
manoeuvre	(1)	108:1
mansions	(1)	220:1
manufacture	(2)	154:1; 231:3
manufactured	(2)	54:3; 230:3
manufacturer	(3)	46:2,2; 135:2
manufacturers	(1)	332:2
manufactures	(2)	47:1; 361:7
many	(41)	4:2; 80:1; 94:1; 105:1; 106:3; 138:2; 151:1; 153:1; 159:1; 161:4; 163:2; 167:1; 175:3,3; 176:4; 187:2; 188:2; 215:2; 221:2; 241:2; 258:2; 268:3; 299:2; 302:4; 309:4; 339:2; 340:3; 341:3; 345:1; 346:1; 354:1,2,2; 357:2,2; 359:3; 364:2; 366:4; 372:2; 381:1; 383:3
March	(4)	101:3,3; 223:5; 353:2
margin	(21)	64:1; 72:3,4; 97:2; 105:1; 111:1; 114:2; 117:2; 120:4; 125:4; 139:1; 144:3,3; 145:1,1,1; 163:2; 251:3; 253:1; 352:2; 375:3
marginal	(365)	5:3,5; 6:2,3,3; 7:1,1; 8:3; 10:1,2; 11:1,2,2; 12:2,2,2; 13:2; 14:3; 15:1,4; 16:1; 17:3; 18:1; 21:4; 26:1; 28:1,2; 29:4,4; 30:2,2; 31:1,1,3,4; 54:3; 55:3,3,3,3,3,5,5; 67:2,2,3,3,3,3,3,3,3,3,3,3; 68:1,1,1,2,3,3,3,3; 69:3,5; 70:1,1,1,3; 71:4,4,4,5; 72:2,2,2,3,3,4,5; 73:2; 83:1; 111:2,3; 112:1; 114:1; 115:1,2; 116:1; 118:2,2,2; 119:1; 120:1,2,4,4,5; 121:1,1,2; 123:2,3,3; 124:1,1;

marginal (cont.)

125:2,3,3; 126:1; 127:1,2; 128:1,1,2,2;
130:2; 135:2,2,2; 136:1,1,2,3,3,3,3,4;
137:1,3,4,4; 138:3,4; 139:1,1,1,1,2,2;
140:1,2,3,4; 141:1,2,2,2; 142:1,1,3,3;
143:1,1,1,2,3; 144:1,1; 145:3,3; 146:1,2;
147:1,1; 149:1,1; 151:2,2; 158:2; 164:3,3;
165:1,1,1,2; 170:1,1,2; 173:1; 174:1;
176:1,1,1,1,3,3,3; 178:1; 183:2;
184:2,2,2,2,2; 187:1,3,4,4; 188:1; 190:1;
192:1,1,2; 193:1,1,1,1; 204:2; 207:4; 210:1;
212:1,1; 214:2,2; 217:2,2; 218:1,1,1,2,2;
219:2,4; 220:1,3; 221:2; 222:1; 223:4;
224:3,3,3,3,3,3,3; 225:1,1; 228:2,2,2,2;
229:1; 232:3,3,4; 234:3; 236:2,3; 238:3;
245:3; 246:1,2; 248:1,2; 249:3; 250:4,5;
251:2; 253:1,3,3; 257:3; 260:2,3;
261:2,2,2,2; 262:2,4; 263:3,3; 264:2;
265:1,2; 266:1,2,2; 268:2,2; 269:2; 270:1;
271:1; 272:3,3,4,4,4; 273:3,3,5,5,5; 274:4;
276:2,2; 278:3,3,4; 283:1,1,3; 284:2,2;
290:2; 291:2,2; 292:1; 294:2,2; 295:2,3;
296:2; 298:2,3; 300:1; 302:2,3,3,3,4,4;
303:1; 306:2; 307:3; 308:2; 309:2;
313:2,2,2; 314:3,3; 315:3,4,6,6;
316:1,1,1,1,2; 317:1,2,3,3; 318:1; 319:2,2,3;
320:1; 323:1; 324:4; 325:3; 344:2; 349:1;
351:3; 352:1,1; 355:3; 356:1; 357:1;
375:1,2,3

marked   (3)   95:2; 249:4; 330:1

market   (73)   8:3; 18:5; 56:1; 57:2; 64:2,2; 85:2; 108:3;
135:2; 137:1; 150:1; 152:1,1; 154:1,1,2;
155:1,1,1,2; 156:3; 157:1,2; 158:2,3; 159:1;
160:1; 164:3; 166:3; 169:3,3;
170:1,1,1,1,2,2,2,2,3,3; 172:1; 175:2;
176:1,1,4; 186:2,2,2,2; 190:3,3; 197:2,2;
198:1,1; 202:1,2; 206:1,2; 223:2,4; 235:1;
277:1,2; 316:1,1,3; 319:2; 320:1; 331:1;
343:1; 364:1

market-price   (2)   135:2; 206:2

market-rate   (2)   202:2; 243:5

marketable   (1)   151:3

markets   (22)   5:4; 149:2; 150:3; 151:1; 152:3; 153:2;
155:2; 157:1; 158:3,3; 159:2; 160:2,2;

may	(Count: 335 − not included)	
maybe	(1)	173:1
maze	(1)	298:1
me	(Count: 25 − not included)	
meal	(1)	215:3
meals	(1)	215:3
mean	(51)	4:2; 11:3; 15:3; 24:5; 26:1; 40:2; 52:2; 61:2; 62:3; 67:3; 74:2,3; 78:2; 79:2; 110:3; 111:1; 139:2; 144:3; 148:5; 152:1,1; 167:4; 174:2,2; 186:3; 188:2; 191:2,2; 207:3; 229:2; 245:2; 254:4; 260:2; 272:4,4; 279:1; 289:3; 290:3,3; 297:2; 301:3,3; 304:2; 306:5; 307:1; 313:3; 314:1,1; 351:2; 375:3; 376:1
meanes	(1)	342:1
meanest	(1)	363:3
meaning	(18)	18:3,5; 40:1; 45:2; 61:2,2; 67:3; 74:2; 76:2; 80:2,3; 135:2; 141:2; 230:2; 272:4; 293:2; 328:1; 345:4
means	(81)	7:1; 17:3; 18:1,5,5; 19:2; 20:4; 29:4; 42:1,1; 44:2; 56:2; 60:1; 61:2; 75:1; 78:2; 80:1; 97:2; 110:3; 130:2; 138:2; 140:2; 143:2; 144:3; 158:3; 162:3; 163:2; 168:2; 173:2; 176:3,4; 187:3; 188:2; 192:3; 193:1,1; 210:1; 231:3; 234:3; 241:3; 247:2; 263:1; 264:2; 266:3; 267:4,5; 270:2; 274:3,4,4; 275:1; 284:1; 304:4,4; 307:2; 314:3; 316:2; 325:1,1; 329:1; 336:2,2,2; 337:1; 338:3; 339:3,5; 340:1; 342:2; 343:4; 344:2,5; 348:4; 354:1; 355:3; 357:2; 374:2; 377:2; 378:1; 380:3; 382:2
meant	(9)	38:5; 61:2; 72:3; 74:2; 77:1,1; 188:2; 315:6; 339:3
meantime	(1)	58:2
meanwhile	(3)	46:1; 187:4; 353:3
measurable	(2)	221:3; 331:2
measure	(23)	31:2; 33:1,2; 38:2; 41:1; 44:1; 53:1; 111:1; 128:2; 152:2; 159:1; 167:2; 172:1; 202:1; 204:3; 209:1; 272:1; 285:3; 306:5; 308:1; 349:2; 373:3; 375:4
measured	(57)	18:1; 30:2; 38:1; 41:2,4,4; 62:3,3; 79:2,3,3; 91:3; 92:1,1; 96:2,3,4; 110:2; 114:2,2,2,2; 116:5; 126:3; 140:1; 151:3; 180:3; 192:2;

mercatoria	(2)	342:1; 345:2
merchandises	(1)	347:1
merchant	(1)	353:4
merchants	(3)	342:2; 344:2,2
mercy	(1)	158:1
mere	(15)	6:2; 9:2; 15:3; 30:3; 49:1; 51:3; 56:1; 64:1; 162:3; 167:1; 212:1; 225:6; 228:3; 298:1; 371:1
merely	(50)	11:3; 42:1,1; 50:3; 69:5; 71:4; 74:1; 76:1; 85:2; 100:2; 115:1; 124:2; 139:3; 141:2; 150:2; 153:1; 162:4; 164:3; 165:2; 178:2; 179:1; 188:3; 194:1; 210:1,2; 211:1; 214:2; 229:2; 239:2; 240:3; 243:2; 245:2; 253:3,3; 288:1; 291:2,2; 299:2; 304:2; 309:1,1,2; 314:1; 325:3; 328:1; 333:2; 351:4; 366:3; 376:2; 383:1
merit	(1)	353:3
met	(6)	186:2; 187:1,4; 221:2; 339:5; 363:4
metal	(1)	349:1
metals	(18)	131:2; 333:1; 334:4; 335:3; 336:1,1,2; 337:1,1,2,2,3; 338:3; 344:3; 345:1; 347:2; 349:1; 358:1
metaphor	(1)	156:2
method	(37)	9:1; 13:2; 43:3; 46:3; 52:2; 58:2; 76:1; 77:3; 78:2; 89:1; 104:1; 119:4; 152:2; 172:2; 187:2; 206:2; 211:1; 216:2; 257:2; 260:1,2; 262:2; 266:3,3; 268:1,1,3,3; 275:4; 282:4; 297:2,2; 298:3; 349:1; 361:5,5; 364:2
methods	(7)	196:3; 208:2; 281:1; 297:2; 309:2; 322:5; 340:1
mettre	(1)	358:3
mid-nineteenth-century	(1)	338:2
Midas	(1)	219:3
middle	(5)	131:2; 345:4; 346:4; 348:5; 365:3
Middlesex	(1)	359:2
midst	(1)	30:3
might	(85)	6:1; 9:2; 19:3; 43:3; 53:1; 60:1,1; 64:2; 66:2; 68:1; 75:1; 78:2; 80:2; 90:2,2; 96:1; 98:1; 99:4; 108:2; 111:3; 125:2; 144:3; 150:2; 154:3; 160:1,2,2; 161:2; 170:3; 182:3; 188:2,4; 190:3,3,3; 192:5; 203:3; 207:3; 208:4; 210:2; 211:1; 221:3;

might (cont.)		232:2,4,4; 233:3,4; 237:1; 238:1,3; 243:3,3;
		247:2; 253:2,2; 267:1; 269:3; 272:4,4;
		276:1; 293:2; 301:3; 302:4; 303:2; 316:2;
		321:1,4; 324:1; 326:1; 327:2,2,2,2; 334:2;
		349:1; 357:2; 359:1; 361:5; 364:2; 369:1;
		376:3; 377:2; 381:3; 382:1; 383:3
mighty	(1)	220:1
mil	(1)	357:1
Mill	(5)	3:2,2; 19:3,5; 364:4
Mill's	(7)	18:4; 19:3; 20:1; 364:2,2,2,4
millennia	(1)	242:1
millenniums	(1)	351:2
million	(5)	139:3,3; 154:1; 188:1; 190:3
millionaires	(1)	220:1
millions	(5)	187:2; 190:3,3; 191:2,2
mind	(28)	57:1; 64:3; 72:1; 80:3; 81:1; 92:2; 106:2;
		144:2; 145:1; 158:2; 160:2; 161:3; 163:2;
		187:3; 195:1; 208:2,2; 243:6; 267:4; 276:2;
		279:1; 290:1; 328:1; 330:2; 344:2; 360:7;
		364:2; 373:2
minds	(9)	91:1; 204:1; 205:1; 212:1; 240:3; 241:2,3;
		264:2; 350:3
mine	(3)	78:2; 149:4; 150:2
mineral	(1)	331:2
mines	(1)	337:1
mingled	(1)	350:4
minimised	(1)	193:1
minimum	(22)	6:1; 8:3,3; 9:3; 10:2; 47:4; 130:1; 145:1;
		146:2; 208:2; 216:2; 219:1,1; 253:3,3;
		254:3; 276:3; 278:3; 303:1; 306:5; 307:1;
		309:2
minister	(1)	354:2
ministry	(1)	101:1
minor	(7)	12:1; 90:2; 196:3; 304:4; 332:2,2; 364:2
minority	(1)	150:1
minus	(5)	174:2; 189:5; 222:2; 223:3; 226:3
mirac'lous	(1)	360:7
miscalculation	(2)	6:2; 108:2
miscalculations	(1)	332:2
miscellaneous	(1)	39:4
misdirected	(5)	189:4; 321:3; 323:1; 327:2; 379:2
misdirection	(1)	189:1
misemploys	(1)	379:2

miser	(1)	359:1
miserable	(2)	218:1; 343:4
miserliness	(1)	108:1
Mises	(2)	192:2; 193:1
misguided	(2)	322:3; 327:2
misinterpret	(1)	320:3
misleading	(6)	3:1; 74:2; 83:2; 174:2; 192:5; 194:1
misnomer	(1)	275:2
Misselden	(1)	342:1
missions	(1)	220:1
mistake	(15)	48:1; 60:2; 142:3; 145:3; 166:4; 182:2; 239:2,2; 242:4; 264:2; 276:2; 332:2; 367:3; 368:1; 383:3
mistaken	(1)	169:3
mistakes	(2)	157:1; 367:3
misunderstanding	(5)	13:2; 95:5; 110:3; 138:4; 315:6
misunderstood	(1)	188:2
mitigate	(2)	163:2; 382:2
mitigated	(1)	231:1
mitigating	(1)	160:1
mitigation	(1)	234:3
mitigations	(1)	220:1
mixed	(1)	150:2
mobile	(1)	277:4
mobility	(1)	14:1
mock	(1)	40:1
moderate	(16)	110:3; 128:1; 226:4; 250:5; 251:1; 252:2,2; 265:2; 266:3; 267:1; 271:3; 277:1,2; 300:5; 352:2,2
moderately	(3)	250:1; 375:1; 377:3
moderates	(1)	331:2
moderation	(1)	338:3
modern	(21)	20:1; 67:3; 81:1; 97:2; 108:3; 119:3; 121:3; 157:1; 160:2; 161:2; 175:1; 220:3; 241:2; 250:2; 331:1; 333:2; 357:1; 368:2; 369:1; 379:1,3
modes	(1)	273:2
modest	(10)	31:2; 49:1; 98:1; 197:2; 204:3,3; 217:1; 233:3; 308:1; 357:2
modification	(4)	47:2; 91:1; 259:1; 274:3
modified	(5)	49:1; 51:1; 148:2; 204:3; 206:2
modify	(4)	93:3; 120:5; 294:2; 372:2
modifying	(3)	92:3; 179:2; 326:1

moment	(11)	8:3; 17:2; 56:1; 72:2; 196:3; 230:3; 274:3; 316:2; 367:2; 380:2; 383:3
momentarily	(1)	324:1
momentary	(1)	324:2
momentous	(1)	365:3
moments	(1)	122:4
monasteries	(2)	220:1; 345:1
monetary	(59)	85:1; 113:1; 119:4; 144:3; 164:3; 177:2; 189:3; 191:1,2,2,2,2,2; 196:5; 202:2; 203:1,1,2; 204:3; 205:1,2,2,3; 206:1,2,2,2,2; 207:1,2,3,3; 217:2; 230:2,3; 267:2,3; 293:1; 294:1,1,1,1; 298:3; 303:2; 304:1; 307:2,2; 308:1,1,1; 316:2; 317:1; 327:2; 337:3; 341:4; 348:3; 349:1; 354:1; 355:3
money	(505)	3:1; 10:3; 11:3; 12:2,2; 13:2; 14:1; 19:3; 20:1,1; 21:3; 32:1,1; 38:2,4; 41:4; 43:2; 49:1; 59:3; 60:3; 70:4; 74:1; 75:1; 77:1,2; 78:1,1,1; 79:2,2,2,3,3; 80:1,3,3; 83:1,1,1,1; 84:3,3,3,3,3,3; 93:2; 95:4; 98:1; 106:2; 124:2; 136:2; 141:2,3,3; 142:1,2,2,2,2,2,2,2,3,3; 143:1; 144:2,3; 147:2; 151:2; 157:1,1; 158:2; 160:2; 161:1,3,3; 166:3,3,3; 167:1,1,2,2,3,3,3,3,3,3; 168:1,1,1,2,2; 169:5; 170:1; 171:2,2,2,3,3,4,4; 172:1,1,2,2,2,2; 173:1,1,1,1,1,1,1,2,2; 174:1,2,2,2; 181:1,1; 182:2,4,4; 183:1,1,1; 186:3,3,3,3; 187:3,5; 188:2,4; 189:2,3; 190:1,3,3,3,3,3,3; 191:1,2,2,2,2,2; 192:4; 194:1,1,1,1,1,1,2,2; 195:1,1,3; 196:2,2,4,5,5; 197:1,1,1,3; 198:1,2,3,3; 200:2,2,2,2,2; 201:2,2; 205:2,2,2,3,3; 206:2; 207:4,4; 208:1,3; 209:1,1,2; 212:2; 213:1,3; 214:1; 217:2; 218:3; 222:1,1,1,2,2; 223:2; 224:1,2,3,3,3; 225:6; 226:4,4; 227:1,1,1,2,2,2,2,2,2,2; 228:3,3; 229:2,3; 230:1,2,2,2,3,3,3; 231:1,1,2,2,3,3,3,3,4,4,5; 232:1,1,3,4,4; 233:2,2,3,3,3,3; 234:2,2,2,2,3,3,3,3,3,3,3,4; 235:1,1,1,1,1,2; 236:4,4,5,5; 237:1,1,2,2,2,2,2; 238:1,1,2,2,3; 239:3; 241:2,2,2,3,4,4; 242:1,3; 243:6; 246:2; 247:1; 248:1,4; 253:2; 258:1,1,1,1; 259:1,2; 262:1,4; 266:2,2,2,3,3,3,3,3; 267:3,3,4,4,5;

money-wages (cont.)		261:2,2,2; 262:2,2,4,6,6; 263:1,2,3,3;
		264:2,2; 265:1,2,2,2,2; 266:2; 267:1; 268:2;
		270:1,1,1,2; 271:3; 276:1,1,1,1,2,2; 284:2;
		285:4,4; 289:2; 301:3,3; 303:4; 305:3;
		306:2
moneys	(2)	224:2,2
monopolies	(1)	150:2
monopoly	(3)	163:2; 268:2; 270:3
montée	(1)	64:2
month	(2)	167:3; 357:1
months	(6)	155:1,1,3; 167:3,3; 332:2
monuments	(1)	362:2
mood	(1)	383:3
moon	(2)	235:2; 292:1
moral	(10)	144:3; 161:4; 208:2,2; 351:2; 352:1; 355:2;
		359:2; 360:3; 361:2
moralists	(1)	362:2
morality	(1)	359:3
morals	(1)	109:3
more	(Count: 283 – not included)	
moreover	(77)	3:1; 9:3; 14:1; 31:2; 39:1; 45:2; 49:1;
		51:1,2; 54:2,3,4; 60:2; 63:2; 67:2; 72:2;
		76:1; 80:1; 82:1,2; 83:1; 95:3; 99:2; 105:1;
		124:2; 130:2; 141:2; 144:4; 145:4; 155:1;
		157:1; 163:2; 169:3; 174:2; 178:2; 190:1;
		192:5; 199:1; 207:3; 210:1; 212:1; 215:2;
		219:1; 232:4; 235:1; 237:1; 239:1; 249:2,4;
		251:3; 252:2; 253:2; 263:4; 264:1,3; 268:1;
		275:4; 277:3; 281:3; 283:2; 284:2; 287:2;
		299:1,3; 302:1; 316:1; 318:3; 320:1; 321:1;
		324:1; 325:3; 329:1; 352:2; 373:1; 374:2;
		376:2; 378:1
morning	(1)	151:1
mortgage	(2)	241:4,4
mortgages	(5)	101:1; 241:2,2,2,4
mortgagor	(1)	241:4
most	(106)	4:1; 5:1; 32:2; 37:2; 42:2; 51:1,1,3; 54:3;
		59:3,3; 70:4; 80:3; 94:1; 118:2; 119:3;
		123:4; 129:2; 138:4; 139:2; 141:2; 144:3;
		148:3,4; 149:2; 152:1; 154:3; 155:2,2;
		156:2; 157:1,1,1; 159:1; 160:1; 161:2,4;
		163:2; 167:3; 178:1; 183:1; 184:3; 187:3;
		192:1; 199:1; 206:1; 207:3,4; 212:1; 214:2;

most (cont.) 215:3,3; 221:2; 222:1; 225:6; 227:1; 229:1;
233:2; 236:2; 237:1; 238:2; 243:2; 261:2;
262:3; 264:4; 265:2,2; 268:1; 270:2; 272:4;
277:1; 279:2,3; 302:3; 309:2,2; 316:1;
320:1; 327:2,2; 329:2; 331:1; 333:1; 338:2;
339:3; 341:3; 342:1; 347:2; 350:3; 351:3;
354:1; 356:2,2; 361:5; 364:1,1,2,4,6;
369:1,1; 370:2; 373:3; 378:1; 380:2,2

mother (1) 353:6
motion (2) 319:1; 332:2
motive (25) 77:1,2; 78:1; 97:2; 108:3,3; 109:1,1,1;
163:1; 170:1; 195:3; 196:3,3,3; 197:1;
231:3; 303:3; 335:3; 362:4; 363:3; 372:2,2;
374:2; 382:3

motives (30) 21:2,2; 91:1; 93:3; 94:1; 97:2; 107:2;
108:2,2,2,3; 109:2,2,2,3; 110:1; 129:4;
166:2; 194:1; 195:1,2; 196:2; 197:1; 253:1;
293:2; 362:4,4; 363:2,2; 383:2

motor-car (2) 61:2; 231:1
mould (1) 176:4
mountain (1) 365:3
mountaineer (1) 365:3
mounting (1) 233:3
move (3) 69:7; 292:1; 373:3
moved (2) 160:2; 382:3
movement (16) 9:1; 49:1; 104:1; 172:2; 199:1; 204:3;
218:1; 254:2; 264:2; 313:3; 314:1; 317:2;
331:2; 332:2; 354:2; 366:1

movement's (1) 355:2
movements (4) 49:1; 204:3; 314:1; 320:1
moving (5) 83:1; 251:4; 252:1; 264:2; 299:2
Mr. (39) 19:5,5; 51:3; 72:5; 75:3; 76:1,1,1; 78:2,2,2;
79:4,4,4; 102:2,3,3; 103:2; 104:1; 113:1;
115:4; 119:2,3; 121:3; 127:2; 143:4;
180:4,4; 187:3; 223:5; 327:1; 349:3; 354:2;
364:2,2; 365:2,5; 366:2; 370:1

much (162) 7:3; 18:5,5; 19:2; 20:1; 21:3; 27:2; 29:6,6;
31:2; 33:1; 39:3; 43:2; 46:1; 47:4; 49:1,1;
54:2,3; 57:3,3,3; 61:1; 64:2; 69:2; 72:2;
76:2; 78:1; 79:2,2; 83:1,1; 91:3; 92:3; 93:3;
95:3,3; 96:4; 99:2; 101:1,1; 102:3; 106:2,3;
107:1; 111:2; 117:2; 118:2,2; 121:3,3;
122:1,2; 126:2,2; 127:1; 128:2; 136:3;

much (cont.)		143:2; 145:3; 149:2; 150:1,2; 153:1; 154:2; 157:1,2; 158:1; 159:1,2; 160:2; 166:2,2; 167:1; 172:2; 175:1; 177:2; 178:1; 187:1,1,3; 188:2; 197:2; 199:1; 203:1; 204:1; 207:3; 209:1; 211:2,2,2; 213:3; 218:3; 227:1,1; 235:1; 237:1; 249:2; 251:2; 253:1,3; 263:4; 264:2; 265:2; 275:2,2; 276:1; 278:4; 287:2; 298:2,2,2,3,3; 300:4; 302:3; 305:3,3; 308:1,1,2; 309:2; 317:3,3; 320:2; 325:2,2; 326:3; 327:1,2,2,2; 331:1,1; 334:4; 339:3; 340:2; 341:5; 342:1; 346:3; 348:3; 353:5; 354:2; 358:2; 359:2; 361:5; 362:2; 363:1; 365:4; 370:1,2; 371:1; 372:2,2; 374:2,3; 375:2; 376:2; 377:1,2; 378:2; 381:2
muddles	(1)	183:1
multiple	(1)	118:1
multiplied	(3)	124:1; 161:4; 258:1
multiplier	(45)	113:1,1; 114:1; 115:3,4,4; 116:2; 117:2; 119:2; 120:3,3,3,4,5; 121:2,2,3,3; 122:2,4; 123:3,3; 124:1,2; 125:1,2,2,4; 126:1,1,2; 127:2; 128:1,1; 248:2,3,3,3; 250:4; 251:3; 252:1; 273:2; 277:1; 298:2,3
multitudes	(1)	360:7
Mummery	(9)	364:2,4; 365:2,3,4; 367:4; 368:7; 369:2; 370:5
Mun	(1)	344:3
Münzwesen	(1)	354:1
music	(3)	156:1,1; 362:2
musical	(1)	156:1
must	(162)	6:1; 11:3; 15:2; 16:1,1; 17:2,2,3; 18:1,3; 21:1,1; 26:1; 27:2; 32:3; 39:3; 41:1; 48:1; 51:2; 52:2; 58:2,2; 61:2,2; 62:1,3; 64:1,1; 66:2; 68:1,1,1,1,3; 69:3; 70:2,2; 73:2,2; 82:1,1,1,1,1; 83:1; 92:2,2; 95:2,2,3; 96:1,2; 97:2; 98:3; 104:1; 105:1; 106:3; 110:3,3; 111:3; 114:2; 118:1; 120:3; 121:2; 137:3; 141:1; 149:2; 156:3,3,3; 157:1,1,1; 158:2,3; 162:3; 166:4; 168:2; 169:1,2; 171:2; 173:1; 174:2; 176:1; 177:3; 178:1,2; 179:1; 183:1; 184:1,2; 194:1; 197:2; 201:4; 204:3; 206:2; 211:2; 214:2,2; 215:2,2; 216:1; 222:1,2; 223:4; 225:3; 227:2; 228:3; 231:6; 235:1;

must (cont.)		238:1; 240:2; 241:4; 243:3; 247:2; 250:2,2; 252:1; 253:2; 254:4; 259:1; 265:1; 266:2; 274:2; 276:1; 287:2; 290:1; 292:1; 294:1,1; 296:3,3; 297:2; 304:1; 313:1; 314:2; 317:2; 319:1; 324:1; 325:2; 329:2; 333:1; 336:3; 338:3; 340:1; 345:3; 347:1; 353:5; 356:1; 361:3,7; 362:4; 363:1,3; 367:2; 369:1; 370:1; 374:2; 377:2,2; 382:3; 383:3
mutandis	(3)	265:2; 266:3; 288:1
mutatis	(3)	265:2; 266:3; 288:1
mutual	(1)	383:1
my	(Count: 96 – not included)	
myself	(Count: 9 – not included)	
mystery	(1)	32:3
mystification	(1)	371:1
nam'd	(1)	361:1
name	(4)	3:2; 89:1; 299:2; 357:1
named	(1)	365:3
namely	(76)	5:2; 15:2; 20:2; 26:2; 29:1; 30:1; 41:2; 53:1; 56:1; 62:3; 66:2; 75:1; 78:2; 90:1,2; 98:2; 106:3; 107:1; 126:1,1,1,1,1; 130:2; 131:2; 144:3; 149:1; 158:2,3; 163:2,2; 166:3; 178:1; 179:1; 181:1,2; 183:1,1,1,2; 192:2; 208:2; 212:2; 225:4; 233:2; 234:2; 236:1; 239:3; 242:3; 243:3; 247:1; 251:2,3; 254:3,4; 261:2; 272:1; 273:1; 278:4; 279:2; 282:2; 283:1; 284:4; 305:1; 314:2,3; 332:1; 339:3; 340:3; 352:1; 358:2; 359:2; 367:3; 375:1; 381:4; 382:3
Nanga	(1)	365:3
narrow	(4)	60:2; 248:2; 252:1; 278:4
narrower	(1)	333:1
nation	(9)	334:4,5; 342:1; 343:4,4,4; 361:5,7; 366:4
national	(44)	4:3; 5:7,7; 21:3; 37:3,4; 38:2,4; 59:3; 80:3,3; 102:2; 103:2; 111:3; 122:2; 125:4; 127:2; 159:1,2; 171:4; 220:1; 245:2,4,4; 246:1,1; 247:1,2; 264:3; 306:5,5,5; 307:1,1; 309:3; 334:4; 335:2,3; 337:3; 348:1,2; 349:2; 359:2; 366:4
nationalisation	(1)	358:1
nationalised	(1)	355:4
nationalistic	(1)	348:2
nations	(7)	345:1; 346:1; 352:4; 361:3,7; 382:3,3

natural	(42)	4:2; 20:3; 33:3; 39:3; 84:3; 94:1; 143:4; 150:2; 183:1,3,3; 213:4; 214:1; 222:1; 235:1,1; 242:3,3,4,4,4; 243:2,3,5; 251:3; 254:4; 315:3; 330:1; 341:3; 342:1,3; 350:1,2,3,3; 354:2; 355:2; 356:4; 363:2; 365:3; 368:2; 381:4
naturally	(9)	62:2; 102:2; 179:1; 301:2; 316:1; 319:2; 342:2; 351:3; 369:1
nature	(30)	4:3; 37:1; 51:2; 90:2; 91:1; 96:4; 118:2,2; 150:2; 157:1; 161:4; 176:1,4; 182:3; 188:2; 250:2; 251:3; 252:3; 259:2; 268:1; 277:4; 297:2; 315:5; 340:3; 343:1,1; 359:2; 366:2; 374:2; 379:3
natürliche	(1)	354:2
near	(8)	125:1; 153:1; 163:2; 203:1; 206:2; 241:4; 272:2; 353:6
near-term	(1)	157:1
nearer	(5)	71:5; 73:2; 118:2; 178:1; 371:1
nearest	(2)	57:1; 276:1
nearly	(8)	156:2; 201:2; 231:3; 333:1; 346:4; 350:2; 364:2; 378:2
necessarily	(62)	8:3; 17:3,4; 18:1,2,2,2,3; 19:1; 20:2; 26:1; 48:4; 63:2,2; 69:3,3,8; 74:1,1; 75:1; 82:1,2; 83:1; 84:2,2,3; 104:3; 105:1; 111:3; 118:1; 128:2; 175:2,2; 177:2; 178:1,1; 182:3; 184:1; 188:2,3,4; 191:1; 206:2; 211:1; 217:3; 228:3; 229:2; 234:1; 236:3,6; 238:1; 258:1; 261:1; 281:2; 289:1; 294:1; 318:3; 335:3; 362:4; 367:2; 375:1; 383:3
necessary	(45)	25:3; 31:4; 40:1; 44:1; 48:4; 56:1; 60:3; 64:2; 72:3; 73:2; 91:1; 98:3; 99:2; 115:5; 117:2; 146:2; 155:3; 158:2; 166:3; 168:2,3; 171:2; 173:1; 177:2; 184:1; 198:1,2; 212:1; 249:3; 254:4; 270:1; 297:2; 300:3; 302:3; 316:2; 332:1; 338:3; 349:1; 363:2; 371:1; 374:2; 378:1,1; 379:3; 382:3
necessitate	(1)	210:1
necessity	(14)	73:2; 84:3; 176:1; 177:2; 180:1; 182:3; 195:1; 196:3; 250:2; 254:4; 347:1; 357:1; 375:1; 379:1
need	(32)	16:2; 23:1; 39:4; 40:2; 43:3; 44:1; 100:2; 124:2; 129:3; 153:1; 162:3; 165:1; 169:2; 170:2; 183:1; 195:1,1; 206:2; 227:2; 243:5;

neufs	(1)	177:1
neutral	(7)	29:5; 183:1,3; 243:3,4,5,6
never	(18)	14:3; 19:3; 20:4; 39:3; 48:2; 168:2; 182:2; 190:1; 198:2; 324:1; 325:1; 339:3; 341:2; 344:1; 346:1; 349:1; 368:2; 378:2
nevertheless	(45)	11:1; 16:1; 19:3; 21:2; 39:3; 48:2; 50:3; 51:2; 53:1; 72:4; 91:1; 110:3; 125:3; 127:2; 128:1,2; 138:2; 143:2; 152:2; 172:2; 190:1,4; 195:1; 199:1; 201:2,3; 221:3; 232:1; 237:1; 249:2; 267:4; 271:2; 287:2; 289:4; 299:1; 316:1,3; 320:2; 322:1; 327:2; 337:3; 340:1; 344:3; 356:3; 370:1
new	(159)	20:4; 28:2; 29:1; 30:2,2; 38:2; 39:1,1; 48:1,2; 49:1,1,1,1,1,1,1,1; 50:2,2; 70:6; 71:3; 73:1; 75:1,1; 78:1; 82:1,1; 83:1,1; 84:3; 89:1; 98:1; 99:2,2,2,4; 100:1,2,2,2; 101:1,1,1; 102:1; 104:1; 105:2,2; 106:2; 117:2; 119:2; 122:1; 123:3; 124:1; 140:2,3; 141:1,2,2; 142:3; 150:3; 151:1,1,3; 158:3; 159:1; 160:2,2; 161:2; 162:3; 165:1,2; 177:1,1; 179:2,2,2,2; 181:1,1,1,1; 184:2,2; 187:4,5; 188:1; 189:5; 192:2,2; 198:1,2; 199:1,1; 200:2,2,2,2,2,2,3; 201:1,4; 202:1; 204:3; 212:1,1,1,1,1,1,1,2; 213:1; 216:2; 228:1; 248:1,1; 250:5; 258:1; 265:1; 271:1,1; 288:1; 290:2; 294:2; 298:2,3; 299:1; 307:3; 315:3; 316:1,3; 317:3; 318:2; 319:3; 320:3; 322:1; 323:1,1,1,1,2; 328:2; 331:3; 332:1; 335:3; 344:5; 349:1; 352:2; 357:1; 358:2; 364:1; 365:3; 366:1; 370:1; 371:1; 381:3; 384:1
new-fangled	(1)	83:2
newer	(1)	333:1
newest	(1)	384:1
newly	(12)	70:3; 81:2; 123:4; 135:2; 136:2; 222:1; 223:4; 228:2; 241:2; 263:2; 277:3; 317:3
news	(8)	153:1; 155:2; 198:1,1,1; 199:1,1; 204:3
newspaper	(1)	156:2
newspapers	(1)	199:1
next	(24)	15:3; 37:1; 47:2; 51:1,3; 56:1; 77:1; 79:2; 91:1; 111:2; 115:2; 125:4,4; 213:2; 276:2; 282:3; 285:5; 289:2; 304:5; 316:1; 317:2; 318:3; 355:3; 364:1

nexus	(2)	21:2; 173:1
nil	(2)	208:2; 226:4
nine-tenths	(1)	116:2
nineteenth	(8)	307:3; 308:2; 309:1,2; 372:2; 380:2; 382:1,2
nineteenth-century	(5)	80:3; 309:4; 314:3; 353:2; 380:3
nipped	(1)	327:2
no	(Count: 301 – not included)	
noble	(1)	362:2
nominal	(1)	207:3
non-causative	(1)	275:2
non-consecutive	(1)	139:2
non-euclidean	(2)	16:2,2
non-exchange	(1)	20:2
non-existence	(1)	350:1
non-existent	(2)	10:2; 241:2
non-homogeneity	(1)	42:1
non-homogeneous	(2)	38:1; 299:3
non-integrated	(1)	55:1
non-manual	(1)	72:3
non-monetary	(3)	190:1; 222:1; 239:4
non-quantitative	(1)	40:1
non-significant	(1)	154:1
non-static	(2)	6:2; 99:4
non-wage-earners	(4)	7:1; 276:2,2; 277:3
non-wage-goods	(8)	7:1,1; 272:3; 274:3,3,4; 275:1,3
none	(4)	155:2; 183:1; 190:3; 327:2
nonsense	(3)	85:2; 179:2; 335:1
nor	(24)	9:3; 11:3; 15:3; 40:1; 47:2; 60:3; 74:2; 99:2,3; 124:2; 137:3; 152:1; 155:3; 156:1,2; 161:2; 178:1; 184:2; 212:2; 242:1; 250:1; 299:1; 318:2; 323:1
norm	(1)	80:1
normal	(43)	9:2; 38:2; 56:1; 61:1,1; 63:1; 68:1; 70:6; 71:1,4; 72:2; 73:2; 77:1,1; 96:3; 114:3; 117:1; 121:3; 123:2; 124:1,1; 125:1; 164:2; 195:3; 196:5; 197:2; 203:3; 228:2,2; 235:1; 237:2; 250:1; 252:1; 264:2; 293:2; 308:1; 317:2; 318:1; 321:1; 322:4; 331:2; 332:1; 368:2
normality	(1)	38:2
normally	(6)	17:3; 54:3; 82:2; 102:2; 226:4; 307:2
not	(Count: 720 – not included)	

number	(25)	43:3; 44:1; 50:2; 55:5; 56:2; 102:3; 114:2,2; 126:3; 127:1; 154:2; 191:1; 195:1; 196:1; 273:1; 274:1; 277:2; 278:4,4; 282:3,3; 296:2; 308:1; 347:1; 358:3
numbers	(1)	116:3
numerator	(1)	224:3
numerical	(4)	41:1; 45:2; 114:2; 125:3
numerous	(2)	347:2; 349:3
o'clock	(2)	216:1,1
o'er-stocked	(1)	360:7
obeys	(1)	274:4
obiter	(1)	186:1
object	(24)	3:1; 14:1; 25:3; 76:1; 89:1; 104:3; 105:2; 127:2; 151:1; 155:2,2; 159:1; 170:2; 235:2; 247:2; 270:1; 280:1; 297:2; 339:1,2; 344:3; 352:2; 367:2; 382:3
objection	(9)	10:3; 13:2; 38:1; 60:1; 90:2; 106:2; 377:2; 378:2; 379:1
objectionable	(1)	221:2
objections	(2)	12:3; 279:3
objective	(14)	60:1; 91:1,1,1,2; 96:1; 97:1; 107:1; 110:2; 203:2; 204:1; 243:6; 339:3; 341:3
objectors	(1)	358:3
objects	(9)	4:3; 39:4; 105:2,2; 107:2; 234:4; 281:1; 293:1; 335:3
obligation	(1)	144:3
obligations	(1)	349:1
obliterated	(1)	340:1
oblivious	(1)	371:1
obscure	(1)	24:4
obscurely	(1)	371:1
obscures	(1)	299:2
obscurity	(1)	189:5
observation	(5)	32:2; 33:2,2; 149:2; 254:4
observations	(5)	8:2; 53:3; 176:4; 258:2; 265:2
observe	(2)	24:4; 33:2
observed	(4)	237:1; 240:2; 250:3; 356:1
obsession	(1)	339:2
obsolescence	(9)	38:2; 56:1,1; 57:2; 73:1; 109:1; 163:2; 318:1; 375:3
obsolescent	(1)	71:4
obsolete	(1)	49:1
obstacle	(6)	15:1; 26:2; 100:2; 106:3; 202:1; 341:2

obstacles	(1)	225:1
obstinacy	(2)	6:2; 111:3
obstinately	(3)	9:3,3; 111:3
obtain	(7)	19:2; 135:1; 138:4; 221:3; 359:1; 376:1,1
obtainable	(8)	71:1; 130:2; 136:2; 138:4; 218:2; 268:1,2; 276:2
obtained	(9)	70:2,6; 129:3; 167:1; 196:3; 325:2; 337:1; 356:2; 377:1
obtaining	(2)	135:1; 196:3
obtains	(1)	64:1
obverse	(1)	17:3
obvious	(36)	5:1,2; 31:2; 41:3; 67:3,3; 72:3; 73:2; 97:2; 104:3; 114:3; 117:2; 118:2; 122:4,4; 127:1; 136:4; 166:5; 168:2; 183:1; 187:3; 204:2; 228:2; 237:1; 258:1; 318:1; 319:3; 350:3,4; 351:1,2; 363:3,3; 372:1; 378:1; 383:2
obviously	(22)	12:2; 16:2; 20:1; 24:4; 33:3; 39:3; 43:3; 59:2; 60:1; 62:1; 64:1; 68:1; 90:3; 91:3; 154:1; 231:2; 287:2; 303:3; 306:3; 319:2; 325:1; 329:1
occasion	(5)	15:1; 40:2; 47:2; 362:4; 364:1
occasional	(1)	109:3
occasionally	(5)	67:3; 75:1; 167:3; 218:1; 315:4
occasioned	(1)	313:2
occasioning	(1)	363:2
occasions	(3)	43:2,2; 241:2
occupation	(1)	139:3
occupations	(3)	14:1; 41:3; 354:1
occupied	(4)	25:3; 37:1; 50:2; 154:3
occupier	(2)	163:2,2
occupy	(4)	31:3; 46:1; 111:2; 313:2
occur	(18)	16:1; 17:3; 49:1,1; 69:4; 76:2; 81:2; 83:1; 117:2; 130:2; 147:2; 161:3; 233:2; 254:2; 261:2; 268:2; 328:1; 370:1
occurred	(11)	82:2,2; 83:1; 121:1; 128:1; 207:4; 324:1; 329:1; 346:4; 347:2; 363:2
occurrence	(2)	197:1; 250:1
occurring	(4)	16:2; 56:1; 97:2; 123:3
occurs	(10)	17:4; 43:3,3; 69:4; 73:2; 76:2; 199:1; 234:3; 331:2; 367:3
October	(1)	4:3
odd	(1)	304:4
odds	(1)	381:1

of		(Count: 7138 – not included)
off	(23)	10:1; 39:1; 57:1; 89:1; 99:3; 100:1; 101:1; 109:1; 126:1,1; 127:1; 128:1; 146:1; 151:1; 173:1; 226:4; 235:2; 269:2; 284:2; 286:4; 317:3; 331:2; 349:1
offence	(1)	359:3
offer	(17)	13:1,1; 18:5; 24:1; 27:2; 47:2,4; 145:1; 206:1; 217:3; 226:2; 233:3; 260:1; 261:2; 287:2; 366:1; 376:1
offered	(7)	11:2; 100:2; 174:2; 186:3; 249:2; 291:2; 302:2
offering	(1)	269:3
offerings	(1)	382:3
offers	(7)	130:2; 192:1; 202:1; 213:3; 224:3; 338:2; 381:4
office	(3)	157:2; 349:3; 357:1
official	(2)	129:4; 235:1
offset	(38)	60:1; 99:4; 110:3; 111:3; 119:2; 120:1,2,5; 142:2; 143:1; 164:3; 177:2; 180:1; 187:3; 198:2; 202:1,1,1; 208:2; 216:2; 217:3; 232:3; 233:3,3,3; 257:3; 263:1; 264:1,2,3; 267:1; 289:3; 314:3; 315:5; 318:3; 320:1; 332:1; 371:1
offsets	(3)	119:2; 121:3; 319:1
offsetting	(1)	288:1
often	(49)	4:2; 13:3; 16:2; 30:3; 33:1; 41:4; 50:4; 51:1; 68:3,3; 72:4; 97:1; 101:1; 110:2; 114:2; 120:2; 122:4; 128:3; 146:2; 149:4; 150:1; 160:2,3; 162:2,4; 163:1; 167:3; 187:2; 198:1; 206:2; 220:1; 223:4; 232:2,4; 233:2; 241:2; 275:4; 279:2; 292:1; 299:2; 308:1; 313:2; 314:2; 315:4,6; 316:3; 338:2; 345:1; 353:3
oiling	(1)	69:3
old	(31)	20:4; 38:2; 39:1,1; 49:1,1,1; 74:3; 75:1,1; 78:1; 94:1; 99:2,4; 107:2; 109:2; 129:3; 141:2; 151:1; 156:1,1,1; 181:1; 187:2,5; 202:1; 212:1; 228:1; 331:1; 381:3; 382:3
old-fashioned	(3)	83:2; 150:3; 343:3
older	(2)	242:1; 333:1
oldest	(1)	69:5
omission	(2)	209:2; 275:3
omit	(2)	50:4; 62:1

omitted	(1)	279:2
omitting	(1)	280:3
omne	(2)	292:1; 376:3
omnipotent	(1)	342:1
on	(Count: 843 – not included)	
once	(22)	12:2; 21:1; 32:2; 60:3; 62:3; 98:1; 112:1; 137:3; 191:1; 203:1; 211:1; 220:1; 230:3; 243:5; 314:1; 317:3; 318:3; 319:3; 325:3; 327:3; 329:1; 353:5
one	(178)	4:3; 5:4; 6:2; 10:1; 12:2; 13:2; 18:5; 20:1; 22:2; 24:4; 25:3; 28:2,2; 38:1; 39:1,1,3,3; 40:1; 42:1,1; 50:4,4; 51:1; 52:3; 53:1,1; 58:2; 61:2; 62:1,1,1; 63:2,3; 68:3; 69:2,6; 75:2; 80:1; 81:2,2,2; 82:2; 83:1; 91:1; 115:5; 121:3; 129:4; 131:2; 135:2; 138:2,2; 139:3; 140:2; 142:2; 145:1; 149:1; 150:2; 151:1; 154:1,3; 158:3; 159:1,1; 161:2; 167:2,3; 169:3; 175:2; 177:1; 179:2; 182:2,3; 184:1; 186:2,2; 188:2; 189:5; 190:3,3; 191:1,1,2; 192:1,1; 195:1,3; 199:2; 200:2; 206:2; 207:4,4; 208:4; 212:1; 213:1; 216:1; 217:3; 224:3,3; 228:1; 229:1,1; 237:2; 238:2,3; 240:1,3; 244:1; 246:1; 247:2; 249:2; 250:2; 251:2; 252:1,1; 257:3; 259:2; 265:2; 269:3,3; 276:1; 286:3; 289:2; 292:1; 293:1,1,1,2; 297:2,2; 301:3; 303:2; 307:1,3; 308:2; 309:1; 314:1,1,3; 317:2; 318:1; 321:1,2; 322:1; 328:1,1; 329:2,2; 333:1; 334:2; 337:1,1; 339:3; 343:1,1,1; 345:1; 346:1,3; 347:2,3,3; 350:4; 351:3; 356:1; 359:2; 362:3; 367:2; 368:1; 369:1; 370:1; 373:3; 375:2; 377:2; 380:3; 382:3,3; 383:3
one's	(2)	156:2; 340:1
one-half	(1)	342:1
one-sided	(2)	81:2; 85:2
one-third	(1)	108:3
ones	(1)	288:1
only	(227)	3:1; 4:3; 7:1,2; 12:1; 16:2,2; 17:2,3,4; 24:4; 28:2,2,2; 29:5; 31:3; 32:2,2; 37:1; 39:3; 41:2; 47:2,3; 48:4; 49:1; 50:3; 54:3; 57:1,3; 59:2; 60:1,2,2; 61:1; 63:2; 67:3; 69:4,4; 73:2; 82:2; 83:1; 91:1; 94:3; 97:2; 98:1,2;

organisations	(2)	241:2; 354:2
organised	(15)	71:5; 150:3; 152:3; 155:1,2; 159:2; 169:3; 170:2,2,2; 215:3; 297:2; 316:1; 320:1; 369:1
organising	(2)	161:1; 164:3
original	(6)	47:2; 80:3; 136:2; 213:3; 345:4; 353:3
originally	(2)	58:2; 142:2
originals	(1)	346:2
originates	(1)	182:2
orthodox	(12)	13:1; 25:4; 33:2; 111:3; 155:2; 348:4; 349:1; 365:3; 368:3,4; 371:1; 382:2
orthodoxy	(2)	365:1; 370:2
oscillate	(2)	254:3; 269:4
oscillation	(2)	49:1; 239:1
oscillations	(1)	332:2
ostensible	(1)	339:1
ostentation	(1)	108:2
other	(266)	5:4; 8:3; 12:2; 13:2,2; 14:1,2,2; 16:1; 18:5; 20:4; 22:2; 23:1,1; 24:1; 25:4; 26:1; 27:1; 28:2; 30:2; 32:1,2; 33:2; 43:3; 47:2,2; 52:1,1,3; 53:1,1,1; 54:2,2,3; 55:1,2; 56:2,2; 60:2; 62:3; 63:2,3; 64:1; 66:2,2,2,2; 67:3,3; 68:1; 70:2; 74:1; 76:1; 80:1,1; 82:2; 83:1,1; 91:1; 94:1; 96:1,2,2; 97:2; 98:1,3; 101:1; 103:1,1; 110:2; 113:1,1; 114:2; 116:1; 117:1,1; 118:2; 119:2,2,4; 120:2,3,5,5; 121:3; 126:1; 128:1,1; 129:4,4; 130:2; 136:4; 137:2,3; 139:1,3; 140:2; 144:3; 148:2; 155:2; 156:2,3; 158:2; 160:1,2; 161:2; 162:4; 166:3; 167:3; 168:1; 170:1; 174:2; 181:1,2; 187:5; 189:2,5; 190:1,3; 191:1; 200:2; 203:2; 205:2; 206:2; 207:4; 208:4; 212:1; 213:1; 214:2; 216:1,1; 222:1; 224:1,3; 225:2; 227:1,1; 228:3,3,3; 229:3; 231:1,2,3,3,4,4,5; 232:1,3; 233:1,1,2,2,2,3; 234:3,3; 235:1,1,1,1; 237:1,2,2; 238:2,2,3; 242:2; 243:3; 244:1; 245:2; 246:1; 247:2; 249:2; 253:2,3; 254:1,2,2; 258:1; 259:1,2; 262:4,5; 263:3; 264:2,3; 265:2; 266:2; 267:1,4,5; 268:1,2; 271:3; 272:3,4; 273:2,5,5,5,5; 274:3,4; 275:4; 276:1,2; 278:3; 279:3; 281:3; 287:2; 288:1,1; 292:1; 293:1,1,1; 294:2; 296:2; 297:2; 300:3,3;

other (cont.)		306:3; 313:2; 322:5; 325:1; 327:2; 328:1; 330:1,1,1; 331:2; 332:1; 336:2; 337:1; 338:3,3; 340:1; 342:1; 343:1; 345:1,3,4; 346:1; 347:3; 352:2; 353:3; 354:2; 357:1,2; 358:1,2; 360:7; 363:3; 364:1; 367:1; 368:4; 371:1,1; 373:3; 374:2; 377:3; 378:1; 380:2
others	(23)	14:1; 42:1; 46:2; 74:1; 82:1,2; 84:2,2; 93:3; 175:3; 184:1; 196:4; 212:1; 217:3; 229:1; 238:4; 329:2; 341:3; 344:3; 345:2,4; 351:3; 381:4
otherwise	(19)	8:3; 59:2; 66:2; 82:2,2; 83:1; 98:1; 101:1; 128:1; 154:3; 193:1; 215:2; 238:1; 258:1; 286:1; 321:1; 324:2; 353:3; 379:1
ou	(1)	364:1
ought	(8)	8:1; 39:2; 119:2; 187:2; 220:3; 276:1; 377:2; 379:2
our	(Count: 202 – not included)	
ours	(Count: 2 – not included)	
ourselves	(Count: 17 – not included)	
out	(129)	16:2; 17:1; 19:5; 20:1,4,4; 23:1,1; 27:1; 30:1; 48:1,2; 49:1; 50:2,3; 51:1; 53:1; 56:1; 59:2; 66:2; 68:1; 69:5; 70:4; 71:3; 74:2,2; 75:1,1,1; 80:3; 90:2; 93:3; 94:1,1; 95:2,3; 98:1; 99:3; 100:1,1; 102:2; 107:1,2; 108:1,3; 110:2; 111:2; 121:1,3; 122:1; 123:2; 141:2; 144:2; 148:3; 151:1,2; 152:1; 156:2; 160:1; 161:4; 166:2,3; 169:1,3; 171:2; 176:1; 178:1,1,2; 179:1,2,2,2,2; 181:1,2; 182:3,4; 191:1; 199:1; 206:2; 207:2,4; 220:1; 223:5; 229:1,2; 234:3; 236:1; 250:1,1; 251:3; 252:3; 253:3; 260:1,1; 261:2; 273:5; 276:3; 297:2; 305:3; 308:2; 309:2; 323:1; 327:2; 330:1; 331:1; 339:3; 344:1,2,5; 349:3; 350:3; 352:2; 355:3; 356:2; 357:1; 359:2; 366:2; 367:1; 370:1; 372:2; 377:2; 378:1,2; 379:2; 382:2,2; 383:3
out-come	(1)	161:4
outbreak	(1)	279:2
outcome	(6)	63:2; 145:1; 154:2; 155:1; 159:2; 377:2
outgoings	(3)	54:2; 66:2; 373:2
outlet	(4)	200:2; 352:2,2; 374:2
outline	(2)	27:2; 383:3

outlined	(1)	215:1
outlook	(2)	185:1; 327:2
output	(287)	5:4; 10:1; 17:3; 20:2,2,2; 21:3; 22:1; 23:1;
		24:1,2,3,4,4,5; 25:2; 26:1,2,2,2,2,2; 27:2;
		28:2,2; 30:1; 31:2,2; 38:1,1,1,1,1,1,1,2;
		39:1,1; 40:1,1,2,2,2; 41:1,1,1;
		42:1,1,1,1,1,2,2; 43:2,2,3; 44:1,1,1,1,2,2,2,2;
		46:1,2,2; 47:1,2,2,2,2,2; 49:1; 50:4;
		51:1,3,3; 52:1,1; 53:1,1,1,2; 54:3; 55:4;
		58:1; 61:1; 62:3,3; 63:2,2,2; 64:1,1,2,2;
		66:2; 67:2,3,3,3,3,3,3,3; 68:1,2,3,3,3,3,3;
		69:1,5,5,5,8; 70:5; 72:3,3; 76:1; 77:1,1,2;
		78:1,1,1; 79:3; 83:1,1,1,1; 91:1,3; 96:2;
		102:2,3; 104:3; 115:2; 117:2; 122:4; 123:4;
		124:1,2; 125:4,4; 126:2; 135:1,1; 139:1,3;
		140:2; 141:2,2,2,2,2,3; 142:3;
		143:1,1,2,2,2,2; 173:1; 177:2,2; 180:1;
		184:2,2; 187:4; 195:4; 196:1; 209:1,2;
		215:3; 220:1; 225:2,5; 226:2; 228:3;
		229:1,1,2,3; 230:3; 231:5; 234:4,4; 236:3;
		237:1,2; 238:1,1; 240:1,1; 243:4; 244:1;
		249:1,1,4; 250:4; 252:2; 257:2,3,3; 259:1;
		261:2,2,2; 268:2; 269:3; 272:3,4,4; 273:2;
		274:3,4; 280:1,1; 281:1,2,2; 282:3,4,4,4;
		283:1,1,2,2,3; 284:3; 285:1,1,2,4; 286:1;
		289:3,3; 290:3; 293:1,1; 294:2,2,2,2; 297:2;
		298:3; 300:1,2,2,3,4,4; 302:4,4; 303:1,1,2,2;
		304:4,4; 318:3; 321:3; 322:4; 325:2;
		326:1,1,1,2; 328:1,1,1,1,1,1; 329:1,1;
		331:1,1; 332:1; 337:1; 344:1; 378:2,2
outputs	(2)	43:2; 55:2
outrageous	(1)	31:2
outright	(1)	336:1
outrun	(2)	105:2; 328:1
outset	(5)	261:2,2; 272:2; 276:2; 317:3
outside	(10)	11:3; 66:2; 69:3,3; 159:1; 189:2,2; 252:1;
		318:2; 378:2
outstanding	(10)	42:2; 149:4; 159:1; 249:4; 254:3; 267:4;
		351:3; 371:1; 372:1; 377:2
outweigh	(3)	214:2,2; 334:1
outweighed	(3)	69:5; 163:2; 329:2
outwit	(1)	155:2
over	(139)	13:3; 16:2,2; 18:2; 23:1; 25:1; 27:2; 28:2;

par (cont.)		260:2,2; 263:4; 284:2; 301:2; 307:1
parable	(1)	356:2
paradox	(1)	30:3
paradoxes	(1)	359:3
paradoxical	(3)	125:2; 142:3; 211:1
parallel	(3)	16:2; 21:1; 344:4
parallels	(2)	16:2; 21:3
parameters	(1)	243:3
paramount	(1)	110:3
Parbat	(1)	365:3
parent	(1)	343:1
pari	(12)	69:3,4; 98:2; 113:1; 122:3; 125:1; 130:2; 143:1; 208:2; 217:1; 228:2; 231:3
paribus	(1)	191:1
parity	(3)	203:1; 259:1; 339:3
parliament	(1)	347:2
parsimony	(2)	363:2,3
part	(106)	14:2; 18:2; 31:2; 32:1; 37:2; 38:3,5; 42:2; 43:3; 48:4; 51:1,1; 52:2,2; 54:4; 56:1,1,1; 57:1; 60:3; 62:3; 63:2; 66:2; 69:3,4,5; 72:3; 73:2; 76:1,1; 89:1; 92:2; 99:3; 102:2; 104:1; 105:2,2; 109:2; 111:4; 113:1; 117:2; 120:3; 122:1; 124:2; 128:1; 130:1; 139:3; 143:2; 144:4; 153:2; 155:2; 160:3; 164:1,3; 166:3; 167:2; 171:2; 174:2,2; 177:2; 178:1; 183:1; 189:2; 190:1; 191:1; 194:1; 199:1; 205:3; 208:1; 215:3; 218:2; 222:1; 233:3; 236:5; 237:1; 278:4,4; 283:1; 287:2; 290:3; 292:1; 299:3; 313:2; 315:3,4; 319:4; 321:3; 330:1; 331:2; 332:2; 336:2; 337:2; 340:1; 346:1; 348:1; 349:1; 355:2; 358:2; 360:3; 362:4; 363:2; 364:2; 369:1,1; 374:2; 382:1
parted	(2)	62:3; 167:3
partial	(3)	275:4; 297:2; 305:3
partially	(4)	68:3; 143:2; 187:1; 319:1
particular	(63)	10:1; 14:1; 28:2,2; 37:1; 40:2; 42:1,2; 43:2,3,3,3; 44:2; 61:1; 72:4; 76:2; 83:1; 95:3; 121:1; 124:2; 135:2; 149:1; 154:2,3; 167:3; 193:1; 196:3; 203:3; 205:2; 206:2; 207:2; 219:1; 232:1; 239:4,4; 249:4; 259:2; 260:1,2; 264:2; 268:2; 270:2; 278:3; 281:2,2; 282:2; 292:1; 294:2; 297:2; 300:3; 303:3; 308:1; 313:2; 314:3; 317:2; 321:3;

perhaps (cont.)		329:1; 334:2; 342:3; 350:2; 353:2,5; 359:7; 364:2; 371:1; 378:1; 380:2
period	(112)	10:1; 12:1; 17:3,3; 38:1,1,2; 46:1; 47:3; 50:3; 51:3; 52:1,2,2,2,2; 53:1,1,1,1,2; 54:3,3,4; 56:1; 58:2; 61:2,2; 62:1,3,3,3,3; 63:1,1,1; 66:2,2,2; 70:3; 72:4; 76:1,2; 91:1; 93:3; 100:1; 105:2; 110:1; 114:2; 121:1; 122:4; 124:2; 136:3,3,3; 142:2; 166:3; 167:1,1,3,3,3,4; 182:4; 191:1,1,2; 201:2; 217:2; 221:3; 225:3; 226:2,2,3; 230:2; 238:1; 239:4; 249:1,4; 251:2; 265:2,2; 270:2,3; 271:1,3,3; 279:2; 287:2,2,2; 303:1; 306:4; 307:1,3; 318:1,2,2,3; 323:1,2; 328:1; 329:2; 341:1,3; 346:1; 348:4; 350:2,2,2; 357:1; 383:3
periodically	(1)	234:2
periods	(17)	19:5; 73:3; 97:1,1; 123:3,3; 130:1; 143:2; 150:2; 153:1,1; 167:4; 170:1; 306:5,5; 340:3; 365:3
perished	(1)	38:2
permanent	(8)	97:1; 106:3; 110:1; 160:2; 191:2; 192:5; 268:2; 327:2
permanently	(4)	190:3,4; 322:2,2
permeated	(1)	20:1
permission	(1)	365:5
permit	(3)	39:1; 276:2; 351:3
perpetrating	(1)	3:2
perplex	(1)	39:3
perplexed	(1)	213:1
perplexing	(2)	222:1; 291:2
perplexities	(4)	37:1,2; 67:3; 213:2
perplexity	(5)	43:2; 106:2; 161:2; 189:3; 350:4
persist	(3)	254:2,4; 314:1
persisted	(1)	350:2
persistence	(1)	204:3
persistent	(1)	338:1
person	(9)	5:4,6; 33:1; 144:4; 188:2; 268:1,2; 269:1; 363:3
person's	(1)	18:5
personal	(12)	111:3; 144:3; 162:4; 170:2; 213:4; 348:1; 365:3; 366:1; 374:2; 380:2,2,2
persons	(7)	5:6; 153:4; 154:3; 268:2; 347:2; 352:2,2
perspective	(1)	158:3

place (44) 32:1; 40:1; 48:2; 64:2; 65:1; 66:1; 69:3; 72:2; 77:1; 80:3; 82:2; 105:2; 121:1,1; 130:2,2; 136:3; 138:4; 171:4; 172:1; 176:1; 177:2; 182:3,4; 202:1,1; 206:1; 236:5; 245:2; 278:1; 281:1,1; 314:1,2; 331:1,1; 343:1,1; 355:3; 358:3; 362:2,3; 363:2; 383:3

placed (2) 178:1; 198:2

placing (3) 3:1; 210:2; 211:1

plain (2) 177:3; 353:5

plainly (1) 340:1

plan (1) 326:3

plane (1) 365:3

planning (1) 366:1

plant (12) 71:5,5,5; 72:3,4; 73:1,1; 100:2; 106:2; 124:2,2; 148:1

plausibility (2) 20:2; 279:1

plausible (12) 9:3; 83:2; 128:1; 154:2; 180:1; 251:3,4; 253:2; 306:3; 329:1,2; 383:3

plausibly (1) 250:2

play (15) 51:1; 76:1; 100:1; 111:4; 150:2; 164:1; 175:2; 233:3; 237:1; 315:3,4; 361:1; 379:3,3; 380:2

played (20) 37:2; 89:1; 128:1; 130:1; 155:3; 156:1; 194:1; 241:2,2; 292:1; 313:2; 331:2; 332:2; 348:1; 349:1; 358:2; 364:2; 374:2,2; 381:4

players (6) 150:2; 156:1,1,3; 374:2; 381:1

playing (1) 196:5

plays (9) 32:1; 76:1; 122:1; 124:2; 141:1; 190:1; 222:1; 236:5; 381:1

plead (1) 366:4

pleasurable (1) 381:4

plentifully (1) 359:1

plenty (7) 30:3; 172:1; 342:1,1; 343:1,1; 345:2

plight (1) 360:2

plot (1) 162:3

plus (8) 24:1; 69:5; 78:2,2; 98:3; 183:1; 226:3; 375:3

pockets (1) 359:1

poem (1) 360:2

point (130) 3:1; 6:3; 8:4; 17:2,2; 23:1; 24:4; 25:3,3,3; 26:2; 29:5; 32:2; 46:2; 51:3; 53:1; 55:2,5; 56:1; 58:2; 61:2; 64:2; 68:2,3,3; 69:1; 89:1;

popular (cont.)		381:4
popularised	(1)	359:2
population	(14)	4:2; 7:3; 48:4; 106:2; 220:3; 221:1; 307:3; 318:1,1; 330:2; 340:3; 363:1; 381:4; 382:3
portfolio	(1)	157:2
portion	(7)	19:2,2; 120:3; 145:2; 194:1; 200:2; 369:1
portions	(2)	115:5; 116:1
portmanteau	(2)	96:2; 368:5
position	(54)	11:1; 12:2,2,2; 49:1,1; 50:2; 75:1,1; 80:2; 89:1; 98:1; 100:2; 120:4; 138:2; 145:1; 159:1; 164:3; 169:5; 179:2; 180:3,3; 181:1; 186:1; 201:1; 217:3,3; 218:1,2; 221:2; 228:3; 232:4; 236:3; 237:2; 249:2; 251:4; 252:1,2; 253:1,2; 254:3,4; 267:3,5; 274:4,4; 278:4; 288:1; 289:3; 291:2,2; 341:3; 343:4; 346:1
positions	(5)	3:1; 179:2; 191:1,2; 301:3
positive	(16)	54:3,3,3; 96:4; 109:2; 128:2; 155:2; 161:4,4; 169:1; 215:1; 217:3; 221:3,3; 356:2; 381:1
positively	(2)	367:1; 373:1
possess	(8)	40:1; 64:2; 81:2; 167:2; 225:4; 241:3; 288:1,1
possessed	(2)	131:2; 327:2
possesses	(4)	18:5; 84:3; 104:2; 343:4
possessing	(5)	44:1; 154:3; 217:2; 239:1; 294:1
possession	(4)	60:1; 205:3; 241:2; 362:2
possibilities	(5)	24:5; 68:1; 176:1; 219:1; 265:1
possibility	(22)	6:2; 9:2; 15:2; 61:1; 84:1; 161:3; 180:1; 207:3; 218:2; 263:3; 275:3; 277:3; 300:3; 308:2; 343:1; 346:3; 353:2; 358:1; 369:1,1; 371:1; 377:2
possible	(63)	3:1; 7:1; 17:1; 33:3; 45:2; 47:2; 52:3; 60:1,3; 75:3; 81:2; 92:1; 95:1; 99:2; 114:2; 116:1; 121:3; 128:1,1; 137:3; 138:2; 141:2; 144:3,3; 177:1; 183:1; 191:1,2; 192:1,1,1; 203:1; 215:2; 216:2; 232:2; 236:2; 257:2; 262:2; 264:4; 270:2; 274:3; 276:2; 277:3; 284:2; 287:2; 288:1; 292:1; 296:2; 299:1; 316:2; 320:2; 323:2; 331:1; 334:2; 343:4; 345:1,1; 353:2; 357:2; 367:1; 368:1; 376:1; 381:2
possibly	(3)	144:3; 192:3; 339:3

post	(2)	357:1; 365:3
post-war	(6)	20:1; 219:2; 329:1; 338:2; 349:3; 353:3
posterity	(1)	131:2
postpone	(4)	70:2; 201:4; 214:2; 215:3
postponed	(1)	220:1
postponement	(5)	123:4; 124:1; 188:3; 214:2; 263:3
postponing	(3)	188:2; 230:3; 269:2
postulate	(12)	6:1,2,2; 7:3; 10:2,3; 11:1; 12:3; 15:4; 17:1,2; 18:2
postulated	(1)	235:1
postulates	(6)	3:1; 5:2; 6:2,3; 16:1; 34:1
potency	(2)	351:1; 383:3
potential	(7)	31:2,2,2; 53:1; 70:6; 226:2,2
potentialities	(1)	379:3
potentiality	(4)	168:1; 205:1,1; 211:2
potentially	(2)	30:2; 31:2
Potosi	(1)	362:1
pounds	(4)	139:3,3; 154:1; 188:1
pour	(1)	358:3
poverty	(4)	30:3; 126:2; 345:1; 365:3
power	(27)	17:4,4; 18:5; 19:5; 65:1; 93:2; 100:1; 108:1; 167:3; 188:1,2; 226:2,2; 230:2; 231:4; 258:1; 268:1; 327:2; 343:4; 344:3; 362:4,4; 363:3; 369:1; 374:2; 376:1; 383:3
powerful	(2)	380:2; 383:3
powers	(3)	18:5; 352:2; 362:4
practicable	(16)	157:1; 164:3; 203:2; 209:1; 218:3; 219:1; 267:1; 268:2; 281:2; 316:2; 320:1; 336:1; 361:5; 375:2; 378:2; 380:3
practical	(38)	3:1; 20:5; 24:5; 29:6; 38:2; 92:2; 99:2; 129:3; 130:2; 148:4; 185:1,1; 206:1; 225:2; 234:2; 243:5; 249:2; 265:2; 277:1; 288:1; 289:4; 301:3; 325:1,2; 327:2; 333:1,1; 338:3; 339:2,3; 340:1,2; 341:3; 351:4; 356:3; 366:1; 383:3,3
practically	(8)	5:2; 12:2; 163:2; 190:1; 207:3; 235:2; 287:1; 325:2
practice	(34)	9:2; 33:1; 43:3; 50:4; 51:1; 59:3; 67:3,3; 94:1; 97:2; 138:3; 148:2; 151:1; 152:1; 157:1,2; 160:1; 163:2; 167:3; 206:2,2; 217:2; 247:2; 258:1; 262:3; 272:4; 273:5,5; 284:2; 334:1; 339:3; 343:4; 357:2; 376:3
practices	(8)	6:2; 59:3; 91:1; 207:2; 240:3; 265:3; 324:3;

preference	(9)	69:5; 129:2; 170:3; 240:3; 242:2; 271:3; 337:2,3; 351:3
preferences	(1)	156:2
preferred	(2)	107:2; 371:1
prefers	(2)	83:1; 207:3
prefix	(1)	3:1
prejudice	(1)	363:2
prejudicial	(5)	359:1,1; 363:1,2,2
preliminary	(3)	89:1; 103:2; 194:1
premature	(2)	326:3; 338:3
prematurely	(1)	362:4
premiss	(2)	19:3; 273:5
premisses	(1)	350:1
premium	(4)	202:1; 235:1; 240:3; 370:1
preoccupation	(5)	12:2; 336:2; 339:2; 340:1; 341:2
preoccupations	(1)	349:2
preoccupied	(1)	335:3
preparation	(2)	48:1; 211:2
prepare	(1)	366:1
prepared	(10)	8:3; 46:1; 117:2; 166:3; 205:3,3,3; 276:1; 285:2; 332:1
preparing	(4)	204:3; 210:1,2; 211:1
prescribed	(1)	234:2
prescription	(1)	357:1
presence	(1)	241:3
present	(79)	10:2; 19:2; 21:2; 50:3; 69:6; 70:1,2; 71:1,1; 77:1,2; 78:1; 93:3; 95:3; 101:1,1; 104:3,3; 105:1; 107:2; 109:3; 110:1; 127:2; 135:2; 137:2,3; 140:3,3; 145:3,3; 146:3,3; 167:2; 168:3,3; 172:2; 191:2; 203:1; 210:1,1,1,1,2,2; 211:1,2,2,2; 218:3; 219:1; 220:2; 224:3,3; 225:6; 228:3,3; 229:1; 242:2; 247:2; 251:3; 271:3; 293:2,2; 294:1,1; 320:1; 322:5; 326:3; 327:1; 334:2; 369:1,1; 374:2; 377:1,2,2; 379:2; 380:2; 383:3
present-day	(2)	146:2; 381:2
present-goods	(1)	93:2
presentment	(1)	279:3
presents	(4)	39:1; 105:2; 170:2; 298:3
preservation	(1)	362:2
preserve	(4)	242:3; 243:2; 274:3; 275:1
preserved	(1)	242:3

preserves	(1)	380:2
preserving	(2)	70:1; 381:2
president	(1)	331:3
pressing	(1)	382:3
pressure	(4)	136:3; 251:3; 301:2; 381:4
prestige	(2)	33:1,2
presumably	(6)	178:1; 219:3; 277:3; 308:2; 329:1; 368:1
presume	(2)	109:3; 190:1
presumed	(1)	41:1
presumes	(1)	11:1
presumption	(10)	41:1; 115:5; 116:1; 163:2; 194:1,1; 230:3; 238:4,4; 253:3
presumptions	(1)	338:3
presumptuous	(1)	339:2
presupposed	(1)	15:4
pretends	(1)	162:1
pretentious	(1)	298:1
pretext	(1)	130:1
prettiest	(4)	156:2,2,2,2
prevail	(3)	252:1; 308:1; 332:2
prevailed	(1)	251:2
prevailing	(12)	97:2; 109:3; 150:2; 156:3; 192:5; 203:1,3; 204:1; 219:2; 302:3; 342:2; 382:3
prevails	(5)	120:2; 150:3; 203:1; 243:4; 372:2
prevalence	(2)	81:2; 204:1
prevent	(9)	37:1; 39:4; 118:2; 128:1; 235:1; 278:1; 290:3; 308:1; 369:1
prevented	(4)	320:2; 363:2; 366:1; 370:1
preventing	(1)	368:1
prevents	(3)	218:3; 238:3; 322:3
previous	(27)	26:2; 50:2; 51:3; 52:2; 53:1; 66:2; 74:1; 76:1,1; 100:2; 101:3; 124:1; 147:1; 166:3; 177:3; 198:2; 218:2; 229:1; 247:3; 261:2; 275:4; 293:2; 303:2,2; 316:1; 323:1; 328:1
previously	(12)	17:4,4; 81:2; 82:1; 105:2; 124:1; 176:1; 243:2; 277:3; 337:1; 342:5; 349:1
price	(157)	7:1,1,1; 8:3; 9:2; 10:2; 15:3; 17:4; 21:3,3; 22:1,1; 24:1,3,4,4,4,4,4; 25:2,3; 26:1,1,1,2,2; 28:2,2,2; 30:1; 39:2; 42:2,2; 44:2; 46:2; 55:3,4,4,4,4; 64:2; 67:2,2,3,3,3,3,3,3,3; 68:1,1,1,1,1,3,3,3; 71:4,5; 72:3,5; 94:1; 98:2; 122:3; 130:1; 135:2,2,2,2; 136:2,3; 137:2,2,2; 139:1;

princes	(1)	345:1
principal	(3)	91:2; 96:2; 287:2
principle	(10)	31:2; 58:2,2; 65:1; 98:2; 122:2; 185:1; 254:4; 271:3; 302:4
principles	(33)	5:4; 18:4,6; 20:4; 52:3; 56:1; 72:3; 91:1; 101:1; 113:1; 129:1,2,3; 139:2; 146:3; 164:3; 175:3,3; 176:1,1; 186:1; 189:3; 190:2; 214:3; 221:1; 242:1; 249:2; 297:2; 334:3,4; 363:3,7; 364:3
printed	(1)	344:2
printing	(1)	200:2
prior	(1)	13:1
priori	(4)	96:4; 149:2; 251:4; 253:2
private	(27)	21:3; 101:1; 106:2; 120:1; 121:1; 129:3,4; 150:3; 154:3; 155:2; 230:2; 316:3; 320:1; 324:4; 339:1; 345:1; 360:1; 361:5,8; 362:2; 371:1; 374:2,2; 378:1; 379:1,1; 380:1
privileges	(1)	163:2
prize	(1)	156:2
pro	(1)	263:4
probabilities	(5)	152:1; 161:4; 169:2; 202:1; 240:2
probability	(5)	24:5; 144:2; 148:5; 201:3; 377:2
probable	(17)	76:2; 98:1; 120:4; 121:3; 130:2; 141:2; 148:3; 150:2; 152:1; 154:3; 232:2; 238:1; 241:2; 260:2,2; 297:2; 300:4
probably	(35)	42:3; 90:2; 93:3; 100:2; 102:1,2; 121:1,3; 128:1; 129:3; 161:4; 214:2; 218:1,2; 226:4; 237:1; 252:1; 258:3; 262:5; 263:1; 267:5; 268:1; 302:3; 307:2; 315:5; 316:2; 317:3; 318:2,3; 321:1; 340:3; 357:1; 358:1; 361:8; 381:4
probe	(1)	213:2
problem	(36)	5:7; 13:2; 29:6; 39:1; 52:2; 55:4; 61:2; 72:3; 101:1; 105:2,2; 153:2; 156:2; 167:3; 184:3; 199:2; 249:2; 260:1,1,2; 275:2; 289:2; 293:1; 308:2; 309:1; 329:2; 348:1; 350:1,1; 364:2; 371:1; 377:2; 379:1; 381:2,2; 383:1
problems	(17)	16:2; 37:1,2; 55:4; 66:2; 89:1; 149:1; 167:4; 176:4; 281:1,1; 293:2; 294:1; 297:2; 346:4; 354:1; 378:2
procedure	(4)	67:1,3; 153:2; 297:2
proceed	(5)	14:1; 90:1; 98:1; 179:2; 275:4

proceeded	(1)	250:1
proceedeth	(1)	345:2
proceeding	(3)	83:2; 250:1; 331:2
proceeds	(33)	14:3; 24:1,1,2,4,4,5,5; 25:1,2,3; 26:1,1; 44:2; 55:2,2,3,3,5; 58:1; 66:2; 67:3; 70:1; 77:2; 89:2,2; 240:1; 261:1,2; 276:2; 330:1; 344:1; 373:2
process	(20)	31:1; 46:2; 48:3; 49:1; 50:2,4; 51:1; 177:2; 214:2; 216:2,2,2; 225:5; 287:2; 290:3; 318:2; 332:1; 367:2; 369:1; 372:2
processes	(18)	46:1; 48:1; 49:1,1,1; 214:2,2,2,2,2,2,2,2; 215:2,2,2,2,3
proclivities	(2)	374:2,2
prodigality	(1)	359:1
prodigals	(1)	190:3
prodigious	(1)	364:1
produce	(47)	4:3; 24:4; 44:1; 46:1,2; 47:3; 51:3; 53:1,1,1,1; 73:2; 76:1; 105:1; 118:2,2; 135:2; 142:3; 203:1; 214:2; 215:3,3; 216:1; 217:1; 225:5,6; 228:2,3; 230:2; 232:3,3; 237:1; 239:2; 250:2; 264:2; 266:3,3; 287:1; 295:3; 303:1; 331:2; 338:1; 362:4; 363:3,3; 370:1; 379:1
produced	(36)	38:2; 58:2; 62:3; 70:3; 81:2; 105:2,2,2; 122:3; 136:2; 141:2,2,2,2; 143:2,2,2; 202:2; 212:1; 213:4; 215:2; 222:1; 223:4; 228:2,3; 230:2,3; 235:1,2; 241:2; 317:3; 321:3; 360:1; 368:2,2; 379:1
producer	(7)	24:4; 46:1,1; 57:1; 63:3; 64:1; 148:1
producer's	(2)	51:1,2
producers	(10)	51:1,1; 192:2,2,5; 193:1,1; 212:2; 213:1; 363:2
produces	(3)	122:4; 303:2; 328:1
producing	(23)	40:2; 49:1; 67:3,3; 117:1; 118:1; 126:3; 135:2; 136:3,3; 148:1; 176:4; 187:4; 216:2; 230:2; 231:4; 232:1; 234:3; 240:1; 252:2; 268:3; 272:4; 339:1
product	(34)	5:3; 6:2,3; 17:3; 18:1,1,3; 31:1; 40:2; 55:5; 69:5; 83:1; 114:2,2,2; 123:3; 128:2; 138:2; 148:1; 176:3,3; 186:2; 191:1; 214:2; 257:3; 258:3; 261:2; 287:2; 289:3,3; 290:2; 295:1; 340:1; 379:1
production	(126)	4:1; 18:3; 19:1,2,3; 23:1,1; 24:5; 25:3;

production (cont.)		31:1,2; 46:1; 47:2; 49:1; 52:3; 53:1,1,2; 54:2,2; 55:1,2; 60:2; 62:3; 66:2,2; 67:1,1,3,3; 69:6; 70:1,1,6; 72:3; 76:2; 117:3; 139:1,2; 141:2; 147:2; 161:2; 176:4; 187:3,3,4; 188:2; 211:1,2; 214:1; 215:3; 216:2,2; 219:2; 225:5; 228:2,3; 229:1,1,1; 230:2,2,3; 231:1,2; 234:3,4,4; 235:1,1,1; 236:3; 237:1; 238:2,3; 240:1; 241:2; 246:1,1; 252:2; 261:2; 271:1; 279:2; 282:4; 287:2,2,2; 288:1,1,1; 290:2; 294:2,2,2; 295:2,3; 296:2; 299:2; 303:1,3; 304:2; 308:1; 315:3,5; 317:3; 341:3; 362:4,4,4; 363:2,2,2,3; 367:2,2; 368:2,2,2; 369:1; 370:1,1; 375:3; 378:1; 379:1,2,3
productions	(3)	18:5; 369:1,1
productive	(14)	18:5; 20:2,2; 48:1; 51:1; 62:3; 63:1; 213:3,3; 244:1; 287:2; 309:3; 356:2; 369:1
productiveness	(1)	176:1
productivity	(17)	6:2; 7:1; 9:3,3,3; 16:1; 29:4; 137:4; 138:2; 139:1; 140:4; 176:1,1,3; 215:2; 268:2; 278:4
products	(19)	4:1; 43:3; 47:2; 221:1; 246:1,3; 286:2,2,2,3,3,4; 287:1,2; 288:1; 329:2; 331:1,1; 332:1
produit	(1)	364:1
prof.	(17)	3:2; 5:7,7; 7:4,5; 20:5; 39:5; 72:5,5; 176:3,4,4; 189:4,5,5; 341:5; 344:5
professional	(7)	33:2; 151:1; 154:3; 155:2,3; 156:2; 157:1
professionals	(2)	154:3; 155:3
professor	(71)	7:1,2; 13:1; 19:3,3; 32:2; 38:1,2; 39:1; 56:1; 59:3; 60:1,1; 72:3; 79:2,2; 80:3; 140:3,3; 141:1; 142:2,2; 143:1; 176:1,1,1; 182:3; 186:1; 188:2; 189:2; 190:1,1; 192:2,2,2; 193:1,1,1; 238:4; 260:1,4; 272:1,3; 273:2,3,4; 274:2; 275:1,1,3; 276:2; 277:1,1,2,3,3,4; 278:3,3,4; 279:2,2,3; 341:1,2; 345:2; 347:3; 350:1; 355:1; 357:1; 358:3; 366:1
profit	(49)	12:2; 23:1,1,1; 24:1; 53:2; 55:2; 56:1; 57:1,1,1,1; 58:1; 60:3,3; 61:1,1,1; 68:1; 69:1; 72:2; 77:1,1,2,2,3,3; 141:2; 150:2,2; 151:1; 162:1; 169:2,3; 170:2; 190:3; 238:1; 261:2; 283:1,1,1; 288:1; 290:3; 335:3;

profit (cont.)		344:2; 370:1,1,1,1
profitable	(8)	157:1; 159:1; 184:2; 196:3; 217:1; 228:3; 229:1,1
profitably	(2)	104:3; 176:1
profits	(17)	17:3; 25:3; 73:3; 77:1,1,2; 123:4; 153:5; 154:1; 156:3; 190:3; 258:1; 261:2; 289:3; 290:2; 362:4; 370:1
profound	(1)	176:4
profoundly	(2)	185:1; 353:3
programme	(2)	120:2; 349:2
progress	(14)	33:1; 37:2; 109:3; 130:1; 150:2; 220:3; 271:3; 275:4; 290:3; 335:3; 340:3; 362:4; 366:1; 372:2
progresses	(1)	313:3
progressive	(6)	120:4; 186:2; 251:3; 279:2; 325:3; 335:3
prohibition	(1)	346:3
project	(2)	148:2; 151:1
projected	(2)	32:3; 51:3
projectors	(3)	352:2,2; 353:5
projects	(3)	108:1; 352:2; 353:1
prolongation	(1)	323:2
prolonged	(2)	323:1; 376:2
prominence	(1)	104:1
prominent	(2)	199:1; 292:1
promising	(2)	161:2; 243:2
promote	(6)	325:3,3; 338:2; 348:2,3; 361:7
promoted	(4)	203:2; 211:2; 328:2; 375:1
promotes	(1)	157:1
promoting	(1)	336:2
promotion	(1)	43:3
prompted	(3)	150:2; 320:3; 321:2
promptly	(1)	186:2
prone	(2)	31:2; 290:3
pronounced	(1)	263:4
pronouncements	(1)	349:3
propaedeutic	(1)	293:2
propaganda	(2)	117:1; 354:2
propelling	(1)	314:1
propensities	(12)	31:2; 91:1; 97:1; 117:2; 118:1; 191:1; 192:1; 242:1; 250:2,2,2; 360:1
propensity	(161)	27:2; 28:2,2,5,5; 29:2,3; 30:1,2,2; 31:3,4; 43:3; 65:1,1; 90:2; 91:1,1,2; 92:1,3; 93:1,3; 94:2; 95:1,2,2,3,4,4; 96:2,3,3; 98:2; 101:1;

proposal	(3)	277:1; 342:3; 357:1
proposals	(1)	234:2
propose	(2)	41:2; 201:2
proposed	(1)	357:1
proposes	(1)	157:1
proposition	(18)	12:2,2; 17:3; 18:1; 20:2; 26:2; 40:1,1; 84:3; 85:1; 115:1; 127:1; 178:1,2,2; 179:1; 205:1; 259:2
propositions	(5)	28:3; 55:3; 85:2; 115:1; 363:3
propounded	(1)	192:2
prospect	(4)	93:2; 213:3; 215:3; 263:3
prospective	(84)	47:2; 51:1; 58:2; 70:2,4; 71:2; 77:2; 130:2; 135:1,1,2,2,2; 136:3; 137:2,3,3,5; 141:2,2; 142:2,2,3,3; 144:2; 145:1; 147:1,1,2; 149:3,3,4; 150:2; 152:1; 153:4; 154:2; 155:1,3; 158:3; 159:1; 163:2,2,2; 170:3; 184:1; 188:1; 206:2; 212:1,1,1,1,1,1,2,2,2,2; 216:2,2,2; 217:1,1,1; 221:3,3; 224:3; 228:3; 229:1; 233:3; 240:2,2; 246:2; 248:1,1; 250:5,5; 252:2,2; 265:2; 288:1; 317:3; 323:1; 368:5; 370:1
prospects	(5)	158:2; 160:2; 162:3; 169:3; 298:3
prospectus	(1)	162:1
prosperity	(7)	33:3; 150:2; 162:3; 338:1; 349:1; 359:3; 382:3
prosperous	(1)	360:2
prostration	(1)	367:1
protagonists	(1)	341:4
protect	(3)	14:2; 109:1; 339:3
protecting	(1)	339:3
protection	(3)	334:2,2,2
protectionist	(2)	334:2; 368:4
protesting	(1)	352:2
prove	(24)	12:2; 98:2; 99:1; 118:2; 160:1; 163:2; 169:2; 170:3; 203:2; 208:2; 219:1; 232:2; 263:4; 264:3; 267:1; 309:2,2; 320:1; 338:1; 339:2; 366:1; 373:1; 377:2; 378:1
proved	(2)	332:2; 340:3
proves	(1)	327:2
provide	(36)	21:2; 31:2; 39:4; 94:1; 98:1; 99:2; 100:2; 104:3,3; 105:1; 106:1; 107:2; 109:2; 136:3; 152:1; 163:2; 187:3; 196:2; 204:2; 211:2; 215:3; 216:1,2; 220:2; 234:3; 251:3; 261:2;

provide (cont.)		275:4; 278:4; 297:2,2; 308:1; 332:2; 367:2; 372:1; 382:3
provided	(28)	33:3; 43:3; 55:5; 61:2; 63:2; 69:2; 95:4; 101:3; 105:1; 117:1,1; 122:1; 127:1; 169:3; 214:2; 221:3; 270:2; 273:3; 276:3; 282:4; 283:1; 304:4; 306:5; 337:2; 338:1; 369:1,1; 375:1
provides	(10)	28:2; 117:2; 204:3; 251:2; 252:2,2; 275:1; 318:2; 337:2,2
providing	(8)	55:1; 60:1; 94:1; 95:2; 105:2; 180:1; 217:1; 375:1
provinces	(1)	366:1
proving	(2)	316:2; 376:1
provision	(17)	98:3; 99:2,2,2,3; 100:1; 101:1; 104:3,3,3; 105:1; 109:1; 128:1; 131:1; 188:2,2; 218:2
provisional	(2)	276:1; 297:2
provisionally	(1)	293:1
provisions	(6)	100:1,1,2; 351:3; 371:1,1
provoke	(1)	308:1
proximate	(1)	248:1
prudence	(5)	100:1,2; 105:1; 109:1; 361:8
prudent	(6)	131:2; 157:2; 352:2; 361:5; 373:3; 374:2
pseudo-mathematical	(2)	275:4; 297:2
psychological	(45)	28:5; 30:1; 57:1,3; 58:2; 60:1; 64:2; 91:1,1; 96:4; 97:1,2; 114:3; 117:1,2; 118:1; 129:4; 147:2; 165:2,2; 166:2,4; 191:1; 192:1; 202:2; 203:3; 217:2; 218:3; 219:2; 246:2; 247:1,1,1; 248:1; 250:2,2; 251:3,4; 252:1; 253:2; 271:3; 277:3; 306:5; 356:1; 374:2
psychologically	(1)	307:3
psychology	(16)	27:2; 116:2; 120:2; 149:2; 154:2; 155:1,2; 158:3; 162:4; 170:1,1; 252:2; 301:3; 307:1; 317:1; 320:1
public	(71)	82:2,2; 101:1,1; 104:2; 106:1,2,2; 113:1; 116:2; 117:1,1,2,2; 118:1; 119:2,2; 121:1,1; 127:1,1,1,1; 128:3; 129:4,4; 154:3; 155:3; 157:1; 159:2; 163:2,2,2; 167:2; 168:1; 173:1; 174:2,2,2; 183:1; 189:2; 194:1; 203:2,2,2; 204:1,3,3; 205:1; 207:3; 218:2; 233:3; 234:2; 235:2,2; 248:2; 261:2; 277:3; 281:2; 306:2; 307:1; 319:2; 323:1; 335:3; 360:1; 363:3; 366:4; 373:2; 378:1; 379:1; 381:1

public's	(1)	194:1
publication	(4)	182:3; 346:1; 365:1; 367:1
publicist	(1)	380:3
published	(8)	101:2; 346:1; 354:1,1,2,2; 365:3,4
puerile	(1)	339:2
pulpit	(1)	367:1
pupil	(1)	334:2
purchasable	(1)	94:1
purchase	(27)	19:2,5; 23:1; 46:1; 61:2,2; 74:3; 75:1,1; 84:3; 94:1; 156:3; 159:1; 160:2; 169:1; 170:1,3; 188:1; 195:4; 196:3; 197:2,2; 206:2; 274:3; 286:2; 337:2; 382:3
purchased	(6)	62:1; 64:1; 67:3; 135:2; 151:1; 357:1
purchaser	(1)	63:3
purchasers	(4)	24:4,4; 316:1; 359:1
purchases	(18)	19:2,2,2; 47:1; 53:1; 62:3; 66:2; 67:3; 69:3,3; 70:2; 135:1; 159:1; 160:2,3; 170:1; 196:2; 383:1
purchasing	(13)	18:3,5; 52:1; 93:2; 153:4; 160:2; 167:3; 169:2; 187:5; 197:2; 231:4; 258:1; 282:3
purchasing-power	(2)	14:1; 330:2
pure	(17)	4:2; 19:1; 68:1; 108:1; 144:4; 145:1,1; 177:1; 182:2; 208:2,2,2,2; 221:3,3; 231:2; 306:5
purely	(5)	39:3; 232:2; 317:1; 355:3; 356:1
purged	(1)	380:2
purported	(1)	242:3
purpose	(34)	37:1; 38:1; 40:1,1; 41:2; 42:2; 43:3,3,3; 46:1; 50:3; 59:2; 127:2; 141:1; 159:1; 165:1; 186:3; 187:5,5; 189:1; 195:1; 204:3; 225:6; 226:1; 227:2; 271:3; 275:2; 305:3; 315:1; 325:4; 341:5; 355:2; 367:1; 374:2
purposes	(14)	33:2; 39:2; 41:1; 42:1; 73:2; 187:2; 195:1; 199:2; 209:2; 227:1; 263:4; 302:4; 315:4; 336:2
purposive	(1)	205:2
pursue	(1)	43:3
pursued	(3)	294:1; 348:5; 361:5
pursuing	(1)	37:1
pursuit	(4)	349:1,2; 352:2; 374:2
pursuits	(1)	352:2
purview	(1)	158:3
push	(4)	29:5; 139:3; 248:1; 350:1

pushed	(8)	104:3; 136:4,4; 140:2; 184:2,2; 337:1; 363:3
put	(9)	15:1; 60:2; 162:2; 220:2; 317:1; 327:1; 344:2; 362:4; 379:2
puts	(5)	104:1; 162:2; 190:2; 347:3; 368:1
putting	(2)	68:3; 269:2
puzzle	(2)	32:2; 359:2
Pye	(1)	354:2
pyramid	(1)	305:2
pyramid-building	(2)	129:1; 131:2
pyramids	(2)	131:2; 220:1
quaesitum	(4)	247:2,2,2; 273:1
qualification	(7)	5:4,6; 81:1; 119:2; 206:2; 231:5; 288:1
qualifications	(8)	6:3; 12:1; 17:2; 114:3; 206:2; 289:4; 290:1; 297:2
qualify	(1)	6:1
quality	(4)	234:2; 245:2; 266:2; 355:2
quantitative	(16)	38:1,2; 39:3,3,4; 40:1; 44:1; 59:2; 113:1; 119:2; 121:3; 161:4,4; 201:3; 281:1; 298:2
quantitatively	(2)	39:3; 241:2
quantities	(19)	6:2; 29:1; 40:1,2; 41:2,2; 44:2; 55:2; 89:2; 90:1; 114:2; 116:5; 185:1; 202:2; 227:2; 230:2; 258:3,3; 300:3
quantity	(240)	4:1,3; 11:1; 12:2,2; 18:2,2; 21:3; 23:1; 37:2; 38:2; 41:1,2,2,2,2,4,4; 43:2,2; 44:1; 45:2; 53:1,2; 54:2,2,2; 58:2; 59:1; 63:3,3; 72:3; 75:1; 79:2,3; 80:1,3,3; 90:2; 109:1; 115:2; 122:3; 126:3,3; 138:3,4; 141:2; 147:2; 167:2,2; 168:1,1,1; 171:2,2,2,2,2,3,3; 172:1,2,2,2,2; 173:1,1,1,1,2; 174:1,2,2,2; 176:3,3; 181:1,1; 182:4,4; 183:1,1; 188:2; 190:3; 191:1,2,2,2,2,2; 192:1; 196:4,5; 197:2; 205:2,2,3,3; 206:2; 208:3; 209:1,1,2,2,3; 213:1; 214:2,2,2; 215:2; 222:2,2; 230:2,2,2; 232:1; 233:2,2,2; 234:3,3,3; 245:2,2; 246:1,1,1,2; 247:1,1; 248:1; 258:1,1; 259:1,1; 266:2,2,2,2,3,3,3,3,3; 267:4,5; 268:3,3; 270:1,1; 273:4; 276:2,2; 285:5; 289:3,3,3; 290:3,3; 292:1,1; 293:1,1; 295:2,3,3,3,3; 296:1,1,2,2,3,3,3,3,3,3; 297:2,2,2,2; 298:2,2,3; 299:1,1,1,1,2,2; 300:5; 302:2; 303:1,2,2; 304:2,4,4; 305:1,2,3,3,3,3;

204

rate (cont.)

166:4,4,5; 167:1,1,1,2,2,2,2,4; 168:1,1,1,2,3;
169:1,1,2,3; 170:1,3; 171:2,2,2,3,3,4,4;
172:1,1,1,2,2; 173:1,1,1,1,2; 174:1,2,2;
175:1,2,2,2,2,2; 176:1,1,1,1,4,4,4;
177:1,1,1,2,2,2; 178:1,1,1,2,2;
179:1,1,2,2,2,2,2,2,2,2; 180:1,1,3;
181:1,1,1,1,1,1,2,2,2,2;
182:2,3,3,3,3,3,4,4,4; 183:1,1,3,3,3;
184:1,2,2,2,2,2,2,2,2,2; 185:1,1;
186:1,1,2,2,2,3,3; 187:1,1,1,2,3,3,3,4,4,5;
188:1; 189:2,2,2,2,2,2; 190:1,2,3,3,3,3,3,3,3;
191:1,2,2,2; 192:1,2,2,2,2; 193:1,1,1,1,1,1;
194:1; 197:1,1,2,2,3,3; 198:1,1,2,2,2,2;
199:1,1,1,3; 200:1; 201:1,3,3;
202:1,1,1,1,1,1,1,1,2,2,2; 203:1,1,1,1,1,2,3;
204:1,1,2,3,3; 205:2,2; 206:1,1,2;
207:3,3,3,3,4,4; 208:2,2,2,2,2,2; 209:1;
211:1; 212:1; 213:1,1,1,3; 215:1; 216:2,2,2;
217:1,1,2; 218:2,2,3,3; 219:1,1,1,1,2,3,4,4;
220:1,2,2,2; 221:2,3,3; 222:1,1,2,2;
224:2,3,3; 225:1,1; 228:1,2,2,2,2,3,3;
229:1,1; 230:1,2,3; 232:3; 233:2; 234:3;
235:1,1; 236:2,3,4,4,4; 237:1; 241:2,2;
242:2,3,3,3,3,3,3,3,4,4,4,4,4,4,4;
243:2,2,3,3,3,3,3,3,4,4,5,5,5,5,5; 245:3;
246:2; 248:1,1,1,2,2,2,2,3; 249:3; 250:5,5,5;
251:2,3; 252:1,1,2,2,2; 253:2,3; 259:2;
260:2; 261:1,2,2; 262:2; 263:4; 265:1;
266:1,3,3; 267:3; 269:2,4,4; 270:1,1,2;
272:1,1,3; 274:4; 275:1,1; 277:1,3; 278:3,6;
281:3; 282:4; 288:1,1; 290:3,3; 294:2,2;
298:2,2,2; 304:1; 306:1,5; 307:1,1,3,3;
308:1,1,1,2; 309:2,2,3; 315:4,4,5;
316:1,1,2,2,2; 317:2; 318:1; 319:3;
320:1,1,2,2,2,2; 321:1; 322:2,2,3,3,3,5;
323:1,1,1,1,1; 324:2; 325:1,3; 326:4;
327:2,3; 328:1,2,2; 329:1,1,1,1,2;
331:2,2,2,2,2; 332:2; 335:3,3; 336:1,2,2,3,3;
337:2,2; 339:2,3,3,3,3; 340:1; 341:2,2,2,2,3;
342:1,1,1,2,3,3; 343:1,1; 344:1,1,2,2,3;
346:4; 347:3; 348:4; 349:1,2; 351:2,3,4;
352:1,1,2,2; 355:3,3,3,3,3;
356:1,1,1,1,1,1,2,2; 357:1; 358:1; 368:1;

rate (cont.)		369:1; 370:1,1,1,1,1; 375:1,1,1,1,2,2; 377:2,2,2,2; 378:1,1,1,1
rates	(49)	28:1; 41:2; 43:3; 111:4; 137:5; 143:2,2; 145:4; 163:2; 167:4; 168:3,3,3,3,3; 169:1; 170:1,1; 172:2; 178:1,1; 182:2; 193:1; 197:2; 204:1; 205:2,3,3; 207:1; 208:4; 223:4,4; 225:2; 235:1; 241:2,2,2; 272:1; 295:2; 302:2; 308:1,1,1; 309:2; 337:1,1,1; 342:2; 356:2
rather	(41)	6:1; 9:2; 39:4; 59:2; 65:1; 83:1; 92:2; 101:1; 102:2; 108:1; 109:1; 120:5; 128:1; 129:2; 140:1; 151:1; 155:3; 161:4,4; 172:1; 194:1; 199:1; 203:3; 216:2; 232:4; 251:1; 253:1; 258:2; 276:1; 306:5; 307:2; 313:2; 329:1,2; 334:4; 342:1; 346:1,4; 352:2; 359:3; 371:1
ratio	(17)	55:5; 93:2; 94:1; 113:1; 115:4,5; 126:4; 138:2,3,3,3; 192:2,2; 201:2,2; 248:2; 299:2
rational	(1)	163:1
rationalise	(2)	152:1; 292:1
rationality	(1)	366:1
raw	(6)	70:4; 73:2,2,3; 331:2; 367:2
re-distribute	(1)	290:3
re-drawn	(1)	281:2
re-embodied	(1)	240:1
re-employment	(1)	121:1
re-estimated	(2)	58:2; 70:3
re-state	(1)	137:5
re-stated	(2)	329:3; 367:1
re-writing	(1)	276:1
re-written	(1)	143:1
reach	(15)	24:5; 48:1,2; 54:3; 68:3; 129:2; 235:1; 264:3; 296:2; 300:3,4; 307:1; 322:1; 338:3; 353:3
reached	(45)	18:2; 31:1; 33:1; 49:1; 64:2,3; 83:1; 98:1; 118:3; 119:1,3; 156:2; 184:2; 192:2; 219:1; 234:1; 236:3; 245:1; 247:1; 252:1; 253:2; 258:3; 289:2,3; 290:3,3; 291:1; 295:3,3; 296:2; 297:2; 300:3,3; 301:1,2; 303:2; 314:1; 322:4; 324:1; 331:2; 353:3; 354:2; 357:1; 371:1; 377:2
reaches	(4)	24:5; 209:1; 218:2; 228:2
reaching	(3)	71:4; 99:4; 212:1

react	(5)	84:1; 142:3; 251:2; 336:3; 377:2
reaction	(11)	142:3; 197:2; 199:1,1; 232:2,3; 263:4; 290:3; 298:2; 355:2; 380:2
reactions	(15)	11:3; 84:2; 92:1; 119:2; 158:2; 162:3; 170:1; 171:2; 206:2; 232:3,4; 264:3,4; 278:6; 287:2
read	(2)	352:1; 366:1
reader	(22)	20:4; 24:4,4; 27:1; 60:3; 66:2; 71:4; 117:2; 136:2; 137:3; 156:3; 184:3; 204:2; 213:1; 222:2; 251:4; 257:2; 278:4; 338:3; 341:1; 353:5; 355:2
reader's	(1)	267:4
readers	(1)	353:3
readier	(2)	10:1; 253:1
readily	(13)	75:1; 129:2; 151:3; 159:1; 184:3; 230:2,3; 235:2; 302:1; 306:5; 308:1; 309:1; 325:3
readiness	(15)	64:2,2; 93:3; 94:1; 142:3; 167:2; 177:2; 178:2; 179:1; 182:4; 185:1; 232:4; 233:3; 319:2; 340:1
ready	(13)	46:1,2; 101:1; 104:2; 172:1; 204:3; 210:1; 226:2; 301:2; 330:2; 334:2; 342:1; 383:3
real	(224)	5:6; 7:1; 8:2,3,3,3; 9:1,2,2,3,3; 10:1,1,1,1,1,1,1,2,2,3,3; 11:1,1,1,1,2,2,2; 12:1,2,2,2,2,2,2,3; 13:2,2,2,2; 14:1,1,1,1,1,2,2,2,3,3,3; 15:3,4; 17:3,3,3,3; 19:3; 20:1; 21:4; 27:2,2; 28:2,4; 29:4,4; 30:2,2,2,2,2; 37:3; 38:1,1,4; 39:1; 40:1; 77:2; 80:3; 81:1; 82:2; 83:1; 91:3,3,3; 92:1; 97:2,2; 98:1; 107:2; 114:2,2,2,2,2,2,2,3; 117:1,2; 119:1; 120:4; 121:1,3; 125:4; 129:2,3; 130:1,1; 142:2; 143:1; 144:3,3,3,4; 153:4; 187:3; 189:2,2,2,2,2,2,4,5; 191:2; 209:2; 212:2; 220:1; 232:4; 233:3; 238:4; 239:1,1,2; 251:3,3,3,3; 258:1; 259:1; 262:4; 263:2; 264:2,3,4; 265:1; 269:3,4,4; 270:1,1; 272:1,1,1,1,2; 273:1,1,3; 274:1,1,1,1,1,2,3,4,4; 275:2,2,4; 276:1,1,3,3; 277:1,1,1,3,3,4; 278:2,3,4,4,4,4,4; 279:1,1,2,2; 284:2,2,2,3; 289:2,2,2,3,3; 290:3,3; 291:2,2; 293:2; 298:1; 299:2; 304:2; 306:3; 330:2; 334:2; 337:2; 338:3; 343:4; 355:3; 356:1; 357:1,1; 358:3; 359:2; 362:1

realignment	(1)	198:3
realisation	(1)	195:4
realise	(4)	89:2; 205:1; 365:3; 379:3
realised	(19)	8:3; 28:2; 47:2; 50:4,4; 51:1,1,2; 60:3; 77:1,2,3; 78:2; 137:5; 219:1; 261:2; 273:5; 299:2; 366:1
realism	(1)	348:3
realistic	(2)	6:2; 42:2
realistically	(1)	15:4
reality	(3)	67:3; 146:2; 258:1
realized	(3)	51:2,3; 161:1
really	(12)	40:2; 150:2; 152:1; 154:2; 155:1; 156:2; 189:3; 190:4; 212:1; 275:2; 344:5; 363:1
reappear	(1)	362:3
reason	(64)	6:1; 11:2; 28:2; 42:2; 43:3; 60:1; 61:1; 95:2; 98:1; 115:5; 116:4; 124:2; 126:2; 145:1; 146:3; 148:2; 149:2; 157:1; 160:2; 169:3; 170:1,3,3; 177:3; 182:4; 187:3; 195:3; 198:3,3; 201:2; 205:2; 206:2,2; 208:4; 213:3; 216:2,2; 219:4; 223:4; 230:3; 254:2; 258:1,1; 263:3; 269:2; 279:2,2; 294:2; 299:2; 301:2; 317:3; 318:1; 320:1; 326:3; 339:5; 342:1; 346:3; 347:1; 352:2; 356:2; 366:2; 376:1; 379:1,2
reasonable	(26)	14:3; 58:2; 59:1; 61:2; 80:2; 148:2; 154:2; 162:1,2,3; 203:2; 208:1; 219:2; 220:1; 278:4; 282:1; 308:2; 315:3; 316:1; 321:2; 323:1; 324:1; 335:3; 338:3; 377:1,2
reasonably	(4)	92:1; 153:1; 307:3; 323:1
reasoning	(6)	126:2; 128:2; 139:3; 193:1; 259:1; 342:2
reasons	(42)	9:2; 10:1; 24:4; 31:3; 51:1; 56:1; 69:3; 72:4; 97:2; 130:2; 148:2; 152:1; 201:3; 202:1; 203:3; 207:3; 215:2; 223:4; 228:2; 232:2; 234:2; 266:3; 269:2; 280:2; 281:1; 288:1; 308:2; 314:3,3; 317:2; 320:2; 331:1; 335:3; 338:3; 340:2; 341:3,3; 358:3; 373:3,3; 376:1,1
rebuilt	(1)	99:3
rebuke	(1)	16:2
rebut	(1)	261:2
recalcitrant	(2)	118:2; 203:1
recalculate	(1)	59:1
recalculated	(1)	59:1

relating (cont.)		366:1
relation	(41)	18:2; 28:1; 44:2; 69:5; 79:2; 81:2; 85:2; 95:3; 107:2,2; 113:1; 135:2,2; 145:4; 147:1,1; 152:1; 174:2; 180:1; 194:1; 199:3; 200:1,2; 201:3,3; 206:2; 212:1; 223:2,4; 243:6; 248:2; 270:1; 277:4; 278:3; 296:3; 297:2; 317:2; 334:4; 343:1; 364:1; 370:1
relations	(2)	120:3; 365:3
relationship	(34)	9:4; 25:2,2,4; 28:2,2,2,5; 68:1; 90:2,2; 92:2,3; 113:1,1; 123:2; 139:1; 169:3; 173:2; 197:2; 205:3; 208:3; 223:2,5; 229:1; 275:2; 278:4; 279:2; 305:3; 306:4,5; 309:3; 318:1; 342:3
relationships	(1)	227:2
relative	(22)	4:1,1; 6:2; 14:1,2,3; 41:2; 43:1; 69:5; 192:2; 193:1; 196:3; 224:3; 225:6; 227:2; 237:1; 238:2; 239:2; 241:3; 252:3; 290:3; 348:2
relatively	(46)	14:1; 15:3; 17:4; 51:3; 78:1; 80:3; 94:1; 111:3; 143:1; 144:1; 147:2; 202:1; 213:1; 214:2; 215:2; 228:3; 230:3; 236:3; 237:1,2,2; 238:3; 239:3; 261:2,2; 262:6; 263:3; 267:3,5; 270:2,2; 277:1,2; 286:4; 287:2; 288:1; 292:1; 301:3,3; 307:2,2; 337:1,1; 345:3; 370:1; 375:1
relaxation	(1)	200:2
release	(2)	232:1; 264:1
released	(5)	19:1; 188:4,4; 210:2; 211:1
releases	(1)	188:3
relegated	(1)	158:3
relevance	(5)	37:1; 39:3; 50:3; 149:1; 180:1
relevant	(26)	40:1; 47:2,2; 57:1; 58:1; 60:1,2,2; 66:1; 95:1; 107:1; 115:5; 116:1,4; 139:2; 144:2,3; 148:2; 149:1; 152:1; 178:1; 205:3; 246:3; 247:2; 281:1; 372:1
reliability	(2)	196:3; 317:3
reliable	(1)	293:2
relied	(1)	201:3
relief	(10)	98:1; 109:2; 121:1; 122:1; 127:1; 129:2; 234:3; 251:3; 318:2; 331:2
religion	(1)	109:3
religions	(1)	351:1
reluctant	(4)	229:2,3; 230:3; 232:2

repair	(1)	166:4
repairs	(4)	100:1; 101:1; 104:1; 128:1
repayments	(2)	101:1; 102:1
repeat	(6)	104:3; 195:1; 279:2; 305:3; 362:3; 381:3
repeated	(1)	187:2
repenting	(1)	220:1
repercussion	(1)	117:1
repercussions	(13)	120:3; 129:3; 161:2; 249:2,2; 257:3; 260:2; 261:2; 262:2,3; 265:1; 278:3; 287:2
repetition	(1)	115:1
replaced	(5)	48:1; 51:2; 71:3; 314:1; 322:1
replacement	(17)	70:2,3,3; 71:2; 73:2,2; 99:4; 100:1,2; 101:1; 135:2,2; 302:3; 321:1; 323:1,1; 324:1
replacements	(3)	100:1; 128:1; 371:1
replied	(1)	342:1
reply	(2)	370:1,2
represent	(4)	52:2; 95:2; 206:2; 262:5
representative	(3)	203:1; 225:1; 303:1
representing	(2)	176:1; 233:3
represents	(17)	34:1; 49:1; 66:2,2; 125:4; 126:2; 175:2,2; 177:1; 189:5; 218:2; 258:2; 279:2,2; 318:2,3; 326:1
reproduce	(1)	365:5
repudiate	(1)	347:2
repudiated	(3)	4:3; 20:4; 351:2
repudiation	(1)	355:2
repulse	(1)	382:3
reputation	(2)	158:1; 359:2
request	(2)	345:2,2
require	(26)	19:3; 61:1; 67:1,3; 101:1; 106:2; 118:2; 120:1; 138:3; 145:1,1; 147:2; 155:3; 166:2; 211:1; 212:1; 214:1; 215:2; 240:3; 276:1; 289:3,3; 293:1; 313:2; 324:2; 374:2
required	(36)	16:2; 27:2; 40:2; 97:2; 100:2; 111:2; 118:1,2; 119:4; 174:2; 190:3,3,4; 191:1; 196:3,3,5; 205:1; 211:2; 214:2; 215:3; 221:2; 231:2; 236:6; 243:5; 267:3; 291:2; 306:5,5; 313:2; 337:2; 350:3; 367:2,3; 368:1; 369:1
requirements	(3)	101:1; 198:1; 200:2
requires	(14)	40:1; 81:1; 124:2; 158:2; 208:2; 211:2; 236:4; 237:2; 301:2; 309:2,2; 353:5; 369:1; 379:3

responsibility	(3)	164:3; 380:1,2
responsible	(5)	278:4; 316:3,3; 365:3; 373:2
rest	(10)	21:3; 54:1; 66:2; 175:2; 257:1; 266:2; 267:5; 270:2; 298:1; 342:1
resting-place	(3)	64:2; 253:2; 304:1
restoration	(2)	124:1; 349:1
restore	(5)	101:1; 253:2; 328:1; 340:1; 370:1
restored	(1)	124:1
restoring	(1)	349:2
restrict	(3)	264:5; 281:1; 377:2
restricted	(2)	75:1; 117:1
restricting	(2)	117:1; 383:1
restriction	(2)	318:2; 338:2
restrictions	(4)	338:2,2,3; 339:1
restrictive	(1)	11:2
result	(101)	3:1; 6:2,2; 14:1; 16:1; 20:2; 30:2; 33:2; 41:1; 44:1; 53:1; 58:2; 59:3; 61:1; 62:3,3; 63:1; 70:2; 79:3; 80:3; 82:2; 83:1,1; 99:2; 100:1,1; 101:1; 105:2; 111:3; 114:2; 117:1; 118:2; 119:2; 121:1,3; 126:1,1; 130:2; 131:2; 136:2; 145:3; 150:2,2; 153:4; 154:2; 155:1,2; 161:4; 162:3; 171:3; 174:2; 179:2; 183:1; 187:1,3; 193:1; 194:1; 195:1; 198:2; 200:2; 202:2; 210:1; 211:1; 217:2; 220:3; 221:2; 228:1; 230:3; 231:3; 232:3; 258:1; 259:1; 260:1; 262:5; 264:2; 267:2,5; 268:3; 269:3; 270:3; 275:4; 277:3,3; 287:2; 290:3; 299:1; 303:3; 314:3; 322:1; 324:3; 327:2,2; 342:1; 346:1; 347:3; 348:1; 350:1; 360:6; 370:1; 378:2; 379:3
resultant	(4)	41:1; 196:5; 201:1; 208:2
resulted	(2)	62:3; 67:3
resulting	(17)	20:2; 23:1,1; 24:1; 28:2; 44:1; 65:1; 77:2; 92:1; 123:4; 252:2; 299:1; 322:1; 330:2; 340:1; 347:3; 368:5
results	(42)	9:4; 12:4; 33:2,2; 44:2; 47:2; 50:4,4; 51:1,1,1,1,2,2; 65:1; 77:2; 78:2; 79:2; 80:1; 99:2; 103:1,2; 109:3; 128:1; 150:2,2,2; 152:1; 157:1; 165:2; 169:3; 172:1; 174:1,2; 183:2; 213:4; 250:2,3; 265:1; 273:5; 333:1; 339:1
resume	(1)	112:1
retain	(5)	20:2; 166:3; 207:4; 234:2; 357:1

rewriting	(2)	116:1; 187:3
rewritten	(1)	187:4
Ricardian	(8)	3:2,2; 4:3; 32:2,3; 190:4; 191:1; 244:1
Ricardo	(19)	3:2,2; 4:3; 5:7; 18:3; 32:2; 190:4; 191:1,2,2,2; 192:1,1; 340:1; 363:5,6; 364:2; 369:1,1
Ricardo's	(4)	4:3; 32:2; 190:2; 367:1
rich	(5)	219:3; 344:2; 372:2; 373:3; 382:3
richer	(3)	31:2; 262:5; 361:5
riches	(1)	343:4
richesses	(1)	358:3
rid	(3)	221:2; 294:1; 347:3
riddle	(1)	105:1
right	(27)	39:1; 60:1; 61:2; 109:1; 129:3; 135:1; 158:3; 159:1; 163:2; 169:3; 183:1; 221:2; 234:2; 269:3; 278:3; 288:1,1; 293:1; 313:1; 317:1; 322:2; 325:1; 352:2; 360:3; 377:2; 381:2; 383:3
rightly	(6)	17:3; 39:3; 76:1; 241:2; 280:3; 308:1
rigid	(4)	266:1; 271:3; 295:3; 339:3
rigidity	(4)	257:1,1; 276:1; 302:2
rigidly	(3)	232:1; 265:2; 337:3
rise	(116)	8:3; 9:2; 13:1,1,1; 15:1,3; 17:4; 71:4; 83:1,1; 91:3; 92:1; 93:3; 99:2; 100:1; 110:3,3,3; 111:2,2,2,2,3; 117:1; 118:3; 119:4; 122:4; 127:1,1; 128:1; 130:1,2; 142:1; 143:1; 165:1; 173:1,1; 187:1,1,1,3,3,3,4,4; 197:2; 198:1,1; 200:2,2; 202:1,1; 204:1; 218:1; 228:3; 230:2; 231:3,5,5; 232:3; 234:3,4; 237:1; 249:1,1,1; 263:4; 265:2; 271:3; 275:2; 277:1,2; 284:2,3; 286:1,1,2; 289:2,3,3; 290:3,3; 294:1; 296:2; 298:3,3; 300:3,4,4; 301:2,2,3,3,3,3; 307:1; 315:4,5; 316:1,1; 326:1,1,1; 327:3; 328:1,1,1,1; 329:1; 340:1,3; 343:4; 351:2,3; 361:7
risen	(3)	101:1; 173:1; 303:1
rises	(20)	17:4; 42:2; 93:3; 111:1,3; 124:1; 142:3; 182:3; 217:1; 230:2; 231:3,3,4; 253:3,3; 304:4; 307:2; 319:2; 336:3; 340:1
rising	(32)	10:1,1,1,1,2; 42:2; 49:1; 97:1; 119:1; 143:1,1; 182:3; 207:4; 228:3; 264:2; 288:1; 290:2,2,3,3; 296:3,3; 299:3; 300:2; 304:2;

rule (cont.)		333:2; 352:1
ruled	(6)	59:2; 309:2; 339:3; 375:2; 382:2; 383:3
rules	(3)	143:2; 223:4; 374:2
ruling	(4)	130:2; 165:1; 168:3; 277:3
run	(18)	50:4; 78:1; 98:1; 136:3; 139:2; 156:3; 157:1; 158:1; 160:2; 192:2; 218:1; 220:3; 253:1; 278:3; 306:4; 319:1; 335:3; 376:1
running	(9)	135:1; 182:2,2; 189:3; 202:1,1; 203:1; 332:2,2
runs	(5)	17:4; 19:3; 72:3; 91:1; 153:1
rush	(2)	235:1; 239:1
Russia	(3)	207:4; 269:3; 353:2
sacrifice	(11)	23:1; 53:1; 66:2; 70:1,1; 81:1; 168:2; 202:1; 309:2; 376:1,1
sacrificed	(2)	53:1; 339:3
sacrifices	(1)	38:1
safe	(15)	50:4; 119:2; 153:1; 162:2; 199:2; 200:3; 201:3; 202:1,1; 217:2; 226:4; 306:3; 351:3; 353:5; 377:2
safeguard	(2)	380:2,2
safely	(8)	32:2; 73:2; 85:2; 169:2; 201:2; 244:1; 249:3; 320:1
safety	(1)	157:1
sag	(1)	265:2
sagging	(3)	265:2; 269:2,2
said	(24)	9:2; 19:2,2,2,2; 43:3; 66:1; 76:2; 139:2; 149:2; 154:1; 160:3; 165:1; 188:1; 197:2; 215:2; 216:1; 229:1; 271:2; 276:1; 321:2; 342:1; 345:4; 363:2
sake	(3)	95:3; 137:5; 360:3
salaried	(1)	41:2
salaries	(2)	41:2; 268:2
sale	(4)	47:2; 75:1; 258:3; 272:3
sale-proceeds	(11)	20:2; 24:5; 46:3; 47:2,2; 51:1,1,3; 67:3; 195:4; 290:2
saleable	(2)	67:2,3
sales	(9)	47:2; 62:1,1,1,1; 160:3; 170:1; 241:4; 382:3
sales-turnover	(1)	66:2
same	(209)	5:7; 10:1,1,1; 12:2,2; 14:1; 15:3; 17:2; 18:1,5; 19:1,1; 20:5; 21:2; 22:2; 23:1; 24:5; 26:1,2; 27:1; 30:1; 38:1; 41:4; 43:3; 47:3,3; 49:1,1,1,1; 55:3; 56:1; 57:1,1; 58:1,1,1; 59:1; 62:3; 63:2; 64:2; 71:2; 74:1; 76:1;

same (cont.) 78:2,2; 81:1; 90:2; 92:1; 93:2; 94:1,1; 96:4;
97:2; 98:2; 99:2; 102:3; 106:2,3; 111:1,2,2;
115:1; 116:1; 117:1; 118:2,2,2; 119:4;
124:1; 126:2; 129:4; 130:2; 137:2; 138:3;
139:2; 141:1,1; 144:4; 145:1; 146:1; 148:5;
149:1; 151:2,2; 156:2; 159:2; 160:3; 168:2;
169:5; 170:3; 172:1,2,2; 173:2; 174:2;
176:4,4; 180:1; 190:1,3; 192:5; 194:1,1;
195:1; 198:1,2; 200:2,2,2; 202:1; 203:2;
205:2; 209:1; 211:2,2; 219:3; 221:1; 222:2;
223:4; 224:2,2,3,3,3,3,3,3; 225:1,2; 227:2;
228:2; 229:2; 234:3; 235:2; 237:1,1;
241:2,2; 247:2; 248:2; 250:1; 251:1; 253:1;
254:2; 259:2,2; 260:2; 263:3; 264:2;
265:2,2; 266:3,3,3; 267:4; 268:3; 270:2;
273:2; 276:2,2; 277:3,3; 279:1; 281:2;
285:2; 286:1,2,2,4; 287:2; 289:3;
295:2,2,3,3; 296:1,1,2; 302:2,4; 304:4,4;
308:1; 314:1; 323:1; 325:3,3; 328:1; 334:2;
336:1,2; 339:5; 341:3; 342:1; 346:1; 348:1;
349:2; 350:1,2,2; 354:1; 360:7; 361:5,5;
373:2; 377:2; 382:3

san (1) 355:1
sanctions (1) 351:2
Sandys (1) 347:2
sang (1) 131:2
sanguine (1) 150:2
sapienti (1) 346:1
satiate (1) 218:2
satiated (1) 219:1
satiation (1) 106:2
satisfaction (6) 97:2; 150:2; 220:1; 232:1; 321:4; 374:2
satisfactory (11) 39:1,1; 41:1; 52:2; 250:1; 282:4; 307:3;
319:2,3; 322:4; 325:1

satisfied (21) 4:3; 8:1; 93:3; 105:2,2; 158:2; 163:2;
218:2; 230:2; 231:2; 236:3,3; 275:2; 282:2;
289:3; 296:2; 304:4; 336:1; 363:3; 374:2;
378:2

satisfies (2) 274:2,3
satisfy (24) 40:1; 44:1; 49:1; 63:2; 97:2; 108:1; 174:2;
196:5; 197:1,1,1,3; 199:2,2,3,3; 212:1;
233:2; 238:1; 244:1; 306:5; 308:1; 328:2;
336:1

satisfying (5) 27:2; 46:1; 105:2; 171:2; 301:2
saturation-point (1) 220:2
Sauerbeck's (1) 308:1
save (45) 19:2; 57:1; 64:2,2; 65:1,1; 81:2;
84:2,2,2,2,2; 92:2; 94:3; 97:1; 101:1;
111:2,3,3,3; 165:2,2; 175:2; 177:1,2;
178:1,1,2; 179:1; 182:4; 187:3; 189:5,5,5;
211:1; 217:2; 218:2; 220:1; 261:2; 347:4;
368:1,5; 369:1; 370:1; 375:1
saved (25) 79:3,3; 80:1,1,1,2; 97:2,2,2; 110:3,3,3;
127:1; 178:1,1,1; 179:1,2,2,2,2; 181:1,2;
182:3; 211:2
saver (1) 212:1
savers (1) 176:4
saves (6) 19:2,2; 83:2,2; 167:1; 212:1
saving (169) 21:1; 31:2; 60:1,1,1; 61:1,1,1,2,2;
62:2,2,2,3; 63:2,2,2,2,2,3; 64:1,1,1,1,2;
65:1; 74:1,2; 76:1; 77:1,1,1,2;
78:1,1,1,2,2,2,2; 79:2,2,2,2,2,4;
80:1,2,2,2,2,2,2,2,2,3,3; 81:1,2,2; 82:1,2,2;
83:1,2,2,2; 84:1,2,2,2; 93:3; 94:1; 95:2;
97:1,1; 100:2; 109:2,2,2,2; 110:1,3,3;
111:1,1,4; 117:2,2,2; 121:1,1; 123:4;
125:2,2; 129:4,4; 165:2,2; 167:1; 175:2,2;
176:1,1,1,1,1; 177:1,2,2,4; 178:1,1; 180:3;
183:1,2; 184:1,1; 192:3,3; 193:1; 210:1,1,2;
211:1,2,2,2; 212:1,1,1,1; 213:1; 217:3,3,3;
218:1; 242:1,3; 248:2; 287:2; 292:1;
328:1,1,1,1,1,1; 358:3; 359:3; 360:2; 361:5;
363:1,3; 365:3,4; 366:1,1,3; 367:1,2,3;
368:2; 369:1; 370:1; 372:2; 373:1; 375:1;
376:1,1
savings (38) 80:1; 81:2; 83:1,1,1; 84:1; 93:3; 108:3;
111:2,2; 117:2; 121:1; 160:2; 166:3; 167:1;
176:4; 179:2; 183:1,1,1,1,1; 188:2,2,2,2,2;
189:4,4; 194:1; 218:1; 220:1; 328:1; 330:1;
352:2,2; 372:2; 381:1
savings-deposits (2) 195:1,2
say (85) 3:2,2; 4:2; 5:4,6; 10:1; 26:1; 28:5; 38:1;
39:1; 40:1,2; 42:3; 43:3; 49:1; 53:1,2; 55:5;
68:1; 69:1; 71:5; 78:2; 90:2; 93:3; 96:4;
109:3; 115:4; 120:4; 121:3,3,3; 126:1;
138:2; 162:2; 178:1; 181:1; 183:1; 186:2;

self-regulatory	(1)	177:2
self-subsistent	(1)	106:3
sell	(12)	64:2; 154:1; 171:2; 197:2; 200:2; 206:1,2; 261:2,2; 345:3,4; 360:3
seller	(2)	85:2,2
sellers	(1)	18:5
selling	(4)	67:3; 135:1; 197:2; 221:1
selves	(1)	163:1
semblance	(1)	131:2
semi-critical	(2)	301:3; 307:1
semi-inflation	(1)	301:3
semi-public	(1)	101:1
semi-religious	(1)	354:2
semi-slump	(1)	322:2
sense	(102)	4:2; 15:2; 16:1; 17:1; 18:3; 21:4,4; 22:2; 24:3,4; 28:2; 38:1; 39:3; 50:3; 52:2; 54:1,1; 57:2; 60:3; 61:1,1,1; 63:2; 66:2; 67:3; 75:1,1; 77:1; 78:2,2,2,2; 79:2,2,2; 80:2,2; 81:2; 91:3; 92:2; 108:1; 118:2; 123:3; 129:2; 138:2; 139:1; 141:1; 142:2; 144:4; 148:2; 151:1; 154:2; 159:1,1; 184:1; 187:2; 191:1; 192:1; 201:2; 206:2; 207:3; 213:3; 225:1; 230:2; 239:2; 240:1,1,2; 241:2; 242:4; 243:3,5,5; 246:1; 274:2; 275:3; 277:3; 282:2; 287:1,2; 289:2; 321:1,1,2,4; 323:1,1; 324:1,1,2; 328:1; 329:1; 349:1,2; 350:1; 365:1; 366:1; 370:1; 375:3; 376:1; 380:2; 382:3
senseless	(1)	338:3
sensible	(6)	51:1; 129:3; 131:2; 155:1; 220:1; 221:2
sensitive	(2)	93:3; 171:2
sensitively	(1)	278:4
sensitiveness	(1)	172:2
sentence	(4)	187:3,4; 188:4; 367:3
sentences	(2)	139:2; 192:1
sentiment	(3)	154:2; 163:1; 316:1
sentiments	(1)	362:2
separate	(8)	65:1; 149:1; 282:2; 286:2; 292:1; 294:1; 352:1; 377:2
separated	(1)	60:2
separately	(3)	91:1; 205:2; 314:3
separates	(1)	104:3
separation	(1)	150:3

sir	(2)	176:1; 347:2
situation	(32)	3:1; 8:1; 9:2; 24:2; 26:2; 28:4; 48:1; 83:1; 92:2; 94:2; 95:4; 96:2; 138:4; 148:2,2; 198:1; 199:1; 207:3; 214:2,2; 218:2; 250:1; 289:3; 293:2; 300:5; 305:3; 316:1; 321:2; 322:3; 324:1; 343:4; 347:2
situations	(1)	72:4
six	(1)	156:2
sixteenth	(2)	337:2; 340:1
sixteenth-century	(1)	358:2
sixth	(1)	354:2
size	(3)	4:2; 118:1; 335:3
skilful	(2)	342:1; 372:2
skill	(11)	41:3; 126:2; 150:2; 154:3; 221:3; 245:2; 375:3,3; 376:3; 381:1,1
skilled	(5)	44:1; 155:2,2; 156:3; 221:3
slaves	(1)	383:3
sleep	(1)	153:1
slight	(2)	55:1; 149:4
slightly	(3)	90:2; 156:2; 342:4
slip	(1)	272:2
slips	(1)	173:1
slipt	(1)	13:2
slop	(1)	231:4
slope	(1)	56:2
slow	(5)	6:2; 109:3; 110:1; 247:2; 331:2
slowly	(12)	110:2; 187:1; 208:2; 228:3,3; 229:1; 236:3; 265:2; 271:3,3; 279:2; 325:2
slump	(23)	71:4,4; 72:4; 100:2,2; 104:1; 128:1,1,1; 144:1; 192:5; 218:1; 316:2; 317:1,3; 318:1,3; 320:2,2,2; 322:3; 327:2; 331:2
slumps	(3)	130:1; 162:3; 322:2
slurred	(1)	137:5
small	(38)	12:2; 13:1; 15:1,3; 68:3,3; 85:2; 110:3,3; 118:2,2,2,2; 121:2; 122:2; 125:2,3; 126:1; 153:2; 172:2,2; 186:2; 202:1; 203:1; 230:2,2; 233:3; 235:1,1; 236:3; 239:1,2; 247:2; 251:4; 289:1; 301:3; 337:1; 345:2
smaller	(22)	69:1; 96:4; 98:1; 107:2; 125:2; 126:4; 127:1; 188:1; 216:2; 218:1; 219:3; 238:1; 248:2; 273:5; 286:1; 287:2; 290:3,3; 324:2; 330:2; 331:1; 358:2
smelliness	(1)	215:2

smelly	(2)	215:2,2
Smith	(6)	352:2,3; 353:2; 361:8; 363:3; 368:2
Smith's	(1)	352:2
smooth	(1)	171:3
snap	(2)	155:3; 156:1
so	(Count: 372 – not included)	
so-called	(6)	97:1; 155:2; 182:2; 239:4; 322:2; 371:1
social	(41)	6:2; 21:3; 33:1,1; 40:1; 91:1,1,3; 93:3; 104:3; 107:1; 109:3; 110:1,2; 144:4; 155:2; 159:1; 161:3; 162:3; 163:2; 164:3; 201:2; 219:3; 221:2; 240:3; 241:2; 245:2; 267:5; 268:2,2; 271:3; 324:3; 325:2,2; 327:2; 335:3; 346:4; 351:2; 355:2; 373:3; 374:2
socialen	(1)	354:1
socialisation	(2)	378:1,1
socialise	(1)	379:1
socialised	(1)	267:5
socialism	(2)	355:2; 378:1
socialist	(1)	365:3
socially	(3)	157:1; 325:3; 352:2
societies	(4)	101:1,1; 324:3; 361:7
society	(26)	3:1; 6:2; 33:3; 104:2; 109:3; 203:3; 208:4,4; 216:1; 217:2,3; 242:4; 269:3,3; 289:1; 335:3; 337:3; 340:3; 351:3; 363:2; 365:5; 366:1; 369:1; 372:1; 378:1; 383:2
solace	(1)	145:1
sold	(12)	46:2; 52:1; 53:2; 54:3; 61:2; 62:3; 64:1,1; 66:2; 67:1,1; 258:3
sole	(5)	8:3; 104:3; 201:3; 214:1,1
solecism	(1)	3:2
solely	(8)	27:1; 148:3; 149:3; 182:2; 191:2; 231:3; 244:1; 286:3
solid	(1)	154:2
solon	(1)	340:3
solution	(5)	37:2; 39:1; 183:1; 326:2,4
solutions	(1)	129:2
solve	(2)	378:2; 381:2
solved	(2)	52:2; 377:2
solving	(2)	350:1; 364:2
some	(189)	5:7,7; 12:1; 15:1; 18:3; 19:2; 20:2,4; 28:5; 30:1; 37:2; 38:1,2; 39:4; 43:2; 48:1; 49:1; 52:2,2; 53:3; 56:1; 61:1; 66:2; 67:3; 69:3,4; 70:2,6; 74:1; 77:1; 79:2,2; 80:2; 81:1,1;

some (cont.)   83:1; 91:3; 92:1; 93:3; 96:1; 98:1; 101:1;
104:2; 105:1; 106:1; 112:2; 116:1; 119:2;
120:3; 122:4; 128:2; 137:3; 138:2,3;
139:1,2; 143:2; 147:1; 149:4; 150:2,2;
153:2,3; 156:1,2; 166:2; 170:1; 171:2;
172:1; 174:2; 178:1; 179:2; 181:1,2; 183:1;
187:2; 188:1; 193:1; 194:1; 196:3; 198:3;
200:2; 204:3; 205:2; 210:1,2; 211:1,2;
212:1,1; 214:2,2,2; 216:1; 217:3; 218:2;
221:3; 225:1,5,5,6,6; 226:4; 228:3,3;
229:2,3; 230:3; 231:3,3,3; 233:1,3,3,4;
234:3; 236:3; 237:2; 239:1; 242:3; 243:5,6;
253:2; 258:1,1,1,1; 259:2; 262:4; 263:4;
270:1,2; 273:3; 278:3; 281:2,2; 282:4;
287:1,1,4; 288:1,1,1,1; 296:2; 299:3;
300:3,5; 301:3; 304:1; 306:4,5,5,5; 307:2;
314:1; 317:2; 319:4; 321:1,3; 322:4,5;
328:1,1; 332:2; 333:1; 334:2; 336:3; 338:3;
342:5,5; 344:3; 346:1; 349:1; 354:1; 355:2;
357:1; 361:5,5,5; 363:3; 371:1; 373:3,3;
375:3,4; 377:3; 383:3,3

somebody   (1)   369:1
somehow   (1)   81:2
someone   (8)   81:2; 82:1,1; 83:1; 84:1,1; 200:2; 212:1
someone's   (2)   200:2,2
something   (15)   16:2; 32:3; 105:1; 130:1; 161:3,4; 175:1;
177:2; 182:3; 226:2,2; 235:2; 241:2; 275:2;
291:2

sometimes   (30)   9:2; 24:1; 46:1; 55:4; 71:5; 135:2;
150:1,3,3; 158:2; 160:2,2; 188:2,2; 194:1;
206:2; 241:4; 246:2; 249:2; 292:1,1; 308:1;
321:3; 328:1; 331:2; 341:3; 363:2; 370:1;
374:2,2

somewhat   (24)   66:1; 92:2; 102:2; 128:1; 144:1; 148:2;
163:2; 164:3; 192:2; 234:3; 236:5; 260:1;
262:4; 268:2; 287:2; 290:3; 318:1; 335:3;
336:1,1; 337:3; 349:1; 362:3; 378:1

somewhere   (1)   118:2
song   (2)   360:3; 366:4
soon   (18)   39:3; 52:2; 72:3; 156:1; 165:2; 219:1;
226:4; 252:2; 264:3; 293:1; 295:3,3; 300:4;
324:1; 338:1; 350:3; 374:2; 384:1
sooner   (4)   48:1; 105:2; 306:5; 307:1

sophisticated	(1)	292:1
sort	(8)	55:3; 129:4; 187:3; 202:1; 279:1; 303:3; 306:5; 363:3
sorts	(4)	152:1; 215:2; 325:3; 332:1
sought	(4)	317:2; 341:3; 365:3; 366:1
sound	(6)	101:1; 130:1; 323:1; 357:2; 362:2; 366:1
sounder	(1)	83:2
soundness	(1)	176:4
source	(11)	94:1; 105:1; 137:3; 144:3; 177:3; 181:1,2; 272:4; 355:2; 366:1,4
sources	(1)	183:1
south	(1)	162:1
Soviet	(1)	354:2
space	(1)	353:3
spaces	(1)	362:2
Spain	(2)	32:2; 337:2
spate	(1)	370:2
speak	(18)	40:2,2; 41:1; 42:1; 47:4; 75:1; 149:4; 155:3; 187:5,5; 210:1; 213:3; 215:3; 216:2; 226:2; 242:4; 247:1; 317:1
speaking	(20)	38:1; 48:2; 56:1; 59:3; 75:1; 90:2; 117:2; 129:4; 152:1; 165:2; 187:2; 205:2; 225:1; 296:3; 297:2; 321:1; 327:2; 333:2; 353:2; 359:7
speaks	(1)	278:4
special	(39)	3:1,1; 9:1; 16:1; 24:4; 25:4; 28:2; 30:1; 37:1; 38:1; 41:2,2; 42:1; 60:3; 61:1; 68:2; 74:1; 77:1; 90:2; 121:3; 153:4; 177:2; 192:5; 205:2; 206:2; 226:4; 229:1,3; 249:3; 264:2; 273:3; 303:3; 306:3; 314:3; 323:1; 328:1,2; 338:2,3
specialised	(9)	6:2; 16:1; 41:3; 42:1,1,1; 46:2; 288:1; 300:3
specialized	(1)	322:4
specially	(2)	67:3; 205:2
specie	(1)	20:2
species	(3)	95:2; 183:1; 323:1
specific	(14)	108:1; 119:2; 122:1; 127:2; 152:1; 161:2; 166:3; 167:4; 210:2; 211:1,2; 212:1,1; 355:3
specifically	(1)	5:7
specified	(10)	80:2; 166:3; 167:1,4; 205:3; 210:1,1; 242:3; 243:5; 247:1

sterling-money	(1)	237:1
stickiness	(1)	238:2
sticky	(7)	232:4; 233:1,1; 237:2,2; 238:2; 304:1
stiff	(1)	101:1
still	(56)	19:3; 20:1; 31:1,3; 42:2; 50:2; 67:1,3,3; 100:2,2; 102:1; 118:3; 139:3; 140:1,1,1,2; 159:1; 164:1,2; 191:2; 195:2; 211:1; 213:1,2; 214:2; 218:1; 221:2,3,3; 237:1; 271:3; 275:3,3; 276:1; 289:2; 295:3; 296:2; 300:3; 319:2; 322:4; 324:2; 325:2,3; 331:2; 332:1; 343:4,4; 345:4; 368:1; 374:2; 376:1; 380:1,1; 382:3
stimulate	(13)	101:1; 113:1; 117:2; 118:1; 177:2; 193:1; 200:2; 212:1; 257:3; 321:1; 337:1; 375:1; 377:2
stimulated	(4)	116:1; 193:1; 258:1; 336:3
stimulates	(4)	141:3; 173:1; 177:2; 193:1
stimulating	(11)	142:3,3; 143:1,1; 164:2; 210:1; 231:5; 234:4; 235:1; 328:1; 338:1
stimulation	(1)	374:2
stimulus	(7)	111:3; 143:1; 193:1; 211:2; 233:3; 257:2; 288:1
sting	(1)	238:3
stipulate	(3)	272:1,1; 277:4
stipulated	(1)	163:2
stipulates	(4)	9:2; 275:4; 276:1,3
stock	(77)	37:3; 38:1,1; 47:2,2; 70:3,4; 75:1,1,3; 76:1,1; 104:2; 130:2,2; 142:3; 143:1,1,3; 147:2,2; 151:1,1,1,1; 157:1; 159:1,2,2; 160:1; 176:1; 186:2,3,3,3,3; 187:1,1,4; 192:5; 194:1; 217:3,3; 218:1,1,1,2,2; 219:1,3,3; 226:4; 228:2,3; 229:1; 230:3; 232:1; 233:3,3,3; 234:1; 238:1,1; 239:4; 317:3; 319:2,2; 325:2; 337:3; 338:3; 340:1,1,3; 344:2; 347:3; 356:1; 375:3
stock-market	(2)	319:2; 320:1
stock-minded	(1)	319:2
stocks	(40)	49:1; 50:1; 51:3,3; 52:1,1; 76:1,1; 124:1,1,1; 207:4; 219:3; 226:4; 235:1; 288:1,1,1; 317:2; 318:2,2,2,2,3,3; 319:1,3; 329:2; 331:2,2,2,2,2,3; 332:1,1,2; 355:3; 356:2; 357:1
stone	(1)	347:3

strong (cont.)		315:5; 318:3; 322:4; 326:3; 337:2; 338:3; 360:5
stronger	(5)	97:2; 204:1; 347:4; 348:1; 383:2
strongly	(2)	264:2; 374:2
structure	(3)	110:1; 245:2; 366:1
struggle	(12)	13:3; 14:2; 252:3,3; 253:1; 341:4; 349:1,1; 381:4; 382:2,3; 383:1
struggles	(1)	267:5
struggling	(1)	348:4
Stuart	(1)	364:2
studied	(1)	194:2
studies	(1)	329:2
study	(8)	141:1; 190:1,1; 247:2; 293:1; 334:4; 347:4; 354:1
sub-normal	(1)	249:4
subject	(42)	3:1; 5:4,6; 6:3; 12:1; 17:2,3; 29:4; 95:5; 110:1; 113:1; 114:3; 123:1; 125:2; 138:2; 144:1; 154:2; 189:2,3; 194:1; 203:3; 208:3; 244:1; 249:4; 266:3; 273:2; 275:2; 277:1; 278:3; 279:1; 281:3; 288:1,1; 293:2; 302:4; 309:3; 314:3; 315:3; 324:4; 340:1; 348:4; 374:2
subject-matter	(1)	37:1
subjected	(1)	247:1
subjective	(11)	91:1,1,1,1,1; 93:3,3; 107:1,2; 109:3; 110:2
subjects	(1)	366:1
sublime	(1)	365:3
subsequent	(10)	47:2; 58:2; 131:1; 143:2; 196:2; 211:1; 331:2; 363:2; 368:5,6
subsequently	(10)	58:2; 97:1,2; 105:2; 141:2; 169:2; 232:3; 301:1; 349:3; 354:2
subsidiary	(2)	32:1; 358:3
substance	(8)	5:7; 7:2; 25:3; 66:2; 190:2; 304:3; 334:2; 358:2
substantial	(24)	93:3; 95:2,4; 101:1; 120:4; 121:2; 126:1; 128:1; 160:1; 163:2; 226:4; 233:2; 259:1; 269:3; 271:2; 300:3; 318:1; 330:1,1; 331:3; 332:1,1; 336:1; 338:3
substantially	(6)	51:1; 130:2; 174:2; 194:1; 249:2; 308:1
substitute	(4)	167:3; 174:2; 231:3,3
substituted	(2)	42:1; 314:2
substitutes	(1)	358:1
substitution	(10)	82:2; 210:1; 211:2; 231:3; 234:3; 236:3;

suddenly	(7)	18:5; 42:1; 99:3; 314:2; 317:3; 360:2; 366:1
suffer	(13)	14:1; 60:1; 91:1; 130:2; 142:2; 212:1; 219:3; 225:6; 253:1; 267:5; 320:1; 347:2; 376:2
suffered	(5)	62:3; 72:3; 104:1; 345:1; 356:3
suffering	(2)	82:1; 94:1
sufferings	(1)	131:2
suffers	(3)	90:2; 102:3; 130:1
suffices	(1)	176:1
sufficiency	(2)	335:3; 358:2
sufficient	(50)	5:6; 14:1; 27:2; 31:2; 48:2; 60:1; 64:2; 100:2,2; 101:1; 105:1; 107:1; 117:2,2; 118:2; 150:2; 152:1; 153:2; 158:2,2; 169:2; 170:3,3; 180:1; 187:4; 201:1; 202:1; 203:3; 236:4; 253:2; 254:2; 266:2; 287:1; 296:2; 300:5; 303:1; 307:3; 308:1; 309:1; 313:2; 318:2; 326:3; 331:2; 332:2; 333:2; 337:1; 362:3; 369:1; 375:1; 378:1
sufficiently	(45)	20:1,4; 30:1; 31:2,3; 38:2; 41:2; 48:1,4; 56:1,1; 61:1; 83:1; 105:2; 111:3; 122:3; 127:2; 160:1,2; 171:2,2; 190:4; 200:2; 214:2,2; 215:2,2; 216:2; 218:1,2,2; 228:2; 234:3; 253:3,3; 278:2; 282:4; 300:4; 308:1,1; 315:5; 318:1; 320:1; 336:3; 376:1
suffix	(2)	285:2; 305:2
suffused	(1)	355:2
suggest	(8)	127:2; 187:4; 192:1; 242:4; 293:1; 313:2; 314:3; 315:4
suggested	(9)	60:1; 75:3; 79:2; 94:1; 180:4; 193:1; 328:1; 329:1; 357:1
suggesting	(1)	119:2
suggestion	(5)	187:3; 194:1; 278:4,6; 279:1
suggests	(5)	128:1; 182:3; 250:3; 313:2; 373:1
suit	(2)	216:1; 360:5
suitabilities	(1)	32:3
suitability	(1)	41:3
suitable	(6)	42:1; 43:3; 129:3; 130:1; 236:1; 341:5
suited	(1)	351:2
sum	(46)	12:3; 21:1; 23:1; 29:1; 30:1; 52:1,1,2; 53:1,1; 58:1,2; 66:2,2; 67:2; 68:1,1,1,2; 77:2; 82:1; 89:2,2,2; 90:1,1,2; 94:1,1; 99:3; 147:2; 151:1; 167:1; 177:1,1; 182:3; 183:1;

sum (cont.)		195:1; 205:1; 211:2; 213:1; 222:2,2; 260:3; 282:2; 285:1
summarise	(2)	247:3; 272:2
summarised	(1)	103:1
summary	(6)	27:1,1; 139:2; 230:1; 249:3; 359:2
summed	(6)	28:3; 56:2; 178:1; 205:1; 207:1; 334:4
summer	(1)	154:1
summing	(1)	96:2
sumptuary	(1)	359:1
sums	(11)	24:4,4; 84:2,2; 117:2; 150:2; 277:4; 341:2; 344:5; 345:2; 360:7
Sunday	(1)	365:5
superfluity	(1)	372:2
superimposed	(3)	50:2; 149:3; 319:1
superior	(1)	154:3
superseded	(1)	203:2
superstructure	(1)	33:1
supervision	(2)	245:2; 375:3
supplementary	(40)	56:1,1; 57:1,1,1,1,3; 58:1,1,2,2,2,2,2; 59:1,1,1,1,2,2; 68:1,1,1,1,1,1,1,2; 69:2,3,4; 70:3,3; 71:1,2; 72:2; 73:3,3; 99:2; 109:1; 131:1
supplemented	(2)	162:2; 381:1
supplementing	(1)	377:2
supplied	(1)	165:1
supplies	(4)	30:3; 106:2; 130:2; 349:1
supply	(187)	6:3; 8:3; 9:1,1; 13:1; 15:3; 18:3,5,5; 21:3,4; 22:1; 24:1,3,4,4,4,4,4; 25:2,2,3,3,3,4,4; 26:1,1,2,2,2; 28:2,2; 29:2,3; 30:1,1,2,2; 41:3; 42:1,1,2,2,2,3; 43:1,1,3,3; 44:2,2,2,2,2,2; 46:1; 55:2,3,4,4,4,4,5,5,5; 56:2; 67:2,2,3,3,3,3,3,3; 68:1,1,1,1,1,3,3; 71:2,4,5; 72:3,5; 89:1,1,1,1; 93:3; 98:2; 115:5; 116:1,4; 123:4; 135:2,2,2; 136:2,3,3; 137:2,2; 139:1; 147:1; 150:2; 165:2; 167:2; 173:1; 175:2,2; 176:1,1; 177:1; 183:1; 186:2,2,3; 187:1,4,4; 189:2; 191:1; 192:2,2; 197:3; 212:1; 213:1,1,3; 224:3; 230:3,3; 232:1; 235:1,1,1; 236:1; 241:3,3; 246:1,1,1; 248:1; 258:3; 259:2; 274:1,1,1,3; 275:1,2,2,4; 280:1,1,1,1; 281:1,1,2,2; 284:2; 287:1; 288:1; 292:1,1,1,1; 295:3,3; 296:2; 300:2,3,3,3,5,5; 302:2; 304:2; 308:1; 309:1;

technique (cont.)   302:4; 339:3,3,3

tell	(7)	111:2; 181:1,1,1,1,2; 246:1
telling	(1)	275:2
tells	(10)	9:2; 115:2,3; 117:2; 162:2; 167:1; 184:2; 298:2,2,2
temperament	(1)	150:2
temporarily	(4)	124:1,1,1; 370:1
temporary	(13)	6:2; 16:1,1; 29:4; 123:2,4; 124:1; 188:2; 189:4; 196:3; 288:1; 289:1; 300:5
tempt	(1)	309:2
temptation	(1)	150:2
tempted	(1)	173:1
ten	(11)	15:3; 40:1; 117:1; 138:2; 149:4; 153:1; 190:3,3; 191:2; 317:2; 369:1
tenable	(1)	367:1
tenacity	(1)	350:2
tenants	(2)	99:3; 241:4
tend	(31)	14:1; 31:2; 93:3; 97:2; 121:1,3; 129:2; 154:1,1; 157:2; 177:1; 185:1; 193:1; 203:2; 210:1; 232:4,4; 233:1; 235:1,1; 248:4; 249:1; 250:1; 251:1; 262:6; 263:2; 296:2; 301:2; 307:1; 314:1; 336:1
tended	(1)	349:1
tendencies	(11)	83:1,1,1; 93:3; 159:2; 254:4,4; 307:1,2; 314:1; 345:1
tendency	(40)	11:1,2; 20:1; 33:3; 60:1; 101:1; 118:3; 120:4,5; 130:1; 168:1; 182:4; 231:3,3; 249:4; 251:2; 259:1; 260:2,2; 262:2; 263:4; 265:2; 271:3; 278:1; 301:2; 304:1; 306:5,5; 308:1; 314:2,2; 315:4; 324:3; 327:3; 328:1; 338:2; 340:3; 341:2; 347:4; 348:2
tender	(2)	167:3; 294:1
tendering	(1)	129:3
tending	(1)	231:1
tends	(15)	172:2; 176:1; 186:2; 206:2; 228:2,3; 230:2; 232:4; 238:3; 301:3; 307:1; 316:1; 319:2; 328:1; 351:2
tenor	(1)	12:2
tens	(1)	346:3
tenure	(1)	163:2
term	(32)	7:1; 24:3,4; 39:2; 52:1; 54:1; 55:4; 68:1,1; 73:3; 75:1; 79:2,2; 80:3; 102:2; 128:3; 139:2; 148:4; 152:1; 155:3; 158:3,3; 170:1;

than (cont.)		100:1; 101:1,1,1,1; 102:2,2; 104:1,1; 105:1; 106:2; 108:1; 109:1; 111:1; 114:2,2,2; 118:2; 120:5; 121:1,1,2,3,3; 122:1,2,3; 124:1,1,2; 125:2; 126:3,4; 127:1,2; 128:1,1,1,1,2; 129:2,2,3,3; 139:3; 140:1; 144:3; 145:3; 148:2; 151:1,1; 154:1,2; 155:2,3; 157:1,1,1; 158:1; 159:2; 161:2,4,4; 162:1,1; 167:1,3; 169:1; 170:2,3; 172:1,2; 173:1,1; 186:1; 190:1,3,3,3,4; 191:1,2; 193:1,1; 194:1; 196:4; 199:1,1; 202:1,1,1; 203:1,1,3; 204:1,1; 206:2,2; 208:2; 211:2; 212:1; 213:3,3; 216:1,2; 217:1; 218:1; 219:2,3; 222:2; 225:2; 228:2,3,3,3; 229:3; 232:4,4; 233:3; 236:3,6; 237:1,2,2,2; 238:1,2,4; 239:1; 240:1; 243:1; 245:2; 249:2; 250:4; 251:1,2,3,3,3; 252:2; 253:1,3; 258:1,1; 261:2,2; 262:5; 263:4; 264:1,2; 265:2; 266:1; 267:2,2,3; 270:3; 271:2,3; 273:5,5,5,5; 276:1,1; 277:1,2; 279:1,3; 281:1; 286:3,3,3; 287:2,2; 289:2,2,2; 290:3,3,3; 291:2,2; 301:1; 302:4; 304:1; 305:3; 306:3,5,5; 307:2,2; 308:1,2; 313:2; 316:1; 317:3; 318:2; 319:2; 320:2; 321:1; 322:1,1; 323:1; 326:3; 327:1,2,2; 329:1,1,2; 331:1; 334:4; 335:1; 338:3; 341:5; 343:4; 344:2; 345:1,3; 346:1,1; 347:4; 348:1; 351:1; 352:2; 353:3; 355:2,2; 356:1; 357:2; 359:3; 361:5; 362:1; 363:2; 364:2; 366:2; 367:1; 368:1; 369:1; 371:1; 373:1; 374:2; 375:2,3; 376:1; 377:1,2,2; 379:1; 380:2; 381:3; 383:2,3
thanks	(1)	347:2
that	(Count: 1571 − not included)	
the	(Count: 9541 − not included)	
Thebes	(1)	361:1
their	(Count: 273 − not included)	
theirs	(Count: 2 − not included)	
them	(Count: 108 − not included)	
theme	(2)	37:1; 89:1
themes	(1)	13:2
themselves	(Count: 37 − not included)	
then	(80)	11:2; 17:3,4; 21:3; 31:2; 39:1; 45:2; 49:1; 53:2; 55:5; 70:1,3; 71:1,3; 79:2; 96:3;

then (cont.)		115:1; 116:2,4; 129:3; 136:1,3; 137:3; 148:3; 151:1; 166:1; 172:2; 179:2,2; 181:1,1; 185:1; 188:1,3; 190:3; 191:2; 192:1,2; 199:3; 202:2; 209:3; 215:2; 219:3; 220:1; 222:1; 224:3,3; 225:2; 237:2; 238:1; 240:2; 243:1; 250:2; 259:1; 260:2; 261:2; 262:5; 269:4; 273:1; 274:1; 283:1; 285:4; 288:1; 289:2; 297:2; 304:4; 307:1; 322:1; 326:1; 335:2; 340:1; 343:1; 345:4; 346:1; 350:2; 359:1; 363:2; 365:3; 366:1; 378:2
thenceforward	(1)	295:3
theorem	(1)	371:1
theoretical	(15)	3:1; 33:2; 39:3; 60:1; 145:3; 184:3; 232:2; 302:1; 325:2; 334:2; 339:2; 340:2; 353:2; 355:2; 361:4
theoretically	(3)	8:2; 266:3; 325:2
theories	(10)	166:4; 183:1; 184:2; 330:2; 341:5; 343:1; 358:2; 364:2; 370:2; 384:1
theorist	(1)	276:1
theorists	(3)	16:2; 333:1,1
theory	(225)	3:1,1,1,1,2,2; 4:1,2,2,3,3; 5:2,7; 6:3; 7:2,2,4; 8:3; 11:1,2; 12:2,3; 13:1; 15:2; 16:1,1,1,2; 17:2; 18:2; 19:1,3,3; 20:1,5; 21:3,3,4; 25:3,4; 26:1,2; 27:1,2; 28:2,3; 29:3,4,5,5; 30:1; 31:3,4; 32:1,1,1,2,2; 33:2,3; 34:1; 41:2; 60:1; 66:1; 67:3; 72:3,3; 85:1,2,2; 93:3; 95:5; 113:1,1; 122:4; 123:3; 124:2; 138:4; 139:1,1,3,3; 140:3,4; 141:1; 142:2,2; 143:1; 146:2; 165:1; 175:1,3; 176:4; 177:2; 178:2; 179:1,2,2,2,2,2; 180:1,1; 181:2,2; 182:2,4,4; 183:1; 184:2; 190:1,2; 191:1; 192:2,4; 206:2; 208:3; 209:1,2,3; 214:2; 215:1,2; 216:1; 222:1; 243:5,5,5,5; 249:3; 250:1; 257:1,2,2,2; 260:1,1,1,1,4; 272:1,2; 275:1,2; 276:1,1,1,1; 277:1,3; 278:4; 279:3,3,3; 284:2; 285:5; 289:3; 292:1,1; 293:1,1,1,1,1,1,1,2,2,2; 294:1,1,1; 295:3; 296:2,3; 304:2; 305:3; 306:5; 313:1,2; 315:1; 329:1,2,3; 330:1,2; 334:2,2; 339:3,4; 340:1,1; 341:2,5; 344:5; 350:1,1; 351:1,4; 352:1; 355:3; 356:2,2,3,3; 357:1; 364:1,2,2,4,4; 366:2; 367:1; 368:3; 370:1,1; 372:1; 373:3; 375:1; 377:3;

thinkers	(1)	367:1
thinking	(14)	12:4; 65:1; 159:1; 258:3; 259:1; 297:2,2; 320:3; 325:2; 340:1,1,2; 348:3; 358:2
thinks	(2)	156:2,2
thins	(1)	360:7
third	(9)	6:2; 15:2; 48:1; 68:1; 125:4; 144:3; 156:2; 234:3; 252:3
thirdly	(4)	37:2; 39:2; 231:6; 233:2
thirty	(1)	384:1
this	(Count: 768 − not included)	
Thomas	(1)	349:3
thoroughgoing	(1)	348:5
those	(Count: 105 − not included)	
though	(Count: 127 − not included)	
thought	(34)	3:1; 12:2; 20:1,1,4,5; 72:3; 98:3; 100:1; 113:1; 130:1; 131:2; 146:3; 162:2; 170:3; 204:1; 297:2; 317:3; 324:3; 325:1,2; 326:2,4; 329:1; 340:1; 341:1,2; 345:2; 358:3; 359:7; 365:1; 368:5; 373:3; 378:2
thousand	(3)	187:2; 188:1; 354:2
thousands	(1)	346:3
threads	(1)	245:1
threaten	(1)	14:3
three	(29)	22:2; 31:4; 37:1,2; 83:1; 138:2; 155:1,1; 167:3,3,3,3; 170:2; 195:1,1; 196:3; 200:1; 225:4; 246:2; 248:4; 260:2; 262:2; 267:4; 274:2; 298:2,3; 309:1; 317:2; 318:2
thrift	(16)	21:3; 279:2; 358:3,3; 362:2; 366:1,4,4; 369:1,1,1,1,1,1; 370:1; 379:1
thrifty	(3)	111:3; 366:3,4
Throgmorton	(1)	159:2
through	(61)	8:3; 19:3; 43:3; 53:1; 55:1; 56:1; 70:3; 72:3; 79:3; 82:1; 94:1; 99:3; 100:2; 101:1; 119:2; 120:2,3; 128:1; 130:2; 141:3; 142:3; 145:3,3; 146:3; 149:1; 176:3,3; 189:1,5; 190:4; 191:2; 196:1; 197:3; 207:3; 225:6; 234:2,3,3; 240:1; 258:1; 260:2; 264:2; 269:3; 274:3; 278:6; 298:2; 308:1; 318:1; 321:4; 334:4; 336:3; 340:1; 344:4; 367:1,3; 370:1; 372:2; 373:1; 376:1; 378:1; 382:2
throughout	(11)	5:7; 68:3; 116:5; 149:3; 279:2; 305:3; 306:2; 347:4; 354:2; 355:2; 356:1
throw	(2)	16:2,2

together (cont.)		114:2,2; 139:2; 173:2; 208:2; 219:1; 245:1; 254:3; 306:5,5; 309:2; 325:3; 349:2; 352:1; 354:2; 361:7; 375:3
told	(3)	159:1; 189:4; 365:2
tolerable	(3)	309:1,2,2
tolerably	(1)	4:3
tolerate	(1)	381:2
toll	(1)	157:1
ton	(4)	71:1,1,1; 73:2
tone	(2)	264:2; 366:4
too	(Count: 36 – not included)	
took	(1)	60:3
topic	(2)	4:2; 287:4
total	(48)	23:1; 27:2; 62:1,1; 66:2; 67:1; 69:5,8; 70:5; 76:1; 84:3; 93:3; 108:3; 113:1; 115:4,4; 116:2; 118:1; 124:2; 126:4; 127:1,1; 151:3; 170:2; 171:2; 187:1,1,4; 194:2; 226:3; 232:1; 270:1; 273:1; 274:1,2; 278:4; 279:2; 280:1; 331:1; 341:3; 343:1,1; 347:3; 348:5; 367:2,2; 369:1,1
totalitarian	(1)	380:2
totally	(3)	190:3; 327:2; 355:2
touched	(1)	265:2
touching	(1)	367:1
towards	(39)	8:2; 11:2; 21:3; 33:3; 93:3; 94:1; 97:2; 109:2; 143:2; 158:2; 159:1; 160:2; 161:2; 164:3; 171:3; 174:2; 176:1; 186:2; 196:3; 205:1; 220:1; 230:2; 234:3; 249:4,4; 283:1; 286:3,3; 287:2; 288:1; 343:4; 350:2; 352:1; 372:2,2,2,2; 373:3,3
town	(3)	106:2; 129:3; 186:2
trace	(1)	241:2
traced	(2)	33:3; 324:3
traces	(1)	364:2
tracing	(1)	177:3
track	(2)	183:1; 234:2
tract	(1)	364:6
trade	(93)	11:3; 15:1,1; 16:1; 20:4; 21:3; 121:3; 122:1; 124:2; 127:2; 139:3,3; 140:1; 144:1; 186:2; 187:2; 262:6; 263:2,2; 267:3; 270:1; 278:4; 279:2,2; 301:3,3; 313:1,2,2,2; 314:2,3,3; 315:4; 316:1; 317:2; 322:2; 326:2,4; 329:1,1,2,3; 330:2,2; 332:2;

unsuitable	(1)	40:1
unsympathetic	(1)	334:2
until	(49)	17:4; 18:2; 31:2; 37:2; 39:1; 48:1; 60:1; 80:2; 84:3; 99:3; 111:3; 117:2; 119:3; 123:4; 130:2; 141:2; 175:1; 184:2; 200:2; 209:1; 216:2; 217:3; 222:1; 229:1; 235:1; 251:4; 252:1; 253:2; 254:2; 257:2,2; 276:1,1; 284:2; 289:2; 304:1; 314:1,1; 316:1; 319:1,2; 324:4; 325:2; 328:1; 354:1; 362:3; 364:2; 365:3; 376:3
unto	(1)	345:4
unused	(3)	76:1; 188:2; 189:4
unusual	(4)	97:2; 242:1; 258:1; 381:1
unusually	(3)	94:1; 145:2; 383:3
unwelcome	(1)	347:3
unwillingly	(1)	98:1
unwillingness	(5)	33:2; 167:2; 207:3; 221:3; 242:2
up	(108)	3:1; 9:1; 12:3; 15:1; 18:2; 23:1; 24:5; 25:3; 26:2; 28:3; 33:2; 37:1; 49:1; 50:1; 52:1; 59:1; 62:3; 70:1,2; 73:2,3; 83:1; 84:2,3; 89:2; 96:2; 98:1; 100:2; 101:1; 105:2; 106:2; 107:2; 108:2; 117:2; 118:3; 119:1; 121:3; 123:2; 129:3,3; 131:2; 136:3; 138:2; 147:2; 151:1; 160:2; 168:2; 175:1,3; 177:2; 178:1; 183:1; 189:3; 197:2; 199:2; 201:1; 203:1; 204:3; 205:1,1; 207:1; 215:3; 217:1; 219:3; 224:3; 225:1,2; 235:1; 236:4; 238:1; 239:4,4; 241:2; 257:3; 258:1; 259:1; 261:2; 262:2; 271:3; 272:2; 276:1; 277:4; 289:1,3; 303:2; 304:2; 315:1; 334:4; 335:1,3; 338:3; 339:2; 341:2; 344:5; 345:2; 348:5; 351:4; 353:5; 358:1; 364:2; 365:3,3; 366:2; 367:1; 372:2; 375:3; 376:1; 381:1
upkeep	(3)	99:2,2,3
upon	(44)	3:1; 7:1; 25:3; 33:3; 46:2; 47:2; 53:1; 96:2,4; 100:1; 147:2; 148:1,3; 149:2; 155:2; 160:3; 162:3; 163:2; 175:1; 188:2; 189:4; 206:2; 220:1; 249:2; 250:1; 286:2,3; 305:3; 316:1; 319:4; 330:1; 331:1; 334:2; 339:2; 340:2; 352:2,2; 361:5,7; 363:3; 366:1; 370:1,1; 372:2
upper	(1)	26:1
upset	(3)	41:3; 232:1; 266:1

upsetting	(2)	162:3; 382:3
upward	(16)	104:1; 252:2; 265:2; 301:2; 303:3; 307:2,2; 309:3; 313:3; 314:1,1,2,2; 328:1; 330:1; 331:2
upwards	(2)	308:1; 314:1
urge	(2)	161:4; 163:1
urged	(2)	106:2; 322:5
us	(Count: 112 – not included)	
usage	(7)	57:1; 60:3; 63:2; 74:2,3; 75:1; 137:4
usages	(1)	61:2
use	(54)	7:1; 19:5; 40:1; 41:2; 42:1,1,1,2,3,3; 43:2,2; 53:1; 54:3; 56:1; 57:1; 61:1,1; 69:5,8; 70:1; 73:2; 77:1,2; 128:3; 138:2; 140:1,1; 168:2,2; 175:3; 176:4; 186:2; 188:2; 215:3; 226:4; 236:1; 240:3; 299:2; 318:1; 320:3; 321:2; 341:3; 342:1; 343:1,1,3; 358:3; 365:3; 367:2,2; 369:2; 375:3; 379:2
used	(36)	4:3; 25:4; 46:2; 53:1; 63:1; 69:4,7; 70:1,2,3; 73:2,2,2,3; 76:2; 79:2; 95:1; 103:1; 137:4; 138:3; 140:1; 181:2,2; 182:2; 187:4; 188:3,4; 190:1; 213:4; 214:2; 225:6; 231:3; 292:1; 339:3; 342:1; 367:2
useful	(15)	74:1; 130:2; 160:2; 205:2; 220:1; 227:2; 243:2; 245:1; 249:2; 250:2; 282:4; 302:4; 321:1; 327:2; 366:1
usefully	(1)	168:2
usefulness	(1)	176:1
uselessness	(1)	176:4
user	(97)	23:1,1,2; 24:4,4,4,4,4,4,4,4; 44:2; 45:1; 53:1,1,1,3; 54:3,3,3,3; 55:3,4,4; 56:1; 57:1; 58:2,2; 62:1; 64:1,1; 66:1,2,2; 67:1,2,2,3,3,3,3,3; 68:1; 69:3,4,5,5,5,5,5,5,5,6,7,7,7,8; 70:1,1,2,3,3,3,5,6; 71:1,2,3,3,4,4,4,4,5,5; 72:1,2,2,2,2,3,4,4; 73:2,3,3,3; 77:2; 99:2; 102:2; 109:1; 131:1; 139:1; 146:2; 290:2; 302:3,3
users	(1)	233:3
uses	(13)	4:1; 69:5; 74:1; 79:2; 139:2; 141:1; 168:2; 186:3; 187:1; 189:1; 232:1; 293:1,2
using	(14)	39:3; 53:1; 66:2; 67:1; 69:3,4; 70:1,2,2; 73:2; 98:1; 138:4; 214:2; 352:1
usual	(22)	40:1; 57:1; 59:3; 60:2; 67:3; 80:2; 93:3;

verbum	(1)	346:1
versa	(2)	95:2; 204:1
version	(2)	20:1; 354:2
vertically	(3)	180:3; 181:1,1
verwirklichung	(1)	354:2
very	(104)	9:1,3; 20:4; 31:2; 39:2; 42:3; 59:3; 69:2; 72:4; 73:1; 74:2; 78:1; 80:2,2; 90:2; 94:1; 100:1,1; 102:3; 103:1; 104:1,2; 116:1; 121:3; 125:2; 126:1; 127:2; 145:1,1; 148:2,3,5,5; 149:4; 151:2; 152:1; 153:1; 157:1; 158:1; 159:2; 161:1; 163:2; 171:2; 176:4; 187:2; 197:2,2; 202:1,1,1; 203:1; 207:4; 214:2; 217:1; 230:2,2; 232:2; 241:2,4; 243:2; 250:4,5; 251:1,2,3; 252:2; 253:1,2,3; 258:1; 264:3; 273:5; 276:2,2; 278:1; 300:4,5; 301:3; 302:4; 307:2,2; 315:3; 318:2,2; 319:2; 322:4; 323:1,2; 329:1; 332:1; 333:1; 342:4; 346:3; 347:1,2; 358:3; 359:2; 362:4,4; 364:4; 370:1; 372:2; 373:2; 375:3
vested	(3)	328:1; 383:3; 384:1
vice	(5)	95:2; 111:4; 204:1; 359:1,1
vices	(1)	360:1
vicious	(2)	264:2; 360:1
victim	(1)	353:5
victor	(1)	156:1
Victoria	(1)	40:1
Victorians	(2)	364:2,5
victory	(1)	32:3
vide	(5)	4:3; 24:3; 38:3; 79:4; 334:3
view	(53)	7:3; 20:1; 23:1; 32:2; 46:1,2; 50:4; 53:1; 74:1; 77:2; 83:2,2; 97:1; 105:2; 121:2; 127:2; 136:3; 137:3; 140:2; 153:2; 155:2; 156:2; 160:1; 177:4; 188:2; 189:2,2,5; 193:1; 199:1; 201:2; 202:1; 203:3; 221:2; 230:3; 239:2; 242:1; 261:2; 277:4; 296:3; 301:3; 304:2; 320:2; 324:3; 325:3; 327:3; 333:1,1; 334:4; 338:2; 344:5; 360:1; 366:1
viewed	(1)	203:1
views	(6)	164:3; 169:5; 172:1,1; 293:2,2
villa	(1)	221:2
violent	(11)	48:1; 122:1; 125:2; 144:1; 239:1,2; 253:2; 269:3; 315:3; 346:1; 354:1

waiting	(18)	167:1; 176:1,1,1; 182:2,2; 186:2; 187:1,1,3; 188:2,2,2,2,4,4; 190:1,1
waking	(1)	292:1
wall	(6)	159:1,1,2,2; 160:1,3
walls	(1)	360:7
Walras	(1)	176:1
wane	(1)	314:1
want	(9)	6:2; 166:3; 235:2; 334:4; 347:2,2,2,2; 362:4
wanted	(2)	295:3; 323:1
wanting	(1)	327:2
wants	(1)	154:1
war	(15)	56:1; 101:1; 117:1; 207:4; 242:1; 307:3; 322:4; 331:1; 348:2,4; 354:2; 370:2; 381:4,4,4
wares	(4)	345:4; 346:1; 347:1; 382:3
warned	(1)	182:3
warning	(2)	249:2; 305:3
wars	(4)	129:1; 130:1; 348:5; 360:3
was	(Count: 210 – not included)	
wastage	(14)	38:1,2; 39:1; 56:1; 67:3; 70:3; 99:2,2,2; 109:1; 128:1; 225:6; 233:3; 375:3
waste	(5)	51:1; 321:1,3; 327:2; 339:2
wasted	(1)	381:1
wasteful	(7)	128:2; 129:2,2,2; 189:1; 220:1; 267:5
wasting	(1)	214:2
water	(3)	106:2; 183:1; 364:1
water-tight	(1)	195:1
waves	(2)	154:2; 162:4
way	(90)	6:2; 14:1; 20:1,4; 21:2,2; 30:2; 34:1; 37:1; 39:3; 45:2,2,2; 53:1; 54:3; 55:1; 57:1; 58:1; 63:2; 66:2; 68:3; 69:3,4,7; 70:3; 71:2; 77:2; 83:1; 93:3; 94:1; 105:2; 124:2; 129:1,3; 142:3; 150:2; 152:1; 159:1; 160:1; 170:3; 173:1,1; 187:3; 193:1; 194:1; 198:1; 199:2; 200:2; 204:1,2,3; 208:2; 216:1; 221:2; 225:1; 227:2; 231:1; 258:2,3; 272:4; 274:3,4; 281:2; 286:3,3,4; 288:1; 297:2,2,2; 299:1; 306:4; 309:1,1; 313:2; 319:1; 320:3; 331:1; 332:1; 334:2; 337:2; 341:5; 345:3; 346:1; 352:2; 353:3; 365:3; 373:1; 374:2; 375:1
ways	(10)	160:2; 189:5; 205:3; 206:2; 234:2; 248:4; 325:2; 332:1; 370:1; 378:1

we	(Count: 687 – not included)	
weak	(4)	31:2; 148:3; 153:2; 370:1
weaken	(1)	106:3
weakened	(2)	93:3; 94:1
weakening	(5)	106:3; 158:2,2,2; 265:2
weakens	(1)	196:3
weaker	(3)	31:3; 192:1; 343:4
weakest	(1)	267:5
weakness	(5)	31:2; 112:1; 159:1; 348:1,1
weal	(1)	345:4
wealth	(106)	4:2,3,3; 19:1,2; 21:1,1; 31:2,2; 48:4; 82:1,1; 83:1,2; 84:1,1; 93:1; 95:5; 109:3; 110:1; 126:4; 129:1,2,3; 130:1,1,2; 131:1,2; 160:2; 167:2; 168:2,2,2; 169:1; 176:1; 211:2,2; 212:1,1,1,1,1,1,1,1,1,2,2; 213:1,1; 218:2; 219:1,1,2; 220:1; 221:2; 232:1; 233:2,3; 234:3; 240:1,2,2,3,3; 241:2,2,3; 242:2; 288:1; 324:3; 334:4,4; 335:3; 336:1; 337:2; 341:2,3,3; 344:2; 348:1,1; 349:1; 351:3; 352:2,2,2,4; 355:3,3; 360:1; 362:4; 363:2,3,3; 366:4; 372:1,2; 373:2,3,3; 374:2,2; 375:1; 381:1
wealth-owner	(1)	309:2
wealth-owners	(5)	227:2; 307:3; 308:1; 309:1,2
wealth-ownership	(1)	374:2
wealth-owning	(1)	93:1
wealthier	(1)	31:2
wealthy	(9)	31:2,2,3; 100:2; 125:2; 126:2; 145:1; 323:2; 366:4
weapons	(2)	327:2; 365:3
wear	(5)	139:3; 250:1,1; 253:3; 273:5
wear-and-tear	(2)	72:3,3
wearing	(1)	100:1
wears	(3)	20:4; 100:1; 360:5
weather	(1)	162:3
weed	(1)	183:1
week	(3)	151:1; 210:1; 357:1
weekly	(1)	367:2
weigh	(1)	240:2
weighs	(1)	326:3
weight	(5)	148:2,5; 164:2; 266:2; 339:2
weighted	(4)	43:3; 44:1; 161:4; 302:4
weighting	(1)	41:2

whole (cont.)		179:2; 181:1; 186:2,2; 188:1; 189:5; 194:1; 200:2; 217:3; 231:1; 243:4; 246:1; 259:1,1,2; 260:1,1,2; 261:1; 262:2,5,5; 263:4; 269:3; 270:2; 271:3; 277:2; 280:1; 281:1,2,2,2; 282:2,3; 283:1,1; 285:2,2,2,3,4; 287:2; 293:1,1,1; 294:2,2,2,2; 295:1; 298:2; 308:1; 321:2,4; 322:4; 334:4; 335:2; 340:1; 341:5; 343:1,1; 355:2; 360:3,5; 361:5,7; 381:1
wholly	(14)	129:2,2; 189:2; 212:1,1; 232:3; 260:1; 278:1; 288:1; 324:2; 329:1; 339:3; 369:1; 371:1
whom	(4)	156:2; 262:4; 360:7; 381:4
whose	(20)	32:2; 33:2; 85:2; 121:1; 156:2; 162:3; 236:2,3; 238:2; 247:2; 258:1; 262:4,5; 268:2; 337:2; 343:4; 349:1; 353:3; 360:7; 381:1
why	(36)	24:4; 31:3; 32:2; 42:2; 98:1; 149:2; 168:2,2; 174:2; 182:4; 187:4; 202:1; 206:2,2; 213:1,3; 214:1; 215:2; 223:4,4,4; 225:2; 230:3; 232:2; 258:1,1; 279:2; 280:2; 314:3; 317:2; 318:1; 356:2,2,2; 373:3; 382:3
whys	(1)	213:2
wicked	(1)	362:2
wickedness	(1)	359:2
Wicksell	(1)	183:3
Wicksell's	(1)	242:3
wide	(11)	9:3; 43:2; 118:2; 163:2; 171:1; 276:1; 278:4; 320:1,1; 378:1; 380:1
widely	(3)	58:2; 116:1; 356:1
widen	(2)	97:2; 248:2
widening	(2)	30:1; 206:2
widens	(1)	380:2
wider	(5)	31:2; 111:1; 145:1,1; 302:3
widespread	(1)	300:5
wild	(2)	128:1; 183:1
will	(Count: 796 – not included)	
willing	(15)	8:1; 13:1; 15:3; 160:2; 167:2; 190:3; 205:1; 206:2; 226:2; 248:2; 277:1; 289:2; 298:2; 379:2; 383:1
willingly	(1)	98:1
willingness	(4)	18:2; 175:2; 207:2; 366:1

windfall	(16)	57:2,3,3; 58:1,1,2,2,2,2; 59:2; 63:1; 92:3; 94:1; 95:4; 288:1,1
winning	(1)	345:4
winter	(1)	154:1
wipe	(1)	350:3
wirtschaftsordnung	(1)	354:2
wisdom	(5)	158:1; 340:1,1,2; 341:5
wise	(4)	16:1; 351:2; 369:1; 374:2
wisest	(1)	325:3
wish	(14)	11:2; 40:2; 41:1; 116:1; 119:2; 120:4; 166:3; 167:2; 172:1; 178:1; 259:2; 304:3; 359:1; 372:2
wished	(1)	382:3
wishes	(1)	212:1
wit	(1)	361:7
with	(Count: 601 – not included)	
withdraw	(6)	9:2; 13:1; 100:1; 187:1; 344:3; 358:3
withdrawal	(7)	8:3,3; 15:3; 277:1,2,3; 290:3
withdrawn	(1)	366:1
withheld	(1)	108:3
withhold	(1)	6:1
withholding	(1)	109:2
within	(36)	8:3; 9:2; 40:1,1; 43:2; 65:1; 98:1; 105:2; 136:3; 151:3; 163:2; 220:3; 246:1,3; 252:1,2; 253:1; 254:2; 267:5; 271:3; 275:4; 276:1,1,1; 302:3; 318:2,2; 324:1; 327:2; 332:2; 341:3; 347:2; 348:5; 357:1; 377:2; 380:1
without	(89)	5:2; 6:2; 9:3; 19:3; 21:1; 26:2; 39:3,3; 40:1,1; 44:2; 51:3; 54:3; 74:1; 81:2; 83:2,2; 85:2,2; 95:5; 107:1; 108:1,3; 117:1; 118:3; 119:2; 122:3,4; 130:2; 139:3; 140:1; 161:3; 163:2; 167:3; 174:2; 175:1; 177:2; 179:2; 183:1; 187:4; 190:4; 191:2; 196:3; 197:3; 198:1; 203:2; 209:3; 210:1; 213:3; 226:4; 234:4; 235:1; 238:1; 249:2,4; 253:2; 259:1; 261:1; 275:1,4; 276:1; 281:1; 285:2; 286:4; 287:1; 292:1; 297:2; 300:3; 303:4; 304:1; 305:2; 316:2; 320:1; 323:1; 326:2; 340:1,2; 345:1; 346:1; 347:4; 350:1; 361:4; 363:2,2,2; 366:1; 368:6; 377:2; 378:1
wits	(1)	155:3
woman	(1)	40:1

worst	(4)	69:5; 118:2; 183:1; 345:1
worsted	(1)	383:1
worth	(25)	24:1; 53:1; 69:5; 70:2; 94:1; 99:4; 127:2; 139:3,3,3; 140:1,3,3; 143:2; 145:1; 153:1; 155:1; 168:2; 192:1; 216:2; 239:3; 274:3; 305:3; 372:2; 381:3
worthy	(1)	106:2
would	(Count: 356 – not included)	
wrestled	(1)	32:2
wriggling	(1)	129:2
write	(14)	29:2; 41:4; 62:1; 100:1; 101:1; 109:1; 115:2; 149:3; 258:2; 279:3; 282:3; 285:4; 304:4; 315:6
writer	(1)	342:1
writers	(13)	16:1; 74:1; 81:1,1; 138:2; 178:1; 180:1; 190:1,4; 243:6,6; 342:1; 345:1
writes	(6)	5:7; 102:3; 140:3; 176:1; 188:2; 383:3
writing	(4)	37:2; 305:3; 346:1; 353:2
writings	(2)	346:4; 366:2
written	(21)	25:2,2; 26:2; 53:1; 56:1; 66:2; 74:1; 99:3; 258:2; 273:1; 276:1; 277:2; 284:4; 342:5; 346:1,4; 355:2; 356:2; 365:2,2; 366:4
wrong	(7)	140:4; 148:3; 182:3; 193:1; 334:4; 350:1; 383:3
wrongheaded	(1)	155:1
wrongly	(1)	76:1
wrote	(7)	329:2; 334:2,2; 345:2; 359:1,7; 361:8
x-curve	(3)	181:1; 182:3,3
x-curves	(1)	182:3
y-curve	(6)	181:1,1,1,1; 182:3,3
y-curves	(2)	181:1; 182:3
year	(27)	40:1; 70:3; 73:2; 99:4,4; 100:1; 101:3,3; 155:1; 168:3; 169:1; 188:2; 210:1; 222:2,2; 223:3; 225:3; 227:2; 265:2; 317:2; 329:2; 330:1,1; 342:1; 346:3; 354:1; 360:5
year-pound	(1)	188:2
year-value-unit	(1)	188:2
yearly	(4)	139:3; 343:1; 347:1; 360:7
years	(42)	3:1; 40:1; 100:2; 101:2; 102:2,3; 128:1; 137:2; 149:4,4; 150:1; 152:1; 153:1; 155:3; 168:3; 169:1,1,2; 175:3; 188:1; 251:2; 307:3; 317:2,2; 318:2; 323:1,2; 324:1; 330:1; 332:1; 333:1,1; 337:2; 339:2;